AF556132

Love, Exile, Redemption

Love, Exile, Redemption

The Saga of Kashmir's Last Pandit Prime Minister and his English Wife

SIDDHARTH KAK
and **LILA KAK BHAN**

RUPA

Published by
Rupa Publications India Pvt. Ltd 2023
7/16, Ansari Road, Daryaganj
New Delhi 110002

Sales centres:
Prayagraj Bengaluru Chennai
Hyderabad Jaipur Kathmandu
Kolkata Mumbai

P-ISBN: 978-93-5702-492-1
E-ISBN: 978-93-5702-470-9

First impression 2023

10 9 8 7 6 5 4 3 2 1

Printed in India

To Bhaiji and Bended,
our most unforgettable characters

∽

This is for you Bhaiji.

The Philosopher

Between the cleft of two great hills,
Mamnyut and Burzakut,
a snow-fed stream, Malhouri,
shrills its descent through ravines.

No traffic here but Bakarwals,
whistling their goats to grass.
Occasional Gujars with their cows,
in summer to a higher pass.

None else, orioles own the birch,
pine and *kikar* trees.
Wagtails strew the meadows,
search for worms beside the stream.

On these solitary slopes and banks,
a cottage whirring with bees;
ravaged by bears and snow
and years, a man ravaged by these.

Grappling with nettles, breaking stones,
growing orchards, unearthing springs,
honeysuckle, jasmine crown this home,
Daman-i-Kosar, skirt of the hills.

He walks alone, reflects,
under this fragrant sky.
Behind him, sacred Mahadev
and the house where he will die.

Except in my heart,
having clutched him stumbling,
the same path, craving
the very mountains, earth and wind,
known to my grandfather;
once king of men,
now among them king.

Contents

THE KAK FAMILY TREE

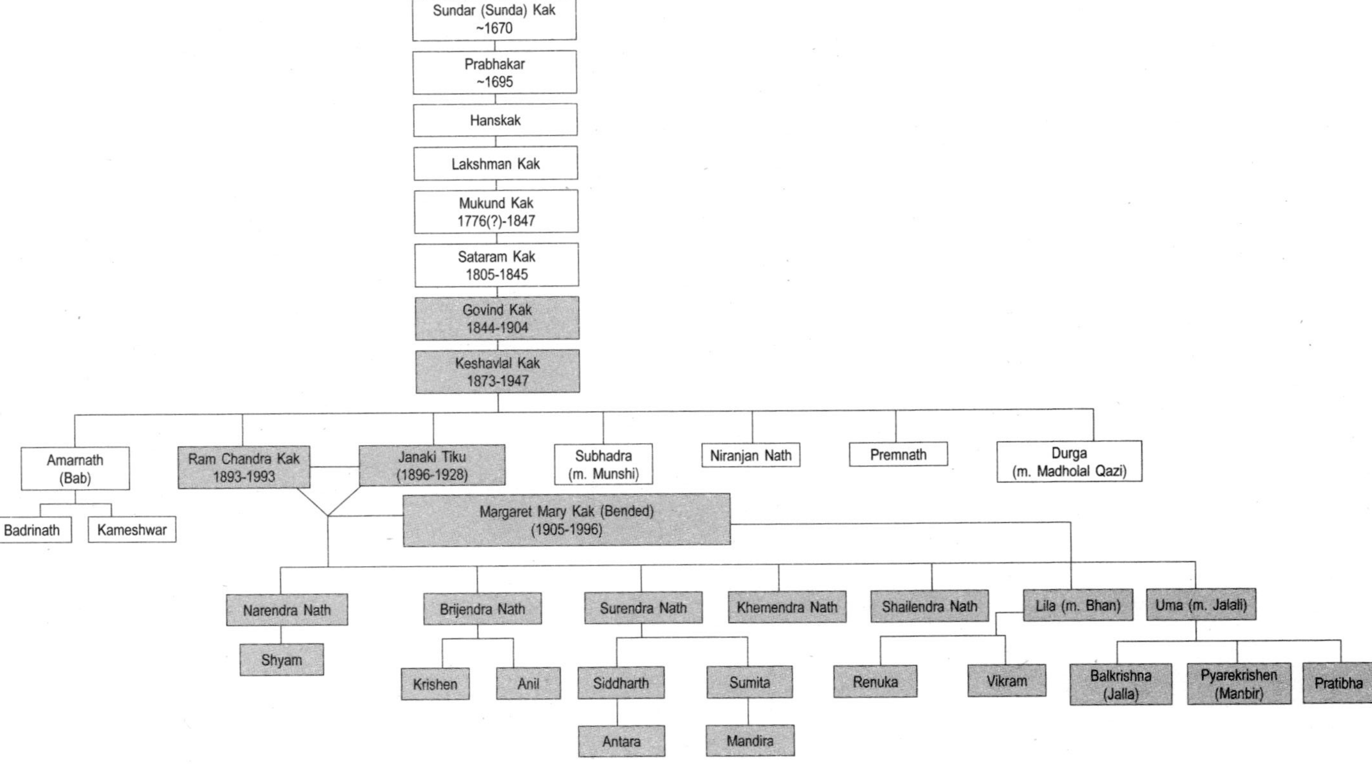

Note: This truncated Family Tree only refers to Ramchandra Kak's family line mentioned in the book for clarity and does not include other members of the extended Kak Family.

Introduction: Happy Walks

It was over half a century ago when I first came to live in Kasauli as an impressionable five-year-old with Pandit Ram Chandra Kak, my grandfather whom I simply called Bhaiji, and Margaret Mary Kak, my step-grandmother lovingly known to me as Bended. I remember the uncluttered beauty of this charming hill station and the rustic simplicity of our lives. I am now 75 but still vividly remember the events that took place 70 years ago—so fundamental were they to my formative years.

I also remember why they were known to us as Bhaiji and Bended. The younger members of our family, out of rebelliousness or mere laziness, refused to call their several uncles, aunts and even grandparents by the charmingly complicated terminologies and conventions prevalent in traditional Indian families, which are indicative of relationships and hierarchy. For instance, a *jija ji* or sister's husband would become *phoopha ji* (respected uncle) to his nieces and nephews. But, in our family, the rule was: once a jija ji, always a jija ji for all members of the family. For instance, my mother, Sarla, was known as jiji (elder sister) by her nieces, nephews and even her parents. My father—affectionately known as Surakak, an abbreviation of his full name, Colonel Surendra Nath Kak—was Surakak to his friends, cousins and their children. My mother's younger sister, Shanta, when she got married, was called *bibi* or wife, and the name stuck. She is still Bibi to our entire family.

Similarly, Bhaiji means respected brother, and this affectionate nickname, first used by his brothers or sisters for my grandfather, made him Bhaiji for us all. Bended or respected sister is the name my grandmother was given in the 1930s, even before she married Bhaiji. And Bended she remained for us, the name becoming synonymous with her smiling face. Thus, an amalgamation of these affectionate names—*Bhaiji and Bended*—was a natural title for this book.

Till the end of his days, Bhaiji loved to walk. Every morning, he would walk up and down the garden outside the porch in his house Bagh Sundar in Karan Nagar, Srinagar. For over an hour or two, he would stride evenly across the garden 50 to 60 times without stopping, lost in his thoughts. He would look up and smile without breaking his stride if one greeted him.

Walking gave him strength and purpose. As he recalls, even when he was held in jail as an ordinary political prisoner after he resigned as the prime minister (PM) of Jammu and Kashmir[1], he walked regularly on the 20-feet patch outside his cell for a year. This was the only outlet for his energy—he even refused all books and magazines.

Walks were special for Bhaiji and Bended. They would take time off from daily chores and the cares of the world to simply imbibe the beauty around them and savour their companionship. They were freeing.

I realised that these walks were the few avenues of enjoyment available to Bhaiji and Bended without a fee that would further deplete their dwindling bank balances. The State had frozen Bhaiji's accounts and denied him his pension while the trial against him went on for nearly 12 years, until the State finally lost the case. Even then, the State denied him his pension arrears. He had to begin his life again from scratch.

We children were happily unaware of this financial crisis. It never felt strange that we would not eat out, visit the cinema or even go shopping for clothes. There was so much else to do! Telling each other stories was our principal pastime.

And then, of course, our walks together every evening before the sun set were my favourites. First, in the charming hill station

[1]The region is henceforth referred to as Kashmir, since that is how the undivided Jammu and Kashmir, including Ladakh, was commonly known during the time discussed in the book.

of Kasauli in the Shimla hills in the 1950s and then, in Kashmir in the 1960s, through the dappled orchards and terraced rice fields around our home in the Dara hills, adjacent to the Dachigam Sanctuary.

Kasauli was a home in exile for Bhaiji, as he struggled, unbeknown to us, and fought for his right to have his pension restored by the Kashmir government. The walks around Dara began only when he returned to Kashmir after winning back his pension, ending his exile and rebuilding his life.

In Kasauli, I was a schoolboy, arguing as I walked, but I was a college-going sophisticate in Dara. By then, I knew that my grandfather had had to face formidable political and personal challenges and risks. Bhaiji was my most unforgettable character.

Bended was a gentle, loving foil to Bhaiji—sympathetic and understanding. I can't remember my grandparents ever having a fight or raising their voices throughout their lives.

During these walks with my grandfather in Kashmir, I embarked on the task of recording his life in long hand. In my mind, they were notes for a powerful book I felt I must write to clear his name. Bhaiji felt no such need. He was happy to be back in Kashmir, the land he loved, and he had much to do to reclaim his life. But he understood my eagerness and indulged my ignorance, patiently sharing his story in bits and pieces. Over a few years, on many walks, I slowly accumulated a few hundred stories from his life.

Then, the world intervened. After college, I took up a job that sent me away to Bombay (now Mumbai). Billy—Lila Kak Bhan, Bhaiji and Bended's beloved daughter and my aunt—had already been teaching elsewhere and our idyllic togetherness was disrupted. The book project and the notes lay forgotten and 50 years passed...

Meanwhile, in a dark attic, Bhaiji and Bended's original documents, personal interviews recorded by me five decades earlier, eye-witness analyses, priceless first-person anecdotes, family history dating back to a 100 years or more, striking observations about Kashmir before and Bombay after Independence, written with insight and respect by Bended, and Bhaiji's deep insights into Kashmir—its people, its historical and political contradictions—languished as life passed by. Miraculously, though, these documents survived the horrifying floods in Bombay, extended migrations across India and the US. Finally, one day, during the seemingly endless Covid-19 pandemic-induced lockdown, the documents were rediscovered, leading to Billy and my resolve to tell my grandparents' story.

Figure 1: Happy walks that Bhaiji and Siddharth took in Kashmir 1970s
Illustration credit: Ira Tuli

The world inhabited by Bhaiji and Bended in the last century was far from idyllic. If we have ebola, AIDS and Covid-19 today, it was tuberculosis, diphtheria and cholera back then, which were equally devastating, snuffing out lives like an evil wind over flickering candles.

Bhaiji and Bended lived through difficult times, perhaps far more difficult than their children ever experienced. They took life-changing decisions, spanning continents, in the teeth of family and social disapproval. Bended sacrificed her comfortable life in England for the love of a partner 12 years senior to her. She undertook a long and uncertain journey that separated her from her near and dear ones and confronted her with unknown challenges in an unfamiliar country. Bhaiji stood by her all his life and made unimaginable sacrifices for his state and family, facing abuse, humiliation and imprisonment in return for his patriotism and unflinching integrity.

It has taken over 70 years for this story to be told—story of the life and sacrifice of two remarkable individuals who lived with simplicity, integrity and affection, never believing they were doing anything exceptional except being true to their principles.

Bended's evocative letters home, now in Billy's possession, and her descriptions of Kashmir and Bombay, can be a book unto themselves, full of unusual insights. Perhaps few Englishwomen of her time were as closely acquainted with the life and politics of India as her, and she wrote her insights with great eloquence.

Bhaiji's sharp mind, erudition and fluency are reflected in the books he wrote about the archaeological monuments of his state, which are classics even today. His analysis of the political state of affairs of Kashmir and the events leading up to his resignation a few days before the battle for Kashmir began and the partition of India erupted will, I hope, provide a never-heard-before eye-witness account, giving a new perspective and understanding of the momentous events not only in Kashmir but across India.

I hope you will, in the telling of this story, realise the immense challenges of the last century, the harsh realities of the times and the essential humanity and wisdom of a couple who faced adversity with fortitude and embraced the little joys of life with a spirit that has percolated down to their children as an eternal legacy of happiness.

Bhaiji once told me, 'If something turns out well, it is good. If it does not turn out well, it is good. Life does not lie in success or failure. Life is in the living!'

1

A Letter That Changed My Life!

I had a rather high opinion of myself when I left St Stephen's College, which was one of the best colleges in India. I had a first class postgraduate degree in History with a rank in Delhi University. Academic prizes! Athletic prizes! The world was waiting for me with bated breath! Or so I thought.

For a year and a half after I left college, I couldn't get a job. I appeared for the Indian Foreign Service (IFS) exam but, in my arrogance, failed the interview. I applied to *The Statesman* and the *Hindustan Times* as a journalist, but there was no vacancy. I applied for teaching posts in schools, but no one offered me History as a subject.

Finally, after several months in the summer, I got a temporary job as a staff reporter with *The Indian Express* for ₹500 a month, inclusive of scooter allowance. My mother was happy, but I was depressed because neither was newspaper reporting the literary career I had been dreaming about nor could I type. I could only manage my daily report by typing with one finger.

Five decades ago, my life went into crisis when one of the stories I had piously researched and laboriously written about homeless children, which I thought was an exceptionally moving effort, was rejected by the newspaper. A senior editor who had assured help also stopped answering his phone. I was inconsolable. My dreams were shattered. I complained and moped all day. My mother was at her wits' end. Then, one day, a letter arrived from Bhaiji, with nuggets of wisdom in English, Sanskrit and Persian.

Bended, my grandmother, had also added her thoughts in the spaces available. It was a letter that changed my life!

> Dara, 30 July 1970
>
> My dear Siddharth,
>
> Just received your letter of the 27th. I know how humiliating it is to have to wait at other people's doors. I have done it myself, even when I was prime minister. I have done it in Kashmir, in India, in England, in France, in Germany and elsewhere.
>
> Once, I had to travel from London to Zurich to see someone, at the instance of a big businessman in India who wrote to me that he had written to the Swiss businessman about an arrangement which was expected to be of great advantage to all concerned, not least myself. When I saw the Swiss gentleman at his office, he received me kindly and invited me to a meal, but said he had no word from our mutual friend about any arrangement!
>
> Once, when I was minister in Kashmir, I had to see the Chief Secretary of the Bombay Government—an ICS [Indian Civil Services] officer of the old sort—on His Highness' business. He didn't ask me to sit down but asked me to see someone else in the office who did what I wanted.
>
> Life is like this, and one has to come to terms with it. One can only grin and bear it.

These were words of advice from a man with 60 years of turbulent experiences, including being the PM of a troubled state, empathising with a callow and self-pitying youth who had almost given up his journey at the first flimsy roadblock. He further wrote:

> No one else can make or mar another man: only he himself can make or mar himself—no father, no mother, no friend however affectionate. They may love you and feel for you or be proud of you but it is you and you alone who can make

you or mar you. As the Gita says, 'Alone one's self is one's friend and one's self one's enemy!'

So it all fell into place.

ᔕ

I shared a special bond with my grandparents because my parents allowed me to stay with Bhaiji and Bended and study at Mrs Bell's school at Waverley Cottage on the Upper Mall in Kasauli when I was six-years-old. My father was an army officer subject to frequent changes in postings. So, they thought I should go to one good school while staying with my grandparents.

My childhood adventures began early under my grandparents watchful eyes—from hillside adventures, chasing butterflies on the way to school, to khudside debacles, chased by monkeys on the way back with the young, local helper Anant Ram running behind, faithfully rescuing my abandoned school bag or water bottle in the flurry of activity and patiently listening to my exaggerated descriptions of encounters with furry creatures. Mrs Bell, a retired British teacher who ran a school in Kasauli where I studied, was not so patient, but she would allow me to stay back after school and colour sketchbooks to encourage my creative streak.

When, in 1957, at the age of 10, I joined Billy at The Lawrence School, Sanawar, a co-educational boarding school popularly known as simply 'Sanawar', I spent every Sunday with my grandparents and Billy during every school term. Billy and I formed a deep bond during these years. Though there was a five-year gap between us, we were inseparable, like brother and sister. Billy was my role model. She was a prefect, champion netball player and star English debater. I wanted to be like her.

So, I was crestfallen at falling short of this dream. In response, Bhaiji wrote to me saying, 'An opportunity missed is missed, no amount of repining can bring it back; the only remedy is not to miss or misuse other opportunities that may arise. Life is a palimpsest: nothing written can be erased, but is possible to overwrite it.' I suddenly realised that my imagined sufferings were nothing in comparison to what my grandparents had been through—banishment, separation, isolation, imprisonment, ridicule and public humiliation. Bhaiji further wrote

> You are coming in contact with the realities of life rather late, unfortunately, but the sooner you recognise the facts the better for you to your future.
>
> ... I remember a Persian verse, which I learnt as a child
>
> *'Hakkam kibbah hakubat,*
> *Dozah barabar asth,*
> *Raftan behoim mardiyeh,*
> *Ham soi dard ishq*![1]'

To these insights, Bended added:

> Cheerio Sid—it would have been indeed scarcely believed if everything had gone so easily that already the plan was plain—believe it or not. I started to 'clarify' my views on poetry (not yet finished) on thinking over what you said regarding modern poetry. Bhaiji has clarified his views on life so you can appreciate your own value as a stimulator! As for the harrowing experiences of these days undergone in horrible heat, I can just imagine how you feel, but it's all 'copy'. If you count up the new experiences you have had, unpleasant they may have been, but in that they are new, they are very valuable. Nobody can write out of an untroubled heart, or out of a comfortably self-satisfied mind. At any rate the product is not likely to be interesting to other people.[...]
>
> Since Bhaiji has given you a quotation, here's one which has impressed me ever since I found it quoted in Burrow's *Lavengro*. This, of course, is from the Psalms:
>
> 'No man can deliver his brother nor make agreement

[1] 'Verily I tell you, going to Heaven through the good offices of some neighbour is the same as having to live everlastingly in Hell.'

> unto God for him. For it cost more to redeem their souls. So he must let that alone forever.'

Even after 50 years, this letter is still with me. Each time I open it, I see the love and hopes Bhaiji and Bended had for me, and how they, along with Billy, shaped me in ways I could not imagine then and continue to do so even now. Bhaiji once wrote:

> The essential thing to remember is that you have to sell what you have written. I lost 10 years in getting *Ancient Monuments* published; the authorities wanted me to eliminate a passage which, in their judgement, had some objectionable overtones. I refused to do so. They refused to give me permission to publish. Eventually, it was published in London, but I eliminated the concerned passage of my own accord—10 years' meditation had made me wiser!

Bhaiji distilled the essence of his life's experiences into five important precepts:

1. 'Nothing that one does goes unnoticed—i.e., unrewarded or unpunished—even though we may not see the result at once.'
2. 'For everything that one wants, one must pay a price, more or less according to the nature and value of the things wanted.'
3. 'Circumstances keep changing: today's friend may be tomorrow's enemy and vice versa. You meet a person for a particular purpose. That purpose may be fulfilled or not fulfilled. If fulfilled, you say thank you; if it is not, there should be no bitter feelings in your mind. Such feelings harm you, without any damage to the other person, who may not even care.'
4. 'Above all, "*Yate krite yadi na sidhyati, kodtre doshahe.*"
   ('"If, having attempted, one fails in achieving ones object, what harm has been done?"')
   'The attempt has been worthwhile, like that of the mountaineers who attempted to scale Mt Everest but didn't reach the top.'

5 'In short, nothing goes waste. Keep on working. The great thing is to keep on keeping on. You have to start life over again and unlearn certain things and learn others. It will be an uphill task but it will be worthwhile as you will see in the course of a few weeks or months. It's dogged as does it! So cheer up; and brace up and greet everybody with a smile!'

Thus, I awoke from my self-pitying slumber. I resolved to live up to my grandparent's expectations. I decided that when I next travelled to Kashmir, I would record my conversations with my grandfather and try and find purpose in my life from his thoughts and career as he rose from being a humble librarian to the PM of a beautiful but flawed state. More so, I decided to learn from how he and his English wife faced his fall from grace, their separation, his banishment and solitary imprisonment and the vindictive freezing of their assets without letting a single word or gesture overwhelm me or Billy with this information. This spoke of the truly exceptional character of Bhaiji, who inspired Billy and me in ways unknown even to us.

2

My Mother's Remarkable Letters[2]

My mother, Margaret Mary Allcock, moved to India from England when she married my father in 1937, taking a huge leap of faith. She adapted to her new life, embracing a new culture and customs with surprising ease. She learnt to drape a sari, cook *haak,* winnow and clean rice and speak basic Kashmiri, never once drawing attention to her British heritage.

One day, fairly recently, we were reminiscing about summers in Kashmir, where the family often congregated for the holidays, 'Billy aunty,' said my niece, Antara, in a confiding tone, 'Bended made me feel comfortable at every age—from the time I was a toddler, to a teen, to an adult! I have always felt she was a friend, an equal! I loved spending time with her, especially "helping" her in her fascinating kitchen, particularly washing up the dishes!' My niece had been a mere three-year-old when she had started visiting my parents—her great grandparents—and forming these memories.

Her words made me think hard about Mummy's interactions with children. Growing up, I had never dissected her personality or traits. I had just taken it for granted that she spoke in the same way with everyone, be it a child or an adult. It had never seemed remarkable; it was just her way! Looking back, it was, indeed, unusual for adults to treat children as sensible equals, more so half a century ago. She certainly had a way with all age groups.

---

[2]This chapter has been narrated by Lila Kak Bhan.

However, as I grew up, I realised that she was, and continues to be, the greatest influence on my life, shaping my decisions, philosophy and interactions. She was able to break through my grandfather's seemingly rigid and conservative Kashmiri Pandit sensibilities, with loving patience and commitment—a feat in itself. Deeply upset at his son's choice of bride, it wasn't too long before my grandfather, Keshavlal Kak or Bhaigash, began to see why my father had made the decision. Above all, Mummy achieved all this without any traces of resentment.

Growing up in an era when class and caste consciousness were heavily prevalent, I have the deepest admiration for my mother's resolve in responding to these hierarchies. I vividly remember how respectful Mummy was of Itwari, one of our helpers who happened to be a sweeper and was considered 'untouchable' in the India of those days. She personally served him tea twice a day. Itwari also cleaned the interior of our house in an era when someone like him would not even have been permitted to enter a home, let alone be in direct contact with the lady of the house. While these little gestures might have been commonplace in my life then, now, many years later, I see how Mummy quietly let her moral compass guide her despite the pressure of the social milieu of those times.

I am certain that there must have been some quirks or differences in Indian culture that might have surprised or even shocked her. But the grace and affection with which she accepted them amaze me. Rather than being critical, she always searched for similarities, and I quote her, 'I revere the possibility and the tradition and the flowering of another culture different from my own but equally authentic.'

Mummy has enriched my life with her passion for learning about people and their heritage. Her living with these beliefs and enveloping me in them has, I realise, been invaluable and core to developing my attitudes. Indeed, life may have been diametrically different from what she had imagined, but she, somehow, found a positive lesson in every encounter. It was only when I entered adulthood and started noticing the things around me that I was able to fully appreciate her, how she marched to her own drum and lived and loved from her heart, regardless of what society dictated. In all this, my father was her greatest support. They were two hearts that beat as one—my greatest influences.

My mother would recount endless tales of her childhood to me. Her vivid descriptions brought everything alive, and I felt I knew everyone she spoke about. It was like a storybook, and many a time, I would ask her to tell me the various stories again and again.

She was 13 when the First World War ended. This was timely in that after graduating from Loughborough High School, she was one of the few women who got the opportunity to study in college. Upon completing her Bachelor of Arts (BA) degree at Westfield College, London, she did a course in nursing and started working at St Thomas' Hospital. Her time there was short. Though shy, my mother was determined to follow her principles and beliefs. The Head Matron at the hospital was a martinet who was most exacting, insensitive and unreasonable. The nurses were regularly summoned to have a ruler placed on the ground near them to make sure the hem of their dress was 8 inches off the ground. If the nurses had short hair, which my mother did, they were required to attach a switch, so that a nurse's cap could be pinned to it, thereby keeping flyways off the neck and face.[3]

Though extreme in my mother's opinion, the rules of the hospital were still bearable. The final straw, however, came when Mummy had the misfortune of getting a nosebleed in the presence of her sarcastic Head Matron, who remarked, 'You are weak, Miss Allcock!' This cut my usually gentle mother to the quick.

---

[3]My mother had a beautiful switch of hair that she had fortuitously saved when her luxuriant tresses had been cut in favour of a stylish bob. It was fascinating for me to hold this mane of thick, long hair. It had a pretty spring to its flow and shone softly when it caught the light. It used to be a treat to have it brought out of its silk bag for me to stroke. Eventually, it was gifted to my friend who had hair of a similar colour and would fashion it into a bouffant on special occasions.

She was shocked and shaken by this lack of common sympathy for a mere nosebleed! She resigned soon after, making sure she informed her uncle, Dr W.S. Handley, a pioneer in cancer research at Middlesex Hospital, about her decision. She preferred he did not hear about the event through third-hand versions. This obviously upset her greatly, for I have heard her recount this episode on several occasions.

I remember the first time my mother shared with me the existence of a bundle of letters from the years 1936 to 1947. Neatly separated by year and meticulously tabulated, the varying blues of the airmail paper had a special feel, smell and appearance. In addition, there were two diaries that she had carefully maintained. The contents were a stunning revelation to me.

Mummy's ability to describe both people and places was phenomenal. She came from an era when letter writing used to be an art and the only way to communicate with people. Mummy wrote every week to her family in England, and so detailed and articulate were her descriptions that they were saved by the family there. This enormous bundle was handed over to her in 1947 when she and I fled Kashmir to live in England for two years. At that time, I had only been five-years-old and it was several years later, when I was about 14-years-old, that my mother first shared the contents of the bundle with me. She started reading extracts from these letters to me about her early years in Kashmir, her entry into the family, the day-to-day life she led and loved through a politically tumultuous decade not only in the world besieged by the Second World War but also in India and, more particularly, in Kashmir. In addition, these remarkable letters were a record of our family history through those years. Listening to anecdotes about the people I knew so well was something I loved. I remember often asking her to read them out to me—the best bedtime story—as we sat by the fire, never feeling I had had enough of the story!

Her writing is unique in that it is not only a record of a decade of politics in Kashmir but also a first-hand observation and history of the tumultuous decade leading up to the partition of India. Recorded from her understanding and point of view, her letters offer a detailed glimpse into Kashmiri life and society as they were when she arrived in the 1930s. As one of my English cousins, upon discovering this pile of Mummy's letters saved by his mother, wrote to me, 'Margaret was a wonderful observer of every aspect of life and her letters do bring alive the sights and atmosphere of wherever she was living together with fascinating insights into the political scene in Kashmir.'

By the time I went off to college, I realised what a remarkable woman my mother was: philosophical, adaptable, observant, devoted to my father and his family and a wonderful writer. A seed was sown in my mind that these letters needed to be woven into a book describing her life. It was a remarkable achievement for her to totally immerse herself in a family so different from her own as a woman who had come on this long voyage across the oceans on an 18-day journey. It was only years later, in 2021, that I, at Siddharth's behest and encouragement and in conjunction with him, finally began to record my parents' unique story through the innumerable letters and the two diaries Mummy had given me. One that my mother had saved from her first daring journey to India, and the second of the year she and I were in England while my father was detained in Kashmir. All her accounts were finally handed over to me in the late 1980s. They were saved just in time from the ravages of terrorism that destroyed all the other contents of my mother's home in Srinagar, including historic photographs that would have had a fitting place in this tribute to two of the most remarkable people.

3

The Kaks: A History by Bended

For years, the joint family home of the Kaks in Zaldragar, near Zaina Kadal, remained a shadowy memory for me until I discovered that my cousin, Jalla, had lived in Zaldragar till he was five and remembered clearly what it had been like—the houses in which they had lived and what their life had been like in bygone Kashmir.

Interestingly, although she never lived with them, Bended wrote extensively about the antecedents of her new joint family, the Kaks. She probably learnt some of these anecdotes in conversation with Bhaiji but most probably gleaned them while sitting with her father-in-law, Bhaigash, once he warmed up to her. As always, she brought a delicate perception to her observations, which she recorded in her elaborate typewritten notes, beginning with a foreword that has partly survived:

> Anything relating to personal experience has often the power to crystallise in the mind from a mass of facts and propaganda, a sense of reality. This is why I want to tell something of the history of the family into which I came at the later end of the 1930s. They were Hindus and, like others of the community, had lived in Srinagar for countless generations. Srinagar was 'Shaihar'—the city—to them; it needed no other name. The river was Jhelum, flowing majestically through the heart of the city. My father-in-law used to say:

> 'Sometimes its waters are white; sometimes they are black, but always the river flows.
>
> 'The story is enacted, the story is finished; remains only a story.'

> His talk was full of such sayings. They must have been rooted in the race consciousness, for his forebears had seen the banks of the great river changing from century to century. They had seen the great stone temples in their glory, later in evil times destroyed. They had seen their shattered remains, their cornices, pilasters and cornerstones, built into the river wall, where they can be seen today. True to their faith, they had lived through good times and bad, but always in Srinagar, always on the banks of the river. On one hand, they had seen the Hari Parbat Hill and on the other the Shankaracharya Hill. The buildings that crowned them had changed, but the hills remained, and beyond the flat levels of the valley, they had looked to the horizon and called it as they saw it, for they knew no other: *Sangamal*—the necklace of peaks.
>
> However long anything survives, it comes to an end one day. It may last so long that it is taken for granted, as the hills and the valley and the river are taken for granted. But when the end comes, the dramatic appeal to the imagination is all the more powerful. The fathers of today's family were nurtured in the Kashmir which had existed essentially unchanged for centuries; the sons saw the old culture all around them and were brought up within it, though they themselves were reaching out to new worlds and modern ways; many of the sons' sons cannot even speak Kashmiri.

Bended's research and reflections, which enabled her to make sense of her adopted family and new life, are invaluable in understanding the history and origins of the Kak family in Kashmir.

> Before the beginning of the nineteenth century, the Kaks are shadowy figures indeed. Only their names remain, recited

> at ceremonials by the family priest. Mukund Kak, son of Lakshman Kak, son of Chetrup Kak, son of Prabhakar Kak, son of Sunda Kak—here are five generations that probably lead us back to the reign of Shah Jahan or thereabouts. But a tradition remains of an ancestor far earlier. His name was Lala Roon (Raina or Razdan). This places him earlier than all the Kaks, for 'Kak' is not a clan name but an honorific, acquired by some ancestor, probably out of respect for his spiritual attainments, which has clung to his descendants ever since. The true clan name of the family is Raina or Razdan, a common name among Kashmiri Pandits derived from the Sanskrit 'Rajankar', meaning 'king's man', and probably denoting that they were officers employed in the service of the state, civil servants as we would call them now. There are many different clans of Razdans. The exact significance of this division is now uncertain, but they maintain certain customs, such as eating no meat during the Shivratri festival, which distinguish them from other families.

Bended recounted an interesting history of the family, which included a boon and a curse, and spoke of their occupation as *kardars* or revenue collectors with the government, under rapacious Pathan rule until Ranjit Singh ousted the Afghan Sunni Muslim rulers in 1819 and annexed Srinagar and Kashmir. Satram Kak was a kardar in charge of the large districts of Brang, Kutahar and Shahabad, and included among its 200 villages, the beautiful spring-fed regions of Verinag, Achabal and Kokernag. An indication of how intimately the role of the kardar was integrated into the life of the local people was that Satram Kak lived alone in the villages of his *kardari* in order to gain the confidence of the villagers and rid himself of the stigma of being a city man. Satram Kak is said to have often come only once a year to Srinagar for the Shivaratri festival in early spring to meet his family. The saying goes that he saw two little children playing in the garden and enquired who they were only to be told they were his own young son and daughter!

Another tale was of Satram Kak seeing a girl bathing naked in the river in his kardari and was outraged to learn that the girl's father had purposely set up the scene in order to curry his favour! Being moralistic, Satram Kak declared that the girl was now like his daughter, got her married off and then punished her father by making him stand in the ice cold river for more than an hour, which established his moral status in the community. However, his being proud and hot-headed led to a dispute, which resulted in the downfall of the Kaks after Satram Kak's early death at the age of 40 in 1843. Bended further wrote:

> In those days, in the better class families when the little brides first came [due to child marriages], they brought with them a Muslim woman servant who stayed with them as a nurse and protector in the strangeness of the new home. These servants, with their husbands and children, would often live in the household permanently, and as need arose, they would act as foster mothers to the family children. In this way, a bond of the strongest kind arose, recognised almost like that of blood, between Hindu families and foster families of Muslims.

Once, a dispute arose between one of Satram Kak's foster brothers and the foster brother from another Brahmin family—the Bhans. Satram Kak intervened on behalf of his foster brother but so did the Bhans, and there was fighting in which least one man was killed. The Bhans swore revenge and when Satram Kak died early, they were quick to strike against his widow, Ganga Ded, and her six young children. They did this by pressing the government to take possession of and dismantle the houses Mukund Kak had built in Ali Kadal in the heart of Srinagar to house the Kak families. They did this to pay off Satram Kak's tax arrears. Ganga Ded, being penniless, had to seek refuge in her brother Thakur Kaul's home in Rainawari. Bended describes the situation poignantly.

To such a household Ganga Ded came, and it was her misfortune that her sister-in-law, and not her mother, was now the first lady of the house. For 14 years, she lived independently in her brother's house. That she found it hard to bear, there can be no doubt. The family tradition was that she would fetch from the kitchen one large *thal* of rice from which she would feed herself and her children. During all the years she was there, she wore the same *pheran* or tunic, in which she had come, rather than be dependent on others for clothes as well as food. But in spite of hardship, she managed, no doubt with her brother's help, to marry her two daughters into good families and to educate her boys.

Of the four sons of Ganga Ded, the two youngest, Deva Kak and Govind Kak, were the most scholarly in inclination. In their uncle's big household at Rainawari, they must have had ample opportunities of listening to *kathas*, and they must have been acquainted not only with great Hindu stories but also with the verses of the fourteenth century mystic poetess, Lal Ded, and with the almost contemporary verses of Swami Parmanand as well as many others. That Govind Kak soon mastered Persian is certain, for we know that while they were still living in their uncle's house, he used to copy Persian manuscripts, and that by doing so he used to earn the money that was necessary to send with his sister, when, after visiting them, she went back to her husband's house. This was known as *attegaat* or 'coming and going money' and is still paid in Kashmir when daughters after staying awhile with their parents return to their married houses.

But as time went on and the boys grew older, their position of dependence must have become more and more difficult to bear. Gula Kak, the eldest, was now married, and it may have been that Ganga Ded, as a mother-in-law, may have felt less able to put up with things than she had when it was only her own prestige that had suffered. Whatever the cause, they decided to go back to their old home in Ali Kadal in spite of all difficulties. There was little left there. The houses had long ago been dismantled, and only about a third of the land they had owned remained, but on that plot, they managed to erect a rough one-roomed hut. With rush matting, they screened off one corner to form a separate room for the young married couple.

It is possible that Thakur Kaul had been piqued by his sister's departure. There is no reason to believe that he was ever anything but kindly disposed towards her, and he may have known little or nothing of the difficulties she had to face in his household, where the women, as in all joint families, had their own politics. He may even have tried to find employment for Gula Kak to the best of his ability. If he had done so, nothing had come of it. But one day, as he was talking with other officers of the administration, the name of Satram Kak was in some connection recalled. 'What had become of the sons? They had been mere children at their father's death, but must by now be grown? How had they turned out, and how were they living in great poverty in their old home?'

There and then Gula Kak was sent for. This messenger arrived at their Ali Kadal house on the third or fourth day of the Anusthan Puja of Wataknath, which the family was performing after several years. A ceremony lasting several days, the Anusthan Puja is considered to be of very great power. The puja demands a very high degree of discipline and mental purity in those performing it and if they fall short of that standard, it is believed that its performance entails great penalties for the presumption that [the performers] seek to obtain that which they are not worthy of achieving. It is, therefore, never performed except after very careful consideration.

Kasha Pandit, a man of the highest character and great learning was conducting the ceremony and under him were

Mahanand Bhai, the family priest, and others. Kasha Pandit had a dream that this puja was to be the turning of the tide in the Kak family's fortunes. And, indeed, it proved to be so. Gula Kak was given a post in the Dharmarth Department, and the long years of misfortune of the Kak family came to an end! Zaldragar and the Kak estate became a reality.

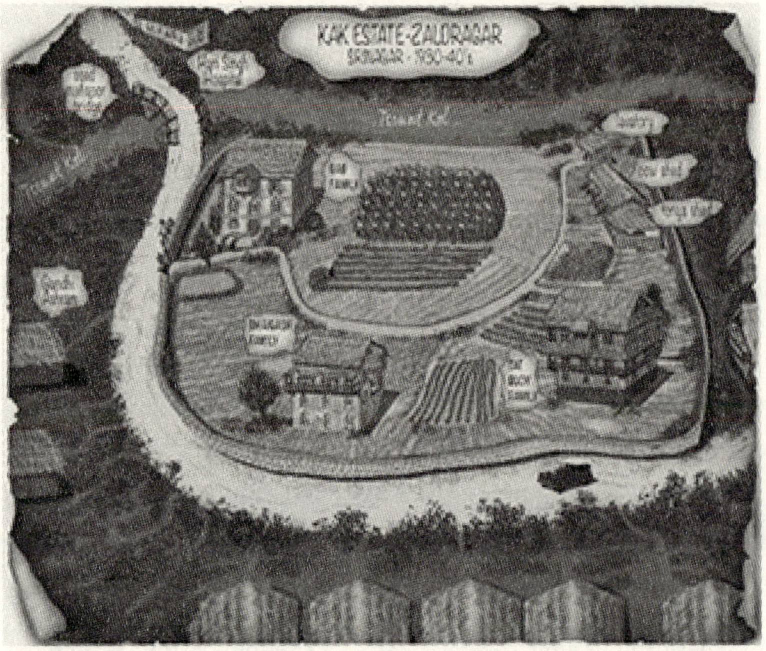

Figure 2: Map of the Kak joint family home at Zaldragar in the heart of Srinagar around 1930s–40s

Illustration credit: Kashmira Tembulkar

In his dream, Kasha Pandit had seen other things too. Cholera had been raging in the city then. In his dream, he saw a fishwife with a basket of fish on her head coming into the lane of Zaldragar Mohalla, opposite the Kak estate. Then, the White Bull of Shiva, had appeared and chased the fishwife out of the lane. This personification of cholera as a fishwife carrying a basket of fish was a common trope in nineteenth century Kashmir. And indeed throughout the period of the cholera epidemic, no one living in that lane fell ill or died of the disease.

The scourge of cholera and tuberculosis, too, ran unchecked in the early years of the twentieth century through the overflowing drains and rotting garbage heaps of an unhygienic city. Life expectancy was short, more so for the women who toiled the most and were short-changed in health and nutrition by a conservative society. The wives and daughters were the first to wake and the last to sleep in the perpetual grind of caring for the family and the procession of guests, relatives, rituals and festivities that were the central occupation and amusement of the Brahmin families of that more primitive age. The women in poor Muslim agricultural families had perhaps less ritualistic responsibilities, but they also laboured all day in the fields.

Bended wrote in her reflections, 'There is no doubt that the young wives of the day, in the first quarter of the century, did often have a very hard discipline to undergo and often they sank under it.' She once told me at Dara:

> The four brothers of Bhaigash all lost their first wives. Though his own wife, Wagri, was, I can imagine, the mildest and most easy-going of mothers-in-law, but even then, there is a poignant story of Bab's [Bhaiji's elder brother] first wife. She had been pouring out hot rice water from a steaming big *deghchi* or utensil. Sensing its balance upset and in danger of falling, she had propped it up with her forehead against the plinth rather than let it fall and had got burnt as a consequence. I am not too sure how that happened, but that is the story! She was Badrinath's mother, but died when he was about three-years-old.
>
> There were two sisters in Bhaiji's family, besides Durga. The elder was just a year younger than Bhaiji. She was married in a Dhar family but died very young and without children. The next sister, Subhadra or Subhri, was said to

> have been very charming in feature and figure. She was Bhaiji's favourite and, according to him, something like Billy, but very slender and graceful! Subhri was his favourite.

Subhri married into the Munshi family and had a little son who died in infancy and then a daughter, Uma, who was only two or three when the Munshi mother-in-law fell ill and died. It was in the depth of winter and for some reason, the elder daughter-in-law left most of the death ceremonies, which entailed going every morning to the river and bathing in ice cold water, to her younger sister-in-law. Subhri fell ill and Bhaiji recalled that when the Kak men, who had not been in Srinagar at that time, returned, they found Subhri very ill and bedridden. They felt maybe that not enough was being done for her in the Munshi household and brought her back home with them. There, in a short time, she died in spite of all their efforts. Bended wrote that before her death, Subhri bound Bhaigash and Wagri to a vow to keep her child, Uma, in their midst. So, Uma never went back to the Munshi's home, was brought up as a Kak and never knew of her relationship, other than as a Kak daughter, until after the day of her own marriage in 1938.

∽

Toil is necessary for success but Kashmiri Pandits often dislike manual work. They also tend to be averse to risk-taking as entrepreneurs. This is perhaps why Bhaigash was not a successful businessman. Kashmiri Pandits are best-suited for clerical and administrative jobs, which are limited in number and scope.

Bhaiji's elder brother, Amarnath Kak or Bab, who later became a top lawyer in Kashmir, began as a humble school teacher earning only a few rupees a month. When Bab demurred at taking the job, Bhaigash said to him, 'At least it will put haak and rice on the table!' So, Bab took up the assignment.

The Kak family members had modest needs, but it was a large family accommodating at least six separate households, sundry cousins, aunts and relatives, not to speak of servants, attendants, gardeners and staff, along with upkeep of livestock and an in-house *tonga* with a pony, equivalent to a car in the garage today, all cheek by jowl with the Kak family estate in Zaldragar.

Meals were cooked and eaten together. Only Bhaiji's grandfather Govind Kak or Lalla, meaning 'loved one', and Bhaigash were served meat. Women and children were vegetarian, often eating the staple haak and *batha*, which came from their vegetable patch rice fields. Haak cooked with meat was sometimes given to the children as a reward. Bhaiji, at any rate, recalled that, as a child, he only got vegetarian food. He and Bab would keep a small hard lump of *nyoth* in their pockets, which they would mix with their food to make it tastier. After their meals would be over, they would dry the nyoth and put it back in their pocket for the next meal!

Bhaiji remembers his grandfather occasionally slipping a piece of fried mutton to him out of affection. The haak and batha ritual was part of the morning brunch eaten at 9.30 a.m. and there would be no lunch for school-going children. They would directly be served *kulchas* at tea time and haak and batha again for dinner at about 7.30 p.m.

One day, this practice took a poignant turn. Lalla had been ailing for some time. He called Bhaiji to his bedside just before he left for school and asked, 'Have you eaten?' Bhaiji said he hadn't. Lalla asked for Bhaiji's food to be brought to his room. The staple rice and haak arrived in a thal. Lalla asked for his favourite fried meat or *kabarga* to be brought. Bhaiji recalled that he ate this delicacy he was unaccustomed to with great relish and felt highly pleased with himself. Then, Lalla said, 'You are going to school now. Remember one thing: time is valuable—never waste it!'

Bhaiji hastened to his school, which was a long walk away, without understanding the significance of what had happened. It was only that afternoon, when a retainer came from the Kak family home and pulled him out of class to inform him that Lalla had passed away, that he realised the importance of that moment. Perhaps Lalla's last words made a deep impression on him because unremitting toil became his watchword.

Bended similarly remembered the last few months of Bhaigash's life:

> In my father-in-law I was privileged to see the flowering of the old culture and knowing him has thrown a new and vivid light on all the knowledge I previously possessed. He knew Sanskrit, Persian and Kashmiri, the last of which I was able more or less to follow. Much I must have missed as I listened, much possibly I misunderstood, but there was enough for me to be able to appreciate the scope and breadth on his mind. He would speak of Aflatoon [Plato] and Sikandar [Alexander the Great]. And as I listened, I realised the unity of human knowledge, how what had travelled from Byzantium to the West had also travelled East and was possibly even earlier and more fully assimilated there. He would recount sayings of his father, many of which were identical in sense with sayings from the Gospels. Yet, it was very certain that he had never read the Bible. He first made real to me the idea of *maya*. He would talk of his father, his childhood, his forebears, but always end with a shrug of resignation, 'Where are they now? Everything is transient, a deceit to the mind. *Khob khayal* [illusory thoughts].'
>
> During the last summer of his prosperity and happiness, Bhaigash was determined to perform a ceremony at Mattan, a famous spring near Anantnag. Perhaps he had some premonition of the dislocations that lay ahead.
>
> One of my most vivid recollections is of seeing him setting out by lorry to Mattan. Several of his daughters-in-law and daughters were with him; several children, his steward, grandson of his own father's steward, the family priests and above all, sitting by his side—both immaculate in white pherans, dupattas and turbans—Pandit Harbat [Hara Bhat] Shastri, his lifelong friend and probably the last of the long line of Sanskrit scholars of old Kashmir, who was to direct

the ceremonies with the aid of his experience and learning.[4] *Chinar* trees in bright sunlight formed a background for the lorry and [...] behind them rose the shoulder of the Shankaracharya Hill with the temple at its summit. In recollection, it has always seemed to me the end of an epoch.

A year of his [Bhaigash's] life remained, but it was one of gloom and increasing weakness. On a snowy evening in February [1948] by feeble lantern light, he saw from the gate of his courtyard his two elder sons being taken into custody by summary order. He turned back to the house, once so full of life, where now only his eldest daughter-in-law remained. All the rest of his families were scattered. Yet, he never faltered. He had always said, 'When the call comes, I am ready. My bedding is rolled. At any moment I am ready to go.' This he had said cheerfully and half-jokingly in prosperity and health. He waited in increasing weakness and blindness, but he was unconquered. He spent money, repaired his compound wall, put everything in order, always believed that in the end, all would be well, though he would never see it. When he felt the end was near, he told the family himself where everything needful could be found. All necessary preparations he had himself made. His eldest son was with him but the second—though he was almost within a stone's throw of his deathbed and unconvicted as yet of charges which, even if proved, were bailable—was not even informed of his life being in danger, and they never saw each other again after the dark February evening when they said goodbye.

∽

[4]Earlier, Bhaiji, Bhaigash, Hara Bhat Shastri and Tota Kak, a highly revered Pandit, had travelled to the sacred shrine of Sharda University, the centre of Sanskrit learning not just for those in Kashmir but all of India too. The ruins of this university now lie in what is known as Pakistan Occupied Kashmir [PoK].

For the Kak family in the 1920s and early 1930s, the events described in Bended's reflections were yet to take place. The weaving of her own life into the fabric of Kashmir was still some years away. Life was pastoral but hard. Her husband to be was still in his traditional home, ensconced in his large orthodox family and had only just stepped onto the threshold of a trajectory that would carry him not just to her but also to the highest point in his eventful career.

The situation for the Kak family changed drastically just a few years later. Partition created two new nations divided by religion, and an armed conflict broke out between the newly formed countries of India and Pakistan. The Kak families evacuated soon after the raiders' attack on Srinagar, probably by October or November 1947. Jalla remembers seeing Dakota planes landing one after the other on the airstrip disgorging soldiers as the family waited to depart. They travelled in a Dakota, which left Srinagar at 6.00 p.m. and reached Delhi at about 9.00 p.m. Nana Kak, Bhaiji's eldest son, came to receive them in his Chevrolet. He had arranged for them to be put up in the Mandi House quarters. My anxious father and mother, Surakak and Sarla bhabi, who had come to Delhi to receive the Kak evacuees, left after a few days for Bangalore (now Bengaluru), where my father had an army posting, taking Bab's daughter, Sushila, with them. I was a few months old when these events transpired.

But before this, Bhaiji had, growing up at the turn of the early 1900s in the Kak joint family in Zaldragar, faced an onerous time, when, in the face of family debts and difficulties, he had to successfully complete his own education and find work to help support the large Kak joint family. It all began with a great adventure.

4

Bhaiji Grows Up

Looking back, the turn of the last century in Kashmir must have been a strange place and time to live in and through. I was born in 1947, but it was not until 1960, when Bhaiji and Bended returned to Kashmir, that I visited with any awareness of what life was really like there. Even then, mine was a blissfully ignorant existence, with a few months of vacations in Srinagar, frequenting its spacious clubs and gardens or staying in the exclusive cottages and holiday resorts of Pahalgam and Gulmarg, far removed from the poverty, illiteracy and superstitions of the rural countryside or the unhygienic maze of the interior city.

The cost of living was comparatively cheap in the mid-twentieth century Kashmir. An anecdotal story of my maternal grandfather, Papaji Wazir, buying a *shikara* full of vegetables for a marriage feast for just ₹3 still circulates. Bhaiji's pension was all of ₹700 a month. In 1969, as a college student, I remember taking an Indian Airlines flight to Srinagar for ₹80. Moreover, the student's concession meant I paid only ₹40! Today, one might not get even a handful of green chillies from the vegetable market for that sum!

The Kaks lived as a joint family in three houses spread over a large estate at Zaldragar on the banks of the Tsunt Kol or apple canal, named after the apple trees growing on its banks. It was a tributary of the Jhelum in the heart of the city that flowed back into the river via a lock regulating the waters of the Dal Lake.

Bhaiji told me that Bhaigash, as was the practice those days, had got married at the age of 15. In 1888, his wife, Wagri, had conceived Bab, Bhaiji's elder brother by four years, at the age of 11. Bhaiji, the second son, had been born in 1893. The year, as Bhaiji recalled whimsically, had become memorable by two events—one was his birth and the other a very large and devastating flood.

Floods were a frequent hazard and occasionally, the Tsunt overflowed its banks, rose over the embankment and flooded the Kak estate, sometimes up to the ground floor. The Tsunt was otherwise an idyllic waterbody in the heart of the city to bathe in or stroll along. The Nawa Bazaar market, where a Muslim bakery coexisted with a paan and cigarette shop and other small shops, selling odd and ends, were nearby. It was a large area with a wall around the entire ground, except its rear, overlooking the Tsunt, which had an embankment with bushes and a few quince trees.[5]

The water on the Tsunt flowed from left to right if you faced it from the Kak estate. However, in the 1930s, there was a big flood and the water from the Tsunt rose over the embankment and completely flooded the Kak estate. Tat Buoy's house (Bhaiji's younger brother) was built on a mound and was, thus, comparatively safe, as was the cowshed. Fields of maize were planted on the side of the road facing the estate. The grassy embankment of the Tsunt was a fine place for the Kak family to take their morning or evening strolls. Karan Nagar and Bagh Sundar—where Bhaiji later built a separate house, first for Bended and then for his family—were about 1.5 or 2 kilometres away, a walkable or cyclable distance, even nearer from the Nawa Bazaar side of Zaldragar.

House No. 1 was near the entrance of the Kak estate. It had Bab's office on the ground floor. A covered external staircase went up to the first floor, where Preya Kak, Bhaiji's brother, lived and the second floor, where Badrinath Kak, Bab's son, lived. House No. 2, where Bab and Bhaigash lived with their families, had a kitchen and bathroom at the back of the ground floor. On the same floor were

[5]I am indebted for this description of Zaldragar to Jalla, son of Uma and Bansilal Jalali, who lived in the Kak joint family home till they were forced to depart during the 1947 conflict. He had been four- or five-years-old at the time but remembers the place vividly.

two long rooms separated by a corridor with a central staircase at the far end that connected the first and second floors.

While the houses were considered modern, the lavatories were primitive and unhygienic, requiring human scavengers to clean them. It was only with the coming of Bended and the building of Bagh Sundar for her, in 1936 in the nearby Karan Nagar, that the first flush system was introduced in the newest Kak family home. Nevertheless, the inconvenient traditional style without an attached bathroom continued in the old houses. One had to traverse through the bitter cold after a bath!

As confirmed by Jalla, the Kaks grew their own vegetables and corn, had some cows and were fairly self-sufficient in providing themselves simple meals of haak, vegetables, *zamadod* and batha. It was necessary to live austerely, as money was in short supply.

∽

In the Kashmir of 1930s, superstitions and rumours would spread like wildfire. The presence of goblins and demons were a fact of life. Miracles happened. Disease and illness were often attributed to wrong conduct or possession by evil spirits. *Hakims* and *sadhus* who could exorcise these evil influences were held in high esteem. Spiritual and religious fervour were accorded great value in society.

Because the Kak family had a reputation for religious orthodoxy, Bhaiji was brought up in this tradition. His father, grandfather and various uncles had their own separate *kut* in the house, where they would conduct their daily prayers, morning and evening, led by the family priest, who would come every day, sometimes twice a day. The Kak family priests, Rishibouy and his son Raghubouy, a pleasant smiling man, together served the Kak family for 75 years. Up until 1947, they used to come every morning to perform the puja at the Thakur Kut and other important ceremonies. There were no fixed fees for performing puja. They would get anywhere between ₹1–₹1,000 for their services. But what they would always get was a meal in the house. Over the years, the ceremonies became fewer and attenuated. An actual marriage puja used to last at least 14 hours. But by the 1960s, it had come down to two to three hours, when Shyam, my cousin, and later, Billy, got married.

Bhaiji told me this story while we were walking:

> 'One morning Bhaigash called out "Raghoa [Raghubuoy]! After me they will not need you. But still you must come regardless on every birthday or *shraddha* day." And Raghubuoy did come, even to Delhi, to perform *mekhal* [thread] ceremonies and weddings in two successive years, in 1966 and 1967, of Billy and Shyam, even though he had more lucrative offers in Srinagar. He got ₹1,100 in cash for the mekhal ceremonies and ₹300 tips in cash, apart from what others gave him for Billy's wedding!'

Whenever Bhaiji and Bended returned to Srinagar from Kasauli after the winter, Raghubuoy would visit them in April and give them all the important religious dates in the Indian *hisaab*. He would perform a puja that day, either in Bagh Sundar or Dara, and would be given a seer of rice for his trouble along with a meal!

As Bhaiji narrated to me amid chuckles, this orthodoxy led to a hilariously unfortunate situation when he was just 16- or 17-years-old in what can be called 'The strange case of the miraculous cure of Hirpur!'

ഗ

From an early age, Bhaiji suffered from digestive problems. He had frequent stomach pains and ate little beyond milk and kulchas. A police constable friend of his volunteered to put it right with certain miracle herbs of which he had heard, as holy men and miracle cures were all the rage in those days. But for that, Bhaiji would have to accompany the police constable to the nearby town of Hirpur, where the herbs grew and where buffalo milk, apparently an essential part of the cure, was also available. Hirpur was about 40 miles from Srinagar, beyond Shopian. Bhaigash gave his assent to the journey, and a pony was borrowed, which Bhaiji saddled and off they went! He was to return within a week.

The first twist in the tale came when the constable was suddenly detailed to find some cattle thieves. Accordingly, a detour was taken, and Bhaiji had to perforce accompany the police party. The police were welcomed at every stop. While the burly police men gobbled up barbecued kebabs, Bhaiji miserably nibbled at some plain rice and sipped a glass of milk. In this way, three weeks passed before they arrived at Hirpur.

As was the custom, the constable took Bhaiji to meet Anandji, a mahatma who lived near Hirpur. They arrived at nine in the morning. The mahatma, on seeing them, promptly turned his back and went to sleep. Two hours passed. Finally, the constable suggested to Bhaiji that the mahatma was showing no signs of awaking, and they had better be on their way home.

Although, so far, there had been no mention of the medicines or herbs, it so happened that Bhaiji had already started feeling much better. His stomach had improved because of the enforced and continuous fasting. He felt an urgency to return to Srinagar because his father would be worried. He wished to put an end to this daily aimlessness. After some persuasion, the constable let him go but pressed upon him a small packet containing food for the journey.

Early next morning, Bhaiji set out. When he had barely cleared Hirpur, the pony began to stumble so much that Bhaiji eventually had to get down and lead the pony. As daylight flooded the valley, they trudged together, Bhaiji in front and the borrowed pony following behind contentedly. In this manner, like Don Quixote and his faithful steed, they neared Shopian, which was not far from Srinagar. Here, he found a group of traders saddling their horses for the ride into Srinagar and beyond. They agreed to allow Bhaiji to accompany them.

About an hour or so out of Shopian, the traders stopped for their meal. Their horses were let free to graze but all of them were on one side of the hill. This happened without a word to Bhaiji. Intending to be clever, Bhaiji thought he would let his pony free to graze on the other side alone, where he would get more grass. Having done so, he was proceeding to the other side when he heard the cry of a shepherd boy. Scrambling back, he found his pony almost up to its belly in a swamp, which was why the traders did not let their horses free on the other side of the hill. Handing his switch to the boy, Bhaiji ordered him to beat the rump of the pony while he tried to pull it out by the reins. After 10 minutes of frenzied exertion and beatings, finally the pony was safely out on the bank, dripping in mud. Convinced now that the traders were utterly heartless men who would knife him at the slightest provocation, Bhaiji waved goodbye and leaping upon his still muddy pony, rode out of sight. Dismounting at a safe distance, Don Quixote and his steed resumed their patient trek to Srinagar, the master grandly in the front, brandishing a willow switch, and the pony stumbling docilely behind.

The trek was interrupted again by a flowing stream, which Bhaiji navigated by jumping nimbly from rock to rock, rein in hand. Midstream, however, the pony stopped and lowered its head for a drink. Bhaiji, interrupted while jumping between two rocks, fell into the ice cold water.

After finally making it out of the stream, the muddy horse and its now dripping master proceeded on the path to Srinagar. They stopped only for some grass to be cut for the pony, which Bhaiji, for lack of anything else, carried in his tussore turban. They sat down together by a spring to have their mid-day meal provided by the constable. The *tsaman* was, however, fiery hot, loaded with chillies, and Bhaiji could only eat it with liberal gulps of spring water. Desperately hungry, he stopped at the nearest village and asked if milk was available. Since he was still an orthodox then, he could not eat the kulcha and *tsotchavur* sold freely in the Muslim shops. After finding some milk, he faced the problem of drinking it from a vessel kept in a Muslim shop. Faced with such a dire situation and extremely hungry, Bhaiji made a spout from his handy tussore turban, spilling three fourths of the milk on the ground and upon his coat, which had dried by then, in the process.

By evening, he was near Srinagar and passing through fields when some pretty and pert Kashmiri peasant girls crossed him and started giggling at the sight of a turban-less boy leading a mud-crusted pony through the fields. Humiliated, Bhaiji was determined to show these irritating girls how virile he actually was! Leaping nonchalantly onto the saddle, he brought the switch down smartly on the rump of the pony. Unused to such ministrations throughout the day, the pony kicked up its heels, sending Bhaiji tumbling into the rice field. Picking himself up with as much dignity as possible, Bhaiji dragged away the cussed pony, his ears red from hearing the laughter of the Kashmiri peasant girls.

Later, Bhaiji met a peasant who was also going to Srinagar and offered to pay him to whip the pony from behind while he dragged it from the front. In this way, they passed the octroi post, where Bhaiji drank a gallon of water. When he finally reached home, he had a gargantuan meal of haak and batha with zamadod before falling asleep, not waking up until the following morning.

Thus ended the tale of the miracle cure of Hirpur—without any herbs or medicines other than a month of enforced fasting, which led to Bhaiji being cured! Eventually, he would also be cured of his early orthodoxy.

∽

The Kaks had made their livelihood as kardars for the government and earned something for themselves as well. However, with the accession of Maharaja Pratap Singh in 1885, the system of administration underwent a fundamental change involving, among other things, the abolition of kardari, which led to a loss for the administration. Govind Kak, Bhaiji's father, was offered a position in the Dharmarth Trust as a compensation for his loss of kardari, but he declined and spent his life as a celibate, in meditation and prayer. He had some liquid assets, out of which he provided sufficient capital to give a head start to his eldest son, Bhaigash, in the money lending and retail business. Govind Kak and his two brothers, Deva Kak and Gula Kak, lived jointly with their respective families as one household, until Gula Kak expressed a desire to separate. Since his wife had died in an epidemic of cholera, his son Sridhar Kak's wife had started exercising greater authority in the household. She insisted on separating their branch from the joint family, where she was still subordinate to the senior ladies, particularly Govind Kak's wife. Govind Kak tried unsuccessfully to dissuade his brother from this course. Finally, he said that instead of Gula Kak leaving, he would leave and stay in the old house nearby. He left all the utensils in the kitchen and the new house to Gula Kak, and started refurbishing his household again from scratch in the old house, along with Deva Kak and his family, who also decided to stay with him. By the turn of the century, in spite of Govind Kak's efforts, fissures had begun showing in the age-old joint family system of the Kaks.

Bhaiji's earliest recollections were from around the age of four. He remembered his parents, Wagri and Bhaigash, his grandparents, and uncles, Deva and Gula Kak. Bhaiji's parents tried to teach him the rudiments of the alphabet at this stage but not very successfully. Bhaiji used to decamp to Deva Kak's room, which no one dared to enter till he had his meal in the early afternoon. Then, Bhaiji used to run out to play, often with a little cousin sister, but would immediately run back to Deva Kak's room at the slightest hint of danger.

Bhaiji and Deva Kak did not make much conversation. The former used to simply sit and, sometimes, the old man used to chat with him. Bhaiji's job then, and for many years, was to prepare *panak* for Deva Kak. The dried leaves would be placed on a paper and heated over a *kangri* till they became crackly. Then, they would be ground on a pestle and mixed with almonds, raisins and cardamom powder, heated and allowed to cool before drinking. Bhaiji was allowed to sip a thimbleful as Deva Kak gulped down his glass. This *bhaang*-like drink would be prepared invariably on Shivaratri for the whole family, but Deva Kak celebrated Shivaratri every day!

Soon, it was felt that Bhaiji should be disciplined and sent to school. This onerous job of escorting Bhaiji back and forth and making sure he stayed in school was assigned to a trusted aide of Bhaigash, called Kish Mam. For this purpose, Kish Mam carried nettles with him, and each time Bhaiji attempted to skip class, Kish Mam spanked his bare bottom with it.

By the time Bhaiji began his senior secondary schooling, he was already outstripping other students and nursed ambitions of writing a book on mathematics. To this end, he devised endless sums featuring addition, subtraction, multiplication and such, in association with a fellow student named Bamzai. The book fizzled out when Bhaiji moved ahead. Around 1905–06, he joined the Hindu High School, where S.P. Moore taught him whatever he knew about English.

Moore would bring a copy of the book *Quentin Durward* by Sir Walter Scott, take it back after class and ask questions based on that reading. By the end of the month, he would set a test with an invariable reference to context, which was naturally difficult, as their books could not be in hand, except during class. Similarly, he would dictate a poem from memory, ask the class to close the book and repeat the six stanzas from their memories. By the time he came to the last few students from the class, they would indeed know the poem by heart. Moore was the principal until Bhaiji finished school and was responsible for Bhaiji's excellent command over English. Eventually, Bhaiji won a scholarship—offered by the Hindu High School—of ₹3 and 8 annas, leaving him a balance of ₹1 and 4 annas after the payment of fees, which were ₹2 a year with 4 annas as sports fees. He placed his first earning with a triumphant flourish before Bhaigash.

Once, in his second year at the Hindu High School, Bhaiji's life was fortuitously saved. He was the captain of the boating team and he happened to go out for a practice boat ride on the Dal Lake with some fellow students. The trip ended in disaster, as the boat overturned around Gagribal point, which is not far from the shore, and the team had to put it right side up again. Bhaiji, however, had been feeling some rheumatic pain in his arms, and he realised that he would not be able to stay afloat for the length of time needed to turn the boat back around. So, he struck out for the bank by himself. Midway, he got so exhausted that he found it impossible to continue. He thought his time had come. To make matters worse, he saw Gyani Ram, the Mathematics teacher with whom he had a long-running dispute, sitting opposite bank and thought, *how this man must be gloating!* Hopelessly entangled in a clutch of weeds, Bhaiji resigned himself to his fate and sank. As luck would have it, his feet touched the ground while his chin still remained just above the water. He was saved! He stumbled gratefully to the bank and was pulled out by Gyani Ram and a few other students who had been watching.

Bhaiji narrated these stories of his childhood to me with a touch of amusement, prompted by my naive questioning, which was more provocative than probing. I should perhaps have interviewed Bended as well, but I think I was unaware of her extensive notes on the history of the Kak joint family. Due to my immature assumptions, I lost her deep perspective not only of family history but also of the social conditions of Kashmir in the 1930s. Luckily, with the discovery of some of her writings and Billy preserving her letters, we still have an invaluable record of those times, which reveal the personal fabric of Kashmir in those days.

In 1913, in order to complete his BA degree from Sri Pratap College, commonly known as SP College, Bhaiji appeared for his final third-year examination, which was conducted at a centre in Lahore. The trip to Lahore and back was an odyssey lasting two or three weeks. This critical examination was to be taken by 13 boys, including the toppers—R.C. Pandita and T.C. Wazir—along with Bhaiji's great friends, Samsar Chand Vaishnavi and Brij Krishen Madan. Bhaiji's elder brother, Bab, was to be their chaperone. Bhaiji, Bab and Samsar Chand set out together with Kesho Ram, the Kaks' trusted cook, in a four-wheeled carriage to their first stop at Rawalpindi. Bhaigash saw them off and told Kesho Ram, 'I have entrusted you with all my wealth—it is for you now to render an account of it!' Though Kesho Ram cooked the food, the boys fetched the wood and laid out the dishes. Cooks had an elevated status then, like family members who had served for generations.

From Rawalpindi, all the boys got on a train to Lahore. Once there, they stayed together in a large hall in Dhan Singh's haveli. It was a tough exam and an anxious time for the boys without their families. Once the examination was over, they all returned to Rawalpindi by train and stayed overnight at a charitable institution, known as Dharampura, run by one Sevak Ram. The next day, they all chartered tongas to take them back home. Bhaiji and Samsar Chand, being the junior-most members of the group, got the most miserable tonga and hack pony. They brought up the rear of the procession.

In those days, there was a very grand *dak tonga* that Bhaiji remembered carrying the mail, changing horses at each stop so that the distance to Srinagar was covered in three days rather than five. Their ponies were well-bred, powerful beasts, and their riders, tall, swashbuckling Pathans, who would blow dramatically upon their bugles, warning of their approach, rather like the piercing klaxons of highway trucks today.

Figure 3: Returning from Lahore in the dak tonga in 1913

Illustration credit: Kashmira Tembulkar

Unfortunately, this sound, or for that matter any sound, panicked the inexperienced pony hitched to Bhaiji's tonga and it reared up and neighed wildly when the dak tonga passed by! The whole tonga procession came to a grinding halt and the occupants of the five tongas sat on the panicked horse to try and prevent it from rearing. This became so frequent and exasperating that it was decided to travel by night, so that the horse would be less disturbed by road traffic. The only danger of travelling at night was that one could fall asleep and fall out of the tonga! This lengthy odyssey to Lahore, full of unexpected adventures, had a happy ending at least for Bhaiji, whose career began unexpectedly after it with a flourish.

5

The Unexpected Archaeologist

In 1913, ironically, Bhaiji crossed paths with another outstanding Kashmiri Pandit, Tara Chand Wazir, who 30 years later, was to become his *samdhi*, or relative, not only being the father of Kamla, Bhaiji's eldest son Narendra Nath's bride but also of Sarla (née Radha), his youngest son Surendra Nath's bride—my parents!

My maternal grandfather, Pandit Tara Chand Wazir, or Papaji as we called him, was an outstanding student and had topped his class. His professor offered him a scholarship to embark on an archaeological career with the first assignment outside Kashmir. Coming from a conservative family where travel outside Kashmir was unheard of because of imagined dangers, Papaji regretfully refused this plum assignment. As luck would have it, the position required mastery over Sanskrit, and due to Papaji's reluctant refusal, Bhaiji got the assignment, although his ranking had been lower. This had far-reaching consequences for Bhaiji's career. He became the very first and only student in Professor Chakravarty's new Master of Arts (MA) class for Sanskrit. Professor Chakravarty, who was the principal of SP college, was so pleased with Bhaiji joining his MA Sanskrit class that he appointed him as the librarian of SP College at the princely sum of ₹50 a month!

This was a large sum in those days and it gave Bhaiji the freedom to do much else because there was not much formal work at the library. Bhaiji said his salary also encouraged Bhaigash to finally quit the money lending and paper goods business in which he had been incurring losses and begin farming in the Rawalpura district, which he continued till the end of his life.

Once Bhaiji joined the Archaeological Survey of Kashmir, he felt he had found his calling. It was his good fortune to receive invaluable training from the legendary archaeologist Sir John Marshall, who was a strict taskmaster and later from another legendary figure, Sir Mark Aurel Stein. Sir John, then director general (DG) of archaeology in India (a post he held for 30 years, refusing appointments as secretary to the government, which he called a clerk's job) was over 6-feet tall, well-built and impressive looking. His manner of speaking was brusque but without malice.

He was extremely considerate and affectionate to his staff. Once, while returning to Takshashila after a tour, he found a large group of people assembled at the railway station to meet him. At one end were Dr Spooner, the famous American polyglot, and Blackstone, deputy DG of archaeology, one step Sir John's junior and so on, down to Kama, the *chowkidar* of his bungalow in Takshashila. Gazing over the heads of the venerable delegation, Sir John spotted Kama and strode directly to him, shaking him vigorously by the hand and booming, 'How are you Kama, how are you? Good old man.' And then going up the line shaking hands, last of all with Dr Spooner.

Bhaiji's archaeological training under Sir John took him to Takshashila, Sanchi and other places in India, where latter was carrying out excavations. According to Bhaiji, his first meeting with Sir John was not a great success. When Bhaiji put it to him that he was training to be superintendent of archaeology in Kashmir, Sir John Marshall barked, 'It will take you 20 years before you are fit to be appointed to the post of superintendent of archaeology!' Bhaiji replied calmly that he was prepared for this, and even if it took 20 years, he had to start somewhere. Sir John eyed him fiercely before striding off wordlessly.

Figure 4: A young bearded Bhaiji interning under Sir John at Takshashila in 1913
Illustration credit: Kashmira Tembulkar

Despite the rocky start, Bhaiji's training began. After three to four days, Sir John noticed Bhaiji roaming aimlessly near a site and angrily demanded, 'What are you doing? Haven't you got any work?' When Bhaiji said he did not, Sir John wrote a note on a scrap of paper he found in his pocket and handed it to Bhaiji. It read: 'Mr Ghosh, give Mr Kak work!' The next day, Mr Ghosh appointed Bhaiji in charge of a gang of men excavating a particular section. In the afternoon, Sir John came on an inspection round and passed by Bhaiji without saying a word. Upon returning, he wrote a note to Mr Ghosh, which read: 'Please hand over all work to Mr Kak,' and deputed Ghosh to work on another site!

Eventually, Sir John had to go on tour, but he did not allow Bhaiji to accompany him. Instead, he asked Bhaiji to draft a five-page letter of instructions to carry out in his absence, which he signed before leaving. Three months later, upon returning, he asked Bhaiji what had been done. Bhaiji replied that they had been working satisfactorily. Sir John snapped, 'I will see whether you have really worked. I will inspect the site this afternoon.'

When he turned up, Bhaiji began to explain the work, but Sir John cut him short, saying, 'You need not explain anything. I can see for myself.' He went around the entire site for one and a half hours without uttering a word, Bhaiji following behind at attention, as it were. At the end of it all, Bhaiji ventured to say, 'Goodbye, Sir.' Sir John curtly responded with a 'Goodbye!' As he started walking away, he suddenly turned around and told Bhaiji, 'Let me tell you this. You have done the work here exactly as I would have done it,' before stalking off.

It so happened that once, at Takshashila, Bhaiji was rude and stand-offish to Sir John in front of a lady friend. Later, John Marshall sent for him and told him angrily that he could have him dismissed for such behaviour. Bhaiji explained that he had walked several miles, though he wasn't well, to a site in response to Sir John's message and said that the latter had not turned up. Apparently, Sir John's message cancelling Bhaiji's visit had not reached him. Finally, Sir John advised him, quite kindly, that it was no good being so thorny and that it might do him good if he occasionally oiled the wheels and was less abrasive. This was an early indication of Bhaiji's uncompromising nature, which was to cause him complications later.

Bhaiji exhibited this uncompromising character even while accepting a report for completing his work in the Central Archaeology Department from his superiors. It so happened that when Bhaiji's term of training came to a close, Sir John was away in England on leave and Dr Spooner was in the hospital. Blackstone, as the officiating DG, wrote Bhaiji's report, but the latter refused to accept it. When Dr Spooner called him and asked him why, Bhaiji explained, 'Well, if you must know the truth, I don't think Dr Blackstone is competent to make a report on my work!'

'He is the DG,' Dr Spooner said.

'[...] If when you are well, perhaps you would write a report and when Sir John returns, perhaps he may also wish to write something?' Bhaiji replied and returned to Kashmir without taking Blackstone's report. Later, both Dr Spooner and Sir John later wrote reports on Bhaiji's work.

Eventually, Bhaiji was appointed the superintendent of archaeology for Kashmir, after having trained with the Archaeological Survey of India (ASI) for roughly three years in the state and two years outside. He proved himself capable well before the 20 years predicted for him by Sir John! As the superintendent of archaeology for Kashmir, Bhaiji also served as the curator of the Shri Pratap Museum and much preferred to sit in the curator's office, which was a large and pleasant room. Being the curator gave Bhaiji unparalleled access to books in English, Sanskrit and Persian. He became proficient in all three, laying the foundation for his archaeological career and his evolution into one of the wisest human beings I have known!

One day, Mr Andrews, the head of the Technical Institute of Kashmir, a rather pompous Englishman, came to see the curator. He did not know that Bhaiji had replaced the earlier curator, Pandit Hiranand Shastri. He was horrified to see Bhaiji sitting in his shirtsleeves in the curator's room, as no Indian could greet an Englishman in his office without a coat. Seeing that Bhaiji was not going to put on his coat, Andrews said abruptly, 'You must leave the room!'

Bhaiji quietly got up and left. Andrews then tried to locate the curator but, naturally, could not find him. At his wits' end, he asked the *chaprasi*, 'Where is the curator?' The chaprasi tilted his head towards Bhaiji, who was lounging outside. Quite baffled and unable to approach Bhaiji with dignity, Andrews marched out in a huff and Bhaiji again quietly entered the office and resumed work. This quiet stoicism was typical of Bhaiji. He never overreacted. I have rarely, if ever, seen him lose his temper. His calm and unruffled temperament enabled him to face abusive actions, threats and even imprisonment with dignity and fortitude three decades later.

Bhaiji was soon promoted to be the director of the newly formed Archaeology and Research Department in Kashmir. He also acted as the director of the local archaeological survey for 10 years, between 1919 and 1929, a term that was attested to by Sir John, who commented on the improved state of the ancient buildings in Kashmir. During this time, he also prepared a scientific catalogue of the collection in the Shri Pratap Museum, Srinagar. While still serving the state in this position, he was appointed as the librarian of Maharaja Hari Singh's private royal library that housed more than 275 Sanskrit manuscripts and 800 rare works prepared with the assistance of Pandit Hara Bhat Shastri, Bhaigash's close friend. As a result of Bhaiji's distinguished services to the cause of archaeology, the Government of India proposed to hire him permanently at the ASI, but the proposal was not agreed to by the Government of Kashmir and the move was dropped.

In 'Ram Chandra Kak: An Intellectual with Integrity', a comprehensive feature on Bhaiji, S.N. Pandita wrote:

> With these pioneering archaeological works in Kashmir, Ram Chandra Kak's research threw light on the earliest period of Kashmir's art and history from the 6th century onwards, the most remarkable results of which came from his work in 1925 A.D. at Harwan near the famous Shalimar Garden in Srinagar. The discoveries made by him here included the findings of foundations of old temples belonging to the 3rd and 4th century [*sic*] and large courtyard of terracotta tiles with features of Central Asian influence. The brief results of this work were however first published by R.C. Kak in the illustrated *London News* in October 1925 and only later in greater details with profuse illustrations in his much acclaimed work *The Ancient Monuments of Kashmir*.[6]

[6]Pandita, S.N., 'Ram Chandra Kak: An Intellectual with Integrity', *Naad*, July 2007, https://tinyurl.com/583jbrmz. Accessed on 11 May 2023.

Bhaiji felt an unexpected affinity with archaeology. It appealed to his innermost instincts. He was a private person, given to reflection and reading. Archaeology gave him an opportunity to consult Persian, Sanskrit and English books without fanfare. He was a patriot and being an archaeologist, in his heart, was an act of patriotism. In his 10 years as the director of Archaeological Survey of Kashmir, he became an expert in the archaeological history of the state. His travels and research resulted in publications like the *Memoirs of the Archaeological Survey of Kashmir: Antiquities of Marev-Wadwan*[7], *A Handbook of Archaeological and Numismatics Sections of Shri Pratap Museum Srinagar*[8], *Memoirs of the Archaeological Survey of India: Antiquities of Bhimbar and Rajauri*[9], among others. His magnum opus *Ancient Monuments of Kashmir*[10] was written in 1922.

The writing and photography of *Ancient Monuments of Kashmir*, a comprehensive work, has been unrivalled in the over 100 years since it was first written. After returning to Kashmir in 1919, Bhaiji toured the entire state on foot or by tonga or bicycle. After three years of hard work, he completed the book in 1921.

In fact, he bought a motorcycle to help him with his travels in about 1920 for ₹600. But, it was more of a hindrance than a help. It kept stopping and breaking down every few miles. The longest trip that Bhaiji could make was to Pattan, which was 27 kilometres away. Later, he realised that the engine was painted red, in contrast to the black body, because it had met with an accident and the engine had to be replaced. Eventually, Bhaiji sold the motorcycle after a few months for a meagre ₹150!

The saga of the *Ancient Monuments of Kashmir* was a lesson

---

[7]Kak, Ram Chadra, *Memoirs of the Archaeological Survey of Kashmir: Antiquities of Marev-Wadwan,* The Archeological Survey of Kashmir, 1924.

[8]Kak, Ram Chandra, *Handbook of the Archaeological and Numismatic Sections of the Sri Pratap Singh Museum, Srinagar,* Thacker, Spink & Co., Calcutta, 1923.

[9]Kak, Ram Chandra, *Memoirs of the Archaeological Survey of India: Antiquities of Bhimbar and Rajauri,* Archeological Survey of India, New Delhi, 1998.

[10]Kak, Ram Chandra, *Ancient Monuments of Kashmir,* The India Society, London, 1933.

in bureaucracy. Bhaiji had found a publisher in The India Society of England and even received permission from the Maharaja to publish the volume, provided he deleted two paragraphs as desired by the Maharaja, which was, perhaps, derogatory to Dogra rule. He refused to do so. For 10 long years, *Ancient Monuments of Kashmir* remained unpublished. Meanwhile, Bhaiji was seconded from the archaeological department to the state's political administration, much against his will. However, his integrity and determination left the Maharaja to grudgingly admiring him.

When Bhaiji was directly serving the Maharaja, better sense finally prevailed on the former and he deleted the objectionable lines from his magnum opus. *Ancient Monuments of Kashmir* was eventually published and remains a classic to this day. There has been no contemporary study of Kashmir's monuments as comprehensive as Bhaiji's!

Commending his epic book, in the introduction of the *Ancient Monuments of Kashmir*, the eminent French archaeologist, Alfred Foucher, attested:

> It seems almost miraculous that after a single generation, one of their [Kashmiri Pandits'] descendants [Ram Chandra Kak] is able to write in English, a work so judicially critical on the antiquities of his country. But the miracle is explained: let us add this to spare the author's personal modesty—first by exceptional intellectual qualities of the race; then by excellent teaching now offered at the Government College of Srinagar affiliated to Punjab University and lastly by the five years of archaeological training (1914–19), which Mr R.C. Kak spent in India under the incomparable direction of Sir John Marshall.[11]

The volume and the way it was written, in some way, are symbolic of Bhaiji, the man. The text is meticulous. The details and historical context are impeccable. There is no humour or storytelling. Just

[11]Ibid.

the facts—bald and clearly stated. This was Bhaiji's personality, even as the PM of Kashmir. A man of great integrity, honesty and austerity, he was devoted to the facts and truth, remote and introspective, distant even from his family and children, who were in awe of him. He acted without fear or favour. This was perhaps his undoing on the political stage.

After Bhaiji took charge of the Shri Pratap Singh Museum and Library on 10 October 1919, the number of visitors went up in the very first year from about 70,000 to 100,000. The archaeological section, which had received little to no attention before, was taken in hand. Especially designed showcases were made for the sculptures and antiquities for an exhibition in honour of the Viceroy Lord Chelmsford's visit in 1921.

Bhaiji's dedication and stern efficiency transformed the museum despite the meagre funds of a few thousand rupees a year being available. The annual budget of the department used to be about ₹6,000, of which over ₹5,000 lapsed in 1917–18. Thus, only about ₹1,000 were left annually for museum upkeep and staff. In recognition of Bhaiji's exceptional services, on 8 April 1921, a confirmation letter was sent to the Home Minister of Kashmir recommending an increase in pay.

Though Bhaiji's career in the archaeological service of Kashmir was on an ascending graph, the Maharaja of Kashmir's appreciation of Bhaiji's stern efficiency, coupled with his disdain for the study of archaeology, was to have a profound impact on Bhaiji's growing archaeological career. The Maharaja did not allow his deputation to the ASI when the request came from the Centre soon after his early publications. Subsequently, another proposal to take over Bhaiji's services completely and compensate the state for all expenses incurred in his training again came from the central government. This time the Maharaja said, 'If he wants to go, let him resign and go.'

At that time, in 1927, Bhaiji's first wife, Janaki Devi, was desperately ill with tuberculosis in Pahalgam. It was impossible for Bhaiji to resign and leave the state considering her condition.

Much to his regret, he had to refuse the offer, which might have changed his career and future standing. Janaki Devi died in 1928.

One day, Bhaiji was summoned by the Chief Secretary George Edward Campbell Wakefield OBE and informed that the Maharaja wanted him to switch from archaeology to civil administration, but he had one condition. That condition was made clear when Wakefield took out a Gillette razor! So it was that Bhaiji shaved and joined the civil administration. He never grew a beard again nor wrote another book on archaeology.

As it turns out, archaeological service is permanent and politics is ephemeral! Had Bhaiji been transferred to the Centre, he would, perhaps, by the time India gained independence in 1947, have risen to become DG of the ASI, like his mentor Sir John, and interpreted many facets of Indian history, instead of becoming a controversial part of that history!

When Bhaiji severed his links with the Archaeological Survey of Kashmir and joined the state administration as political secretary in 1929, he had no idea that he had set in motion a series of steps that would inevitably lead to his becoming embroiled in a critical period of India's history in 1947.

6

The Iron Man

One day, while cataloguing the works in the Maharaja's Sanskrit library, Bhaiji happened to run into the then Foreign Secretary of the Maharaja, George Wakefield. Wakefield was an Anglo-Indian civil servant, who eventually served as the PM of Kashmir between 1929 and 1931. A tall and jovial man, he requested Bhaiji's help in drafting the annual reports, which had fallen six years in arrears. Bhaiji agreed and, in some days, made the necessary summaries. Bhaiji recalled that for the final reports, he took Madho Ram, his servant, in a shikara and went out to Telabal, where the Dara stream meets the Dal Lake, and wrote all day sitting in a willow grove while Madho Ram prepared tea and food. The reports were handed in next day, much to the satisfaction of Wakefield.

Wakefield became quite fond of Bhaiji and appointed him in charge of catering arrangements for the visits of the Viceroy Lord Irwin in 1924 and 1927, as well as for the Maharaja's coronation in 1925, during which there were huge separate princely camps—Jodhpur, Gwalior, Bikaner, Baroda, Kutch, etc.—with a senior state officer in charge of each camp reporting to Bhaiji for catering.

This brought Bhaiji close to the Maharaja's administrative camp. An impressed Wakefield told Bhaiji that the Maharaja felt he should leave archaeology and join the administrative service as a foreign secretary, which involved liaising with the Government of India. Bhaiji was reluctant and said he would join on the condition that he continued to hold charge of the Archaeological Survey of

Kashmir. A month later, however, someone else was appointed foreign secretary. Nonetheless, Bhaiji continued to occasionally work for Wakefield, whenever required.

Figure 5: Bhaiji writing the annual reports in a shikara at Telbal, near Dal Lake, for Wakefield, then foreign secretary of Kashmir, 1928
Illustration credit: Kashmira Tembulkar

For the Viceroy's visit in 1927, Bhaiji was requisitioned, because of his excellent knowledge and drafting skills, to write a general introductory note on Kashmir. Bhaiji recalled writing 60 or 70 pages, which were much appreciated by P.K. Watal, then private secretary to the Maharaja.

But there was a problem. The Maharaja did not approve of the draft. In short, he wanted the history of Kashmir to start from the reign of his forefathers. There was consternation. It was past 11.00 p.m. then. Bhaiji sat up till 4.00 a.m. and wrote the full new draft in one sitting while his assistants provided him tea and dinner and sat with him. Eventually, they walked back

4 kilometres to their houses on the Canal Bank in Jammu. Next morning, Watal was full of praise saying, 'Only Bhaiji could have done such a thing!' Bhaiji was a serious worker and developed a reputation for efficiency and integrity. This came to the notice of the inner circle of the Maharaja, but there were several false alarms about Bhaiji's elevation to the Maharaja's administration.

The Raja of Poonch, Sukhdev Singh, needed a strong man to replace McDermott, his resident officer at Poonch in 1927. Following the precedent, the Government of India wanted a British officer. But the Raja of Poonch insisted on an Indian officer. Finally, it was agreed that if Bhaiji went to Poonch as the Resident, it would be acceptable to the Kashmir government. Watal apprised Bhaiji of the situation and told him that the appointment would be discussed and confirmed with the Maharaja upon his return from a shooting expedition in Ladakh. Meanwhile, Bhaiji's replacement had arrived from Gilgit but had to hang back, as Bhaiji refused to relinquish his office till he got formal posting orders. When the Maharaja arrived, the transfer was confirmed and Bhaiji was ready to go. The Raja of Poonch went back from Srinagar to Poonch to celebrate his birthday along with McDermott. Bhaiji was to join him the following week. The Raja of Poonch was a heavy drinker and, unfortunately, died during his birthday celebrations. The whole matter was then dropped, and Bhaiji's replacement returned to Gilgit. Such was the uncertainty in administrative affairs in those days.

In 1929, Watal made another proposal to appoint Bhaiji to the higher administrative post of secretary to the council. The understanding was that Bhaiji would get the post, the proposal being a formality. Bhaiji himself drafted the proposal for Watal's signature. The proposal came back with the Maharaja's comment the next day. Watal was too embarrassed to see Bhaiji all morning. Finally, he sent for him in the afternoon and pointed to the Maharaja's comment, which read: 'Pandit R.C. Kak may be appointed director of archaeology!'

The Maharaja was under the impression that this was a higher post whereas the other one carried both higher powers and pay. The Maharaja did realise his mistake later and Bhaiji was appointed foreign secretary, relinquishing charge of the archaeological survey and four months later, becoming foreign and political secretary, with the individual post of foreign secretary being abolished. Leaving behind his first love, archaeology—which he had served for 10 years, till 1929, both as superintendent and as director—Bhaiji's political and administrative career took off. Now answerable directly to the Maharaja, a new adventure began.

Bhaiji learnt the ropes and displayed exceptional administrative abilities. From being the political and foreign secretary (1929–31), he was appointed as the inspector general (IG) of customs and excise (1932–37), chief secretary and political adviser to the Maharaja (1937–41) and army minister and minister-in-waiting from 1941. The wait was long! Finally, in 1945, he was appointed the PM of Kashmir.

Wakefield's fondness for Bhaiji became a liability. His useful drafting skills made Wakefield reluctant to allow Bhaiji's transfer as IG customs and excise, even though he had been nominated for it. Wakefield offered Bhaiji a pay rise from ₹700 to ₹1,000, which he refused, as the IG's post carried a salary of ₹1,500.

Bhaiji was also good friends with Colonel Colvin, who headed political services and later took over from Wakefield as the PM of Kashmir between 1932 and 1934. Colonel Colvin helped Bhaiji get a transfer from the post of political secretary to the superior post of IG customs in spite of Wakefield's objections.

In those days, Kashmir was a haven for retired civil officers, such as Colonel Colvin, Colonel Miller, the chief medical officer of Kashmir who had formerly been the DG of medicine in India, and Sir Peter Clutterbuck, the forest minister, among others. Theirs were prize posts, with good houses in pleasant settings offering good fishing and leisure. So they would often come to Bhaiji when he was IG customs, and he would help them clear their baggage through customs.

Bhaiji told me a number of stories of the circular nature of the

Kashmir administration. For instance, when Bhaiji was still political secretary in 1931, Raja Hari Kishan Kaul, who had been PM for a few months and did not like Bhaiji's demeanour, refused to give him work apart from preparing the daily situation report, which could only be done after all the reports came in the evening, at about 8.00 p.m. All day, Bhaiji used to sit idly and then have to stay back in office till late at night to complete the report. Once, a letter came for the Maharaja from the chairman of the Council of Princes and the Maharaja, as was his wont, scribbled that Bhaiji should draft a reply. Raja Hari Kishan passed the letter on to Bhaiji for reply but refused to let him see the file, saying it was confidential. Annoyed, Bhaiji said that in that case, Raja Hari Kishan could tell the Maharaja that he would not draft the reply and that this was another example of his unfairness, the other being kept without work deliberately for the past month. Raja Hari Kishan had to give in because of the Maharaja's express instructions.

Raja Hari Kishan was PM for less than a year and did not do too well. Bhaiji explained to me the difference between working for the British Government of India and for a princely state. Raja Hari Kishan worked for Punjab Provincial Service as finance commissioner and won much praise. Rules were set for everything and if they were followed, a successful career was assured. Besides, in Punjab administration, there was stability. A Patwari knew he had the administration's support, right up to the chief secretary. In Kashmir, however, the only rules were made at the whim of the Maharaja and if there was a slip up, there was no backing or support. For good work, the credit went to the Maharaja and for bad work, the subordinate got sacked. In the changed circumstances, Raja Hari Kishan fared poorly and lasted a very short time.

Administration, as might be imagined, was more the art of procrastination veiled under the guise of executive action. Bhaiji perhaps realised he was enmeshed in this cynical web, and sometimes used it in the game of one-upmanship indulged in by the Kashmir administration. Bhaiji's proud approach and ability to manoeuvre within bureaucratic norms ruffled quite a few feathers. For instance, the then Chief Justice and officiating PM of Kashmir, Sir Burjor Dalal, the first Parsi ICS and a judge of the High Court, had irritating *burra sahib* mannerisms, such as getting extremely annoyed if other cars did not stop while he was passing by. Bhaiji and Sir Burjor detested each other. One day, when questioned if he was going to Bhaiji's place to attend a ceremony being held for his elder brother, Bab, Sir Burjor snapped back, 'Go to that damn fellow, never!' Bhaiji found Sir Burjor's quirks amusing and got the better of him several times using both the system and simple logic.

Once, Bhaiji had just returned from England after six weeks, having attended a round-table conference, and found an order from Sir Burjor appointing an anti-corruption commission. The order stated that all the names and records of the personnel in his department were to be handed over to Sir Burjor by the end of the month. Bhaiji waited for a month and then sent a letter to Kartar Singh, the finance minister and his boss, referring to the order and asserting that he had the full authority to deal with corruption in his own department without a second party interfering. Sir Burjor wrote back a furious reply that he had been authorised by the Maharaja to carry out an investigation, that this was rank insubordination and that he had the authority to dismiss officials higher than the IG Customs (that is to say, finance minister Kartar Singh himself) and that the information must be handed over in a month. Kartar Singh, who was in on the game, passed on this letter to Bhaiji, without comment.

Bhaiji waited a month and then went to personally see Sir Burjor. 'Yes,' said Sir Burjor testily upon seeing Bhaiji. 'What is it?' he demanded.

Bhaiji explained that there was no corruption in his department and since he knew his men and had the authority, he would not tolerate any corruption in the ranks. Any corrupt man would be dismissed at once.

'What do you want then?' Sir Burjor almost shouted, becoming apoplectic.

Bhaiji said he would reply to Sir Burjor's letter stating that he had explained the matter to Sir Burjor and there was no need to proceed with the matter.

'Alright,' said Sir Burjor gruffly, concealing his embarrassment at having lost the round.

If indeed the commission on corruption had been as important as Sir Burjor had made it out to be, the officiating chief minister would most certainly have taken some action during the two or three months it took to resolve the issue, supposedly on the suggestion of the Maharaja. Such was the chaotic state of affairs under a whimsical administration.

Once, Bhaiji even had a run in once with N. Gopalaswami Ayyangar, who was the PM of Kashmir for six years, from 1934 to 1939—the longest tenure for a PM of Kashmir. Bhaiji had been hospitalised for six weeks, having been operated on for a fissure. For some reason, no one attended to his files during his absence and, on being discharged, he found six trunks full of files awaiting his scrutiny, even for trivial matters. By this time, Bhaiji was chief secretary and, in due course, he sent up the files to Ayyangar who was absolutely furious at the delay, scribbling in the margin: 'What has the chief secretary been doing all this time? Why have these files not been disposed of earlier?'

Bhaiji went to see Ayyangar, who vented without allowing Bhaiji to speak. Bhaiji finally got a word in, explained that he had been in hospital and the files could have even been seen by the deputy secretary and perhaps even Ayyangar himself. Ayyangar then cooled off but did not expunge his remarks nor did Bhaiji ask him to. The remark went into the file, where it remains till date.

On another occasion, while Bhaiji was still the chief secretary, Ayyangar asked him to make a full report on tourism development in the state. When submitting the report, Bhaiji, in his covering note, added, as a courtesy to Ayyangar, 'Kindly incorporate anything else you may deem fit.' The report was sent at about 4.00 p.m. to Ayyangar's residence by dispatch rider and came back in an hour with Ayyangar's angry comment, which read: 'The Chief Secy has been wasting my time. I have no time to go through incomplete reports. The full report must be submitted to me by tomorrow!'

Apparently, Ayyangar had looked at only the covering note and not the report itself. Bhaiji tore up the paper and comments and wrote a fresh, formal note and had the report sent back with the same dispatch rider. The updated note read: 'Sir, I have the honour to submit the Tourism Development Report, complete in all respects [...]'

Later, he met the minister Chetram Chopra and asked how the Tourism Development Report was getting on. The Minister threw up his hands and exclaimed, 'Kaksaheb, you have finished us. Once you finished your report, there was nothing else for us to do. Whatever we have been doing is contained in it.' Later, the report was printed as an official note, but nothing ever transpired from this elaborate administrative charade based on the misunderstanding of a courtesy covering letter!

Another case when Bhaiji had to do work at short notice was while making arrangements for the new Viceroy Lord Linlithgow's visit to Kashmir. Ayyangar thought Bhaiji to be the only man capable of doing the job that needed to be completed successfully in the fortnight before Lord Linlithgow's arrival. Ayyangar asked Bhaiji to go and see the Maharaja for any instructions. Bhaiji announced himself to the Maharaja at 4.00 p.m., and the Maharaja's cronies, Effendi and Haksar, among others who were already ensconced in the ring of courtiers, looked at Bhaiji, the intruder, with considerable surprise.

Bhaiji sat with them, sipping tea till 6.00 p.m., at which time drinks were brought in. No business was discussed and when, at 10.00 p.m., the Maharaja called for dinner, Bhajii rose to go. The Maharaja then produced the cyclostyled programme of Linlithgow. Bhaiji, without seeing it, said he would carry it out. The Maharaja was surprised at this okaying without seeing the contents. Bhaiji explained that since the Maharaja and the Viceroy had approved the programme, how was it of any consequence if Bhaiji made any suggestion!

From Bhaiji's anecdotes, I can only conclude that the Kashmir administration under the Maharaja resembled an elaborate ritual dance. Each person performed a move and waited for a counter-move. Commissions were set up. Reports were submitted and filed. As in a dance, the movement was sometimes languorous, sometimes vigorous, but at the end of it, the players all moved in circles and remained where they were. All the while, the Maharaja, being the absolute fount of all power, remained largely absent, on vacation abroad, racing horses in Bombay or engaged in elaborate hunting expeditions across the state. Meanwhile, his administration conducted an elaborate charade of activity without action, making notes in their files without result, putting on stage performances with only the principal actors as the audience.

Only the PM had any access to power but had to tread carefully if he wanted to survive. All this ended one day as the rising tide swept away the painted actors of make believe, replacing them with shriller and harsher voices that installed their own version of reality.

7

Falling in Love[12]

History and circumstance had an important role to play in the meeting of my parents—Bhaiji and Bended—and the cementing of their relationship in England. My father visited London for the first time as part of the Maharaja's official delegation to three round-table conferences held in 1930, 1931 and 1932. This was fortunate because it was only in the previous year that he had been transferred from the archaeological to the political department. The Maharaja, it is said, delivered an electrifying speech on behalf of the princely delegation at the first round-table conference. Since travelling to England was time consuming and cumbersome—about three weeks each way—when the delegation reached London, it stayed for a few weeks, sometimes a few months, before returning to India.

My mother had done a secretarial course, in addition to her BA in English and nursing degree. Once she resigned from her job at St Thomas' Hospital, she decided to work in India House just for the duration of the round-table conferences my father was attending from 1930 to 1932. Colonel K.N. Haksar—who served as a senior member of the Chamber of Princes, with offices in the Savoy Hotel—was in charge of interviewing and appointing staff. He hired my mother as a secretary.

The whiskered and courtly Colonel Haksar was quite a charming gentleman for the ladies. It was he who first took my mother to

[12]This chapter has been narrated by Lila Kak Bhan.

see St James' Palace, otherwise not accessible to ordinary folk. Haksar also, it is believed, took his staff, mostly composed of women, out to a nightclub. One of them was apparently quite sweet on him. My mother told me that she admired Haksar but more from the point of view of exoticism. My father, however, gave her quite a lot of that. He humorously recalled that perhaps that was why she transferred her attention to him!

Before my mother was assigned to the post, my father's secretary in England was a cousin of Sir Dinglefoote, a Member of Parliament from the Labour Party. One day, while returning to his hotel, my father spotted her walking along the kerb near Piccadilly Circus. Since he had some instructions to give, he stopped the car, leapt out, spoke to her for a few minutes and left. My father, apparently, presented quite a picture on the busy streets of London, as he was wearing tight white pyjamas (Jodhpurs), a black *achkan* and a flaming red turban. No doubt he wore his clothes well, even the humblest variety. His secretary later informed him that he had accosted her near her college, where several of her friends had been hanging out of the window and seeing the episode had got greatly excited, questioning her no end about the Indian raja she was keeping company with!

Sometime after this incident, Colonel Haksar asked my mother if she would work for my father while he was there for the round-table conferences. She agreed on the condition that she would be allowed to leave if she got a permanent job elsewhere. Haksar's responded to this saying, 'Well I don't suppose he will break his heart over it!' But, by the time my father returned to India in 1931, it seemed probable that he would! There was an interest on both sides, but it was nothing too serious. They began an initial correspondence.

This is how my parents met and were drawn to each other, cementing their acquaintance over the years of the conferences, starting in 1931 and later, through a prolific correspondence—a relationship that finally culminated in marriage. In the early years, when my mother's father opposed the relationship, she would destroy my father's letters after reading them. Finally, after five long years, her father told her, 'For goodness sake, marry him or break it off!'

∽

When they first met in 1931, my father asked my mother out to watch a film. It was apparently a noteworthy event for him. I am intrigued by this recollection because, to my knowledge, I do not recall my parents ever seeing any films in later years. I have often wondered what they did outside work. I know they would go for the occasional plays and see some of my mother's friends and relatives.

Figure 6: Bhaiji and Bended courting—a tryst at India House, London, 1933
Illustration credit: Kashmira Tembulkar

Their relationship wasn't all smooth sailing by any means. My father was 37 years old when they first met. He was a widower with four sons and a daughter (his niece, in actuality, whom he took as his own after his favourite sister's death). He was in a responsible job, on an upward trajectory in the Government of Kashmir and devoted to his family. My mother was 25, young, charming and very friendly with her sister-in-law's brother—a solid army officer from a well-established family like hers. It was all 'just right', which was a strong consideration in those days. She broke off her engagement with the army officer after she met Bhaiji at the consecutive round-table conferences because his unusual personality and levels of interest were very appealing to her. She decided to introduce him to her family.

The introduction of my father to the Allcocks is predicated on a rather hilarious incident. When my father went to Loughborough to spend a night and visit the family, a splendid spread had been prepared for high tea. Five o'clock rolled around and my grandfather, great-aunt, father and mother gathered round the table. Everyone, except for Bhaiji, filled their plates and tucked into the delicious offerings. They continually offered the various meat pies (carefully omitting any beef), scones, a delicate array of pastries and, of course, cheeses to my father. My father took an exiguous serving despite everyone pressing him to have more. After a couple of hours of pleasant conversation, it was bedtime. My mother took him up to his room, where he found a cup of hot milk and some biscuits, neatly arranged on a beautiful bone china plate next to it, along with a container of Horlicks. Around 9.00 p.m., as my mother was at the door, about to go to her room, he suddenly sprung a question at her, 'Don't any of you eat dinner?' My mother was surprised and responded, 'Of course we do. What do you think all the delicacies at high tea were? We kept pressing you to have some, but you scarcely ate anything.' He was really hungry by bedtime, but all the food had been cleared away and my mother jokingly told him, 'Next time, eat when you see everyone else enjoying the food! We were all imploring you to eat!' In India, dinner is served late, often at 9.00 p.m. or 10.00 p.m., sometimes even later. In England, it is done by 6.00 p.m. or 7.00 p.m. at the latest! This remained a private joke for decades.

Figure 7: Bended's father, Edward Thomas Allcock, and Auntie Tantes with Bended and Bhaiji, in the middle, in 1933

Illustration credit: Kashmira Tembulkar

Another observation that my father made was the long duration of baths in England. He told my mother how unhygienic he thought it was to 'Wallow in your own dirty and soapy water!' He dealt with this by using his shaving mug—which was usually home to his bristle shaving brush, shaving soap and razor—to pour a few mugfuls of 'clean' water over himself before emerging from the bathtub!

Bathrooms featured prominently in my father's list of priorities, since he had a Brahminical attachment to bathing and cleanliness. This led to an unexpected crisis at the Savoy Hotel, where he was staying. He found some strange basins and gadgets in his bathroom; he twiddled some knobs and taps to no effect before leaving the bathroom, bewildered. A few hours later, he went to answer a furious knocking on the door. When he opened it, a gang of plumbers fell in, gasping, 'What have you done? You have flooded the whole dining room!' Apparently, while twiddling the gadgets, he had inadvertently opened an internal tap and the water had leaked through the ceiling of the lower floor and had begun to drip on to the dining room tables below.

London was a cultural learning experience for my father over the six years he happened to visit it for the round-table conferences and later for the King's coronation. The first time he came, he stayed at the posh Mayfair Hotel in central London. All his bills went into his room account and to settle them at the end, he gave a tip of only half a crown or five shillings at that time. Remembering this act caused him great embarrassment later, when we realised how disproportionately small the tip had been to the bill. Similarly, while staying in an exclusive flat on St James' Street, where he first met my mother, with St James' Palace at the end of the road, the manageress, Mrs Collins, came up to have a word with him about leaving his money and change on his dressing table, which was likely to be pinched. My father, thinking perhaps of his house full of faithful retainers in Kashmir, said that he would not complain if his money was pinched. Mrs Collins replied, 'Well I don't mind if you don't love money, but the girls who work here are poor people and it is unfair to expose them to the temptation.' Thereafter, he never left his change outside on the dressing table.

These cultural differences never came in the way of my parents' relationship. In fact, they cemented their understanding and love further, becoming the basis for a humorous and much deeper understanding of the commonalities that we all need to recognise in one another. I remember many occasions when they teased each other about such funny incidents! I was blessed to grow up in such a harmonious and loving atmosphere.

My parents were both very open with each other right from the beginning. While Bhaiji was very clear that his children's welfare was his primary occupation at that point, he was also certain that he loved my mother deeply and dearly. He suggested she visit Kashmir and meet his family. He wanted my mother to see for herself if she would be able to accept a dramatically new culture and way of life and make it her own. Not only would this give her a clear idea of what her life in Kashmir would be like but would also, very importantly, give his family time to meet her and come to terms with his decision. He might not have been a very demonstrative man, but his actions clearly showed his concern for my mother, his children and his immediate family. After nearly seven years of courtship, amid many agonising moments of 'Will it work?' or 'There's no one I've loved more, or by whom I have been as intellectually stimulated', their trust and love prevailed.

One day, on my father's invitation, my mother decided to travel to India and introspect if she really wished to adopt this man, his family and his land as her own. It was a leap of faith. 'Billa,' Mummy once called me, using her special name for me which is a derivative of Billy, 'despite all the troubles we have had to go through, I would choose to live my life the same way again, with your father.'

This statement is an amazing testimony to my father and mother's relationship. I can see her and hear these words clearly as I write them. They truly were the most compatible couple I have ever known. Who made more adjustments? Was it the times? Whatever it was, it led to an amazing partnership. I am not exaggerating when I say I cannot recall an argument between them. They were very democratic, and listened to and respected each other's opinions. They gave and took advice and shared so many interests! In a moment of loving indiscretion, my mother confided in me, 'London was strewn with our kisses,' for they had had six years of courtship!

8

Voyage into the Unknown[13]

A regular correspondence was all my parents depended on for three years after the 1933 round-table conference. In 1936, my mother took the plunge and visited my father in India. The journey itself was about 18-days-long one way on the P&O liner *Strathmore*. She left from Dover, England, felt rather seasick in the rocky Bay of Biscay, entering the Mediterranean Sea with a stop at the towering Rock of Gibraltar. It was an exciting voyage with well-known dignitaries, like Lord Linlithgow and Lady Bonham Carter, on board. Though the passengers did not mingle with them, they certainly proved to be a point of interest and observation. She arrived in Bombay on 17 April 1936. It was an exciting day, as Bended narrated in her diary from the time:

> One of the longest and newest days in my life. I got up at 5.15 and was up on deck by a quarter to 6.00. It was still almost dark. Three boats of the Indian Navy were already escorting us. They are very small and elegantly painted pure white with their lights glistening in the half light, they were a pretty sight. We could just see a range of hills that was very faint. The waning crescent of the moon was still bright and the morning star stood above it. As we came into Bombay Harbour, the sun rose above the hills. There were innumerable fishing boats, very tiny with brown slanting

[13] This chapter has been narrated by Lila Kak Bhan unless stated otherwise.

sails. We moved up onto B deck and watched the launches delivering magnificent officers in scarlet topees, then the civilian gentleman who arrived in a launch, which belched out filthy black smoke, but which was to me appointed with an opulent magnificence which seemed in direct descent from the spacious days of John Company. There were little white tables set out with waiters in attendance in white with bright green turbans and sashes.

First in the Viceregal party came the daughters and lady-in-waiting and a covey of aides-de-camp [ADCs] in white and scarlet. They all packed into the launch and a very gay load it appeared to be. The Viceroy and Lady Linlithgow went ashore in a Royal Indian Navy launch alone. As the boat drew away from the ship, the band played 'God Save the King', and they both stood and faced the ship meanwhile. From B deck, he looked a very small figure with a very big future ahead.

As soon as the Viceroy had departed, passports were examined and my famous and quite irrational bogey, that mine was not in order, [was] disposed of. Breakfast and the final clearing up of my affairs [happened] down below, then began an anxious half hour or so, when I tried and failed to find any American Express courier. I walked all over the boat, getting hotter and hotter, followed by a representative of one of the less important agencies who evidently hoped I would weary of the search and turn to him on the rebound. Finally, I met one of the ship's officers, noted before for his attractive smile. He advised me to go ashore, where I would certainly find someone from American Express. With some misgivings, I regarded the gangway and wondered whether to exchange the *Strathmore's* shelter for this unknown land, but, finally taking my courage in both hands, I brought out my passport and ventured forth!

Almost immediately, an American Express man appeared, and on hearing my name, bustled around. Madho Lal, Durga's

> husband, appeared and welcomed me very effusively. With the help of the American Express, I was soon hustled through the customs, and though a benevolent old man in white with a white turban and a greying beard insisted on my unlocking one trunk, he did not delve very deeply.

Once united with her brother-in-law to be, Madho Lal, who was studying medicine in Bombay, they met the son of Professor K.T. Shah. He was a great friend of Bhaiji's and had, interestingly, been one of the chief contestants for the first President of India. Describing Madho Lal, my mother wrote:

> He had a very thin and silky black beard as a sign and token of his intellectuality, which certainly was astounding. He has a much more comprehensive knowledge of Modern English and American literature than I have myself. He was very friendly and the two of them led me to a waiting motor car driven by a chauffeur.
>
> The streets of Bombay, through which we drove to the GPO, seem to me very nice, flat, wide and pleasant. The sunlight and bright clothes, to my English mind, seem appropriate only to a particularly successful bank holiday. There were policemen solemnly directing the traffic under the shade of their big umbrellas.
>
> We drove on until we came to the Colaba district, which is pleasantly suburban with tree-shaded streets. The Shahs' flat is on Laburnum Road. It seems very cool and airy. The door opens directly into a large room with big windows on one side shaded with a hanging glass bead fringe. Immediately opposite the door, more windows open onto a little verandah, also shaded by fringes from the sun. The room is furnished very simply with chintz-covered settees and chairs. The floor is covered with a cashmere carpet in dark attractive colours and in the middle of it stands a small inlaid Indian table. A long dark passage runs from this across a small patch of bright sunlit courtyard into the kitchens

> beyond. Two servants clad in white gleam, came from time to time in this small, sunlit space and up and down the dark passage. In through the sunlight and into the kitchen walked the widowed aunt, who keeps the house. She was dressed in a black blouse with her thin red sari wrapped over [her head] and her walk was particularly graceful. Opening out of the sitting room was another large room with two white mosquito-canopied beds standing in the corners, and in the middle, slung from the roof, a swing bed. We sat and talked. Madho Lal, though quiet, is very keen on his medical studies and is humorous and friendly.

I admire my mother's non-judgemental approach to her adopted land from the first day of her arrival. It is very fascinating to read her observations of the Shah household, made a mere four hours after she reached Bombay. Her own words best illustrate her ready acceptance and sense of curiosity—traits that led to her being loved and accepted by her Indian family and reciprocating her sentiments in an unadulterated way. Bended then described her first meal in India:

> Lunch was served in the dark dining room halfway along the kitchen passage. The tablecloth was spotless, and each place was set with a scoured-coloured metal dish with three or four tiny metal pots set up on it. Little piles of condiments were placed around the edge and in the middle were small, thin cake-like pancakes. The others ate with their hands, but I was given an assortment of implements out of which I eventually chose a teaspoon. Eating with hands is not the messy business that English people imagine. The right hand only is used and [that too] just the fingers. Afterwards, a servant brings soap and water in a metal ewer and pours the water for each guest to wash. The Shahs are vegetarians. In the little pots were curry, curds, potatoes cooked with seasoning and some sort of chopped green vegetable, perhaps gherkin. There were little dishes of sweetmeats at the centre of the table.

> The meal showed me that a good housekeeper is recognised the world over—cleanliness and order, good cooking and well-trained servants. After more talk, the party retired for rest. I to one of the big, white-canopy beds. It was very hot, but the sounds in the street, cars and children calling, and men selling silk, 'stop me and buy one', were tinkling their bells, seemed not unlike the sounds of a hot summer afternoon in England.

This was Mummy's first meal in India—it was a traditional Gujarati meal, complete with *thalis, katoris* and *phulkas*—the unleavened delicious, fresh, hot 'pancakes' she referred to! Throughout her 60 years in India, my mother's close and astute observations were almost always compared and connected to England, always sharing the commonality rather than the differences. As I grew older, I realised how special this attribute was and how it contributed to her unique and everlasting love and connection to wherever she lived in India.

After her welcoming break at the Shahs', it was time for her to leave for the railway station to board the train, which would finally get her to the destination for which she had come all the way. Madho Lal and the eldest Shah drove her to the station, and the former gave her a huge wicker basket full of fruit for the journey to Wazirabad, where Mummy was hoping my father would be waiting for her as he had promised. This fruit she shared with the whole carriage, much to their great comfort and delight. Bended wrote of her train journey too:

> By the time I got on to the train, I felt dead tired, my brain full to saturation point with new experiences. We settled down as quickly as possible. I took two aspirins and, though I woke fairly often during the night, I slept much more than I have ever done before on a train. It was hot at first but deliciously cool in the early morning. I had breakfast with Mrs Allen, the remaining occupant of the carriage. She was pleasant but not my type. By the time we got back to our compartment, it was

just getting frightfully hot and I retired to my bunk, where I slept off and on, feeling incredibly dirty and incredibly hot. I enjoyed looking out the window after sundown and watching the tiny villages we passed, where the people were settling down to their cooking and relaxing around tiny glimmering fires. Others were driving home cattle lumbering along the bullock carts. We saw a group of women coming from the well with water pots balanced on their heads, there was a lovely afterglow with stars gradually emerging.

Delhi railway station was the noisiest, vividest sight I have ever seen. Hundreds of different types, hundreds of different clothes, all bustling, all excited, all clamouring. We had to watch for a long time, for we were at the station between 30 and 45 minutes, but it did not seem too long. One train, labelled Lahore, was packed to bursting point. There were open carriages crammed with every type and description of people, mostly fanning themselves with palm-leaf fans. We left it as we found it, still packed and still waiting.

The second morning we were in Punjab, much more fertile country, beautiful in parts, like English parkland but still parched and dusty. My appreciation was, by this time, dimmed by a sickly feeling in the stomach and silly fears that I might not be met at Wazirabad. At last came Wazirabad and I saw RCK's [Ram Chandra Kak's initials—one of the ways Bended referred to him] face very set in a yellow turban. He was in a white suit with white jodhpurs. Brij Lal [Brijendra Nath Kak, also known as Brija Kak, Brija or BNK] was with RCK and to him I was handed over while RCK dealt with my trunks. I said goodbye to Miss Newnham and Miss Gomery, both of whom were to become very good friends of ours in Kashmir. I would have introduced them to RCK, but in the pressure and excitement of arrival, there did not seem many opportunities. Brij Lal took me out to the car. RCK, still very set, came along and, motioning Brij Lal into the back of the car with me, he took the wheel with the Sikh driver beside him and off we set for the 50 miles to Jammu. The extent of my communications with RCK during the journey were some quizzical glances relayed in the driver's mirror!

Figure 8: Bended travelled by the Frontier Mail from Bombay to Wazirabad in 1936

Illustration credit: Kashmira Tembulkar

Though my father scarcely spoke to my mother when she reached Wazirabad, their love and faith in each other was phenomenal. Bhaiji had made detailed preparations, and it must have been a huge feat and leap of faith to tell his sons and relatives about Mummy's impending visit in a society where a European woman had probably never been inducted in a 'typical' family. You must remember, he did not cut away, he chose to induct her into the joint family to a certain extent! Such trust and faith in spite of not having an effusive welcome on arrival! How much deeper, more meaningful and unique their love seems in so many ways!

Although, of course, in the India of the 1930s, it was taboo to show any public display of romantic affection. Bended continued her description of the journey thus:

> Anyway, on from Wazirabad to Sialkot—a big English cantonment. The gardens are lovely and there is a wonderful shop, belonging to Messrs Goolam Kadir & Co. which stocks, English groceries, English toilet preparations, table silver, scent—a most amazing collection. There I bought, under RCK's instruction, a packet of grape nuts, a tin of Huntley & Palmers Osborne biscuits and a jar of Hartley's bittersweet marmalade.

I love this list, for my father so obviously asked her to buy these items to remind her of home and encourage her to find some familiar tastes on her sojourn to Kashmir. These actions are so indicative of my parents' sensitivity and care for one another. One has to put oneself in their shoes and into the India of 1936 to truly understand their story! Anyway, Bended continued:

> Beyond Sialkot is the Kashmir Customs barrier through which we sailed in lordly style with officials *salaaming* on all sides. Further towards Jammu, we passed mimosa trees with lovely perfume. We saw the town raised up on the plateau among the foothills and beyond mountain peaks, some snow-capped but very dim and misty. Finally, we drove to the dak bungalow in the town and then the three of us had lunch, but I wasn't hungry. We had an English meal of soup, fried freshwater fish from the river Tawi, fried cutlets, chipped potatoes, green peas and onions, cornflour pudding and coffee. Soon after, they left me to rest (a little to my secret dismay). Bishambar Nath, an anxious-eyed customs guard, for the moment acting as a servant, was on guard. I rested, did my nails and wrote home to catch the mail. My domain consists of three rooms, a large bedsitting room, a dressing room and a lavatory, all whitewashed and lofty. The

> big arched doorways have reed curtains over them. I still feel rather in the public eye unless these are drawn. There are doors as well but the curtains are cooler.
>
> RCK came back at 6.00, and we had an hour or more to ourselves, which was the best rest. Then, we went in the car to their house. It is built in a rather pretentious way with a columned entrance and a turret. It was dark when I saw it but the general impression was very pleasant. The front door opens into a large sitting room with a huge chandelier and the portrait of the owner of the house above the mantelpiece. RCK's bedroom is to the left with a door out into the garden. We decided to sit outside. There is a brick platform where our chairs were placed. There were lovely smells. It was very brilliant starlight and innumerable fireflies darted here, there and everywhere. So we sat, Brij Lal, RCK, the scoutmaster who lives with them and a cousin, Prithi Nath, who has a handsome, shy and serious face. Later, I went with RCK to explore the orange grove with the aid of a flashlight.

This was Bended's first day in India with my father. Her consistent curiosity, interest and positive reactions were to be the hallmark of her 60 very satisfying years in India. Her observations accurately describe the norms and expectations of the society she was choosing to meld with.

From Jammu, they went to Srinagar. As the day to move arrived, Mummy was packed and ready to leave the dak bungalow for the house where the family was living. The family Jeeves, Kashinath aka Koshiah, our major domo, was running hither and thither, organising the bulk of the luggage into a lorry. This move between Srinagar and Jammu happened twice a year, and Koshiah was a pro! Mummy wrote this of the rather adventurous journey to Srinagar:

> About three miles out of Jammu, the car was held up by Dina Nath and Neelkanth, who garlanded me and [attempted to

do so for] RCK with something which looked like orange flower buds. Up to lunchtime, I sat up and took notice and tried to miss nothing. It is a strange country. Hills covered with scrub, huge watercourses, dried up and dusty, rocks that are not rocks, but blocks of white crumbling shale. The scale is so vast that it can't be compared to anything in England, Scotland or Wales.

By and by we came to the Chenab running in a vast gorge-like valley between towering hillsides. At one point where the valley widens is a huge hill standing actually in the valley with river gorges on three sides. It is capped by a fortress where the political prisoners of Kashmir state were erstwhile kept. One can't imagine walking in such countryside and to live in it would be hell, but the road maintains a civilised easy air.

RCK took the wheel. Like some other drivers I know, he is nervous while sitting behind and hates being swooped around corners, but he doesn't expect the back passengers to notice swoops while he is driving! Brij Lal and I tried to sleep in the back seat. When I roused myself, we were passing over the bridge crowded with flocks of goats, which were being driven up to the summer pastures.

From that point, the drive took on a rather nightmarish air—great swerves of road[14], terrific depths below, towering hillsides above, torrents dashing down, threads of road pointed out to me miles away and miles up where we must soon pass, and a head which felt it had been lifted off and a tummy which heaved ominously.

After a night in a dak bungalow [probably at Banihal before the Pass into Kashmir], I woke to a lovely, sunny

---

[14]Though the roads have been widened over the 80-odd years since Bended wrote this description, this journey was one of the great excitements when Siddharth and I travelled to Kashmir by bus for our summer holidays. Of course, flights soon became a viable alternative, but those gaping ravines and high roads resulted in our clinging to each other, screaming and laughing simultaneously as we drove along those giddying roads, not daring to open our eyes to look at the drops on one side of the road!

morning. We went up onto the paddy fields which rise up behind the little bungalow. The valley looked lovely in the morning sun. We started by 7.45. At the end of this valley there was the tremendous rampart of mountain which had to be crossed. The road climbed it in great sweeps. The gradients were still very mild, but the loose stone and shale above the road looked ominous. The last few hundred feet were tunnelled through the shoulder.

On the other side was brilliant sunshine with white clouds swimming in the valleys below. Great banks of snow rose above the road, the side cut sheer to keep it open. There were tall pine trees growing on the mountainside. The road wound down and down. The vegetation began to look like home, the trees and the grass and the whole atmosphere even though there were lovely strange wild flowers and flowering shrubs and thorns. In one place, there were deep orange-crown imperial lilies growing. There was a very charmingly situated dak bungalow at Munda which I marked down as a lovely place for a holiday. Below Munda, the road branches off to Verinag[15]. We walked round the octagonal tank of green water. It has a lovely garden and the enclosure is flanked by two lines of poplars.

In the [Verinag] shrine, we were invited to see more images. Removing my shoes, I entered the House of Baal for the first time in my life. It didn't seem permeated by evil or brooding with horror or any of the other things that I have been told. There the images were, some with flowers stuck upon them or wreathed with a garland and sticky with ghee with which they had been libated. I missed the smell of our village churches, dust and lamp oil and old wood, but there was a smell which no doubt to an Indian is just as full of association...

---

[15]The Verinag spring and Mughal Garden are sources of the Jhelum, one of the key rivers of Kashmir, which bisects the entire valley.

In preparation of Mummy's arrival in Srinagar, my father had two houses built on a large plot of land that he owned. One was where he would stay and, about a three-minute walk away, he had a brick house constructed with a casing of mock Tudor wall panels on the outside to give Mummy a feeling of home. Interestingly, this was the first house in the region, not belonging to officials or the British, that had a bathroom with a flush. My mother's bedroom had one western-style lavatory while all the others were Indian-style in both houses. Her 'guardians' were my big brothers, who each had a room in what was named the 'The Red House'. And so began my mother's reconnaissance visit, a year before my parents got married in London, thanks to King George VI's coronation in 1937, which my father attended.

My maternal grandfather had felt greatly reassured after meeting my father and had said to my mother, something like, 'Margaret, were he English, he would have been all I would ask for.' On the other hand, my paternal grandfather, Bhaigash, was very worried and stopped talking to my father for about three years and my mother for nearly six years! Mercifully, my half-brothers[16] and their generation were wildly excited to meet my mother.

My mother had lots of interesting meetings with family and friends, learning new nuances about a different way of life while being rejected by her soon-to-be parents-in-law. Apparently, my brothers would go and visit their grandparents regularly and relay stories about the 'lady from England'. My grandmother, Wagri, was most curious to hear about all the happenings at Bagh Sundar, which was the enclave Bhaiji built for my mother and his flock. I bet, that given half a chance she would have visited Mummy and probably even encouraged her to come over to Zaldragar estate, where the Kak joint family stayed.

It was my grandfather who refused to even speak to my father and mother for a few years. One day, after the initial rapprochement between him and Bhaiji, my parents were having

---

[16]I henceforth refer to them as my 'big brothers' in the book.

a deep conversation about Greek philosophers. By this time, my mother knew a smattering of spoken Kashmiri and could understand it well. I remember she said that she was fascinated by Bhaigash knowing all about Plato. My grandfather was well versed in Persian and Sanskrit, in addition to Kashmiri. With time, Bhaigash and Mummy were drawn closer and closer to each other. He finally paid her the ultimate compliment conveyed in the simplest, purest and most down to earth words, 'I now see that there is no difference between you and me/us except that you eat beef and we don't.' My mother was deeply moved, reassured and thrilled with his total acceptance of her. So simple but clear that, in fact, there are no differences in the essence of people who seem different. Despite his initial rejection of my parents' relationship, when Bhaigash did relent, he could not have been a more accepting and complimentary father-in-law.

During the years of rejection, my father would go every single day to sit with my grandfather, on his way from his office to Bagh Sundar. He would take off his shoes, sit down on the expanse of material covered by *gabbas,* with bolsters bordering the room.

I imagine this scene so: Bhaigash would sit propped against the wall, with bolsters to make himself comfortable, near a carved wooden window. When my father would enter the room, my grandfather would turn his face away, not uttering a word, ignoring his very presence. After a little while, Bhaiji would take his leave. This was a daily ritual. However, the love Bhaigash had for his son never diminished. I remember being told that he would make subtle enquiries with the youngsters of the family about the Bagh Sundar household. They were constantly there, curious, interested and protective. It resulted in a familiarity and understanding that grew and made Mummy's entry into the family a year later so much more natural and easy.

Soon, the day for Bended to return to England arrived. Although she was excited at the thought of describing her sojourn to her family, she was wistful at the idea of leaving Kashmir, which she now considered home, and the family. She wrote:

There was a crowd to see me off. RCK first of all appeared to see if my trunks were all ready. Then came the boys and then Ramji's [Ram Chandra Kak's] brothers. I finished my packing before I dressed for the journey while they looked on. Soon, the girls arrived. It was a very gay breakfast with Prem Nath and RCK at their most vivacious, arguing about the plant *datura* and its botanical name! I said goodbye to the girls and all around. I didn't know whether to shake hands, do *namaskar*, or what to do. Finally, I bowed and smiled and got somehow into the car.

We set off into a delicately grey morning with the sun not far behind. The first few miles were occupied by anxious conversation with RCK as to whether my goodbyes had been satisfactory. He finally promised to make good any deficiencies himself and to explain that, in the excitement of the moment, I had not thanked them all as I would have wished. I also sent letters from Jammu.

By the time we reached Qazigund, I was enjoying every minute. The rice fields were in the process of being reaped and the parts which were still uncut made a lovely pattern of green, tawny green, brown and yellow. We had lunch at Kud, in my room. The sun was sparkling on rain-washed trees and hillsides and we set off for the Pinewood, which we had watched through all the vicissitudes of the morning's rain. It turned out to be a lovely place. After the interlude, we travelled on to Jammu. RCK stopped the car where the road, in the fading light, looked like an English lane running through the high banks of a common. By the roadside, under a *bodh* tree was a spring. Steps led down to the circular spring, which were covered because of the rain. We finally reached Jammu and stayed at the dak bungalow.

Next morning, we left for Wazirabad and got there an hour sooner than we had thought we would. So, we sat in the ladies waiting room. The train arrived and I got into my carriage, and there was Mrs Allen, with whom I had

> travelled up. The surprise of this rather took off the edge of my parting from Ramji. But, in any case, what could we do with the eyes of the whole station on us and what could we say that had not been said already? So, the train steamed out and I smiled from my seat and he lifted his hat and smiled, it was rather like a deep cut that you don't feel for days after. The *Strathaird* was waiting in the Bombay port to take us to Marseilles from where the passengers had to take a boat train to Victoria Station.

My mother's voyage into the unknown from England to Kashmir in April 1936 successfully transformed what had, until then, been an unknown way of life for her into something she understood and indeed came to love. She had behaved quite the blushing bride when she prepared to return to England from Kashmir!

However, after she returned, there was still no definitive date on which the couple had committed to marry. The continents that separated them were daunting. This procrastination may have continued with unknown consequences had the tides of history not, once more, begun to flow in their favour. As luck would have it, my father received an opportunity the very next year to visit London, along with the Maharaja of Kashmir, to attend the coronation of King George VI in May 1937, following the unexpected abdication of his elder brother Edward VIII in the winter of 1936.

This opportunity was as unexpected as it was momentous. For my parents, it was now or never.

∽

A foreign woman had never been a bride in my grandfather's orthodox joint family.[17] Neither was this a decision that tradition allowed him to make, as he was not the head of the family. Besides, Bended and he had met only for a few months over three years of his trips to England, which scarcely gave confidence for a lasting

---

[17]This section of the chapter has been narrated by Siddharth Kak

relationship—separated as they were by culture and continents—that may have sparked a novelty for either of them but hardly foretold a lifelong affair. In fact, Bended had already been engaged to a suitable boy in England and her parents were unfamiliar with India and Indian customs—they could scarcely be expected to agree to the match. So, when Bhaiji invited Bended to Kashmir for a few months to decide if she could make this strange new place her home, neither realised the extent to which it was a decision fraught with the gravest consequences.

Bhaiji had to build a home in Kashmir to house his bride to the standards she had been used to in England. Funds had to be set aside, a year had to be assigned to build a separate house for her in Srinagar, with a Western-style toilet, which had been non-existent in the average Kashmiri home in the 1930s and certainly did not exist in the Kak joint family home in Zaldragar. There was no central heating, even in the new house, unless one counted the old Bukhari system as a traditional form of central heating.

This house, which took a year to build in Chattabal, adjacent to Kak Sarai (a landing place for trucks and trade between Delhi and Ladakh) gradually grew into the verdant complex much loved by us all—Bagh Sundar. It was a large tract of land and included vegetable patches, a small trestle of vines, which, in my memory, only yielded sour grapes, and two lawns bordered by delightful flowerbeds. In later years, my parents lived on the ground floor of what came to be known as the White House. My father's elder brother, Narendra Nath, lived with his wife Kamla on the first floor of the White House. Another beautiful house had been built next door called the Red House, where Bhaiji and Bended initially lived when in Srinagar. Outhouses were built for the staff to tend to the family and the gardens. Bagh Sundar was a delightful oasis in an otherwise crowded area, complete with a marketplace offering everything—provision shops, grocers, butchers, bakeries, auto garages, a post office, banks and tongas for hire—just around the corner!

Bhaiji spoke to me extensively about how, when Bended

first came to Srinagar in 1936, she lived alone in the Red House. He would visit her every morning on his way to work and in the evening while returning. During the day, she would occupy herself with reading, writing letters to her father and her beloved Aunt Tantes in England or walking in the ample garden. Bhaiji's young sons or the wives of his brothers sometimes visited her during the day, curious to see how the *mem* who had developed an attraction for their Bhaiji, was passing her time and what it was that he saw in her! They would return to the joint family home, about a mile away, with gossip and stories of the alien ways of this unusual white woman who had dared to join their family, who spoke no Kashmiri but often broke into a friendly broad smile to tide over the awkward pauses while they stared at her. Not knowing English, they too reciprocated with awkward smiles and gestures!

Orthodoxy ruled in the early years of the last century. Till Bhaiji shifted to his own home in Bagh Sundar in 1933 at the age of 40, he did not retain a penny of his salary. As with all his brothers, who were the only earning members, all his money went to Bhaigash, who ran a trading and moneylending business and spent the money as he thought best for the family. Without the patriarch's consent—in this case, Bhaigash's father, Govind Kak—no marriage alliance could be sanctified. Under the circumstances, Bhaiji's defiance was a threat to tradition and the wrath of the patriarch was visited on the apparently scheming white woman who was held responsible for Bhaiji's defiance.

9

An Unusual Bahu[18]

Even after my mother's return to England in 1936, my parents did not have a definitive plan for the future of their relationship. They both knew each other's families and backgrounds and seemed to feel at ease despite the cultural differences. They definitely cared deeply for each other, but beyond that, no conclusion had been reached. However, as it turned out, King George's coronation in May 1937 was a fortuitous event for them. My father came to attend the coronation as a member of the Maharaja's delegation, and it was there that he was presented with an ultimatum by my usually timid mother! In no uncertain words, she told him he needed to decide if they would get married or part ways. My father was worried if the Maharaja would agree, so Bhaiji sent Nawab Khusro Jung to meet my mother and the deed was done.

On 7 August 1937, Bhaiji and Bended got married in Kensington, London. My father hosted a party in London after that for the delegation. Shortly after, the newlyweds set sail for India. This led to almost half a century of an amazing life together. In addition, one must constantly bear in mind that their cultures had different outlooks in many ways. The East could be considered conservative in certain ways and, therefore, difficult to understand for a Western mind. Fortunately, both Bhaiji and Bended looked beyond superficial reactions and had no problem

[18]This chapter has been narrated by Lila Kak Bhan unless stated otherwise.

understanding the reasons for the diverse evolution of the two thought processes. The extracts from my mother's letters and the conversations and reactions of my father illustrate why this remarkable union was such a success.

The following excerpts from Mummy's letters to her family in England describe the very first months of married life. Her power of observation was startlingly detailed and so was the candidness, warmth and depth of her relationship with her parents. She painted a vivid picture of a family and the atmosphere in the Kashmir of the 1930s and 1940s, almost an anthropological study. The different people, superstitions, customs and thinking were all revealed through her writing. Clearly, her second journey to India was in great contrast with her first trip, now that she was secure about why she was going and with whom.

> We arrived last night after a good journey and made up for the awful heat of the ship by having a comparatively cool journey, but even then it was dusty and I was thankful we got off at Lahore. The first snag was that, owing to a lack of accommodation, the heavy luggage had been put off the train at Delhi and was to be sent by the following train. When it will arrive I don't know, but I hope it doesn't take forever. We were met by the working manager of the Nanda bus company, an extremely good looking KP [Kashmiri Pandit] who took us to his office to arrange things and then to his lodgings above the office. We went up a steep wooden loft ladder to three little rooms on the second floor. A kitchen, a little place to sit, a bedroom with a big electric fan whirring above the bed and a little verandah opening out of the room. The floors were red brick and there was scarcely any furniture but the general effect was neat, clean and pleasant. There were two children, a little girl and a boy of about five two and half years old [respectively] and a smiling pleasant wife who was very shy at first but eventually opened up. She served us tea and sweetmeats and a kind of

salted pancake thing. We set out of Lahore at about 9.30. It was too far a journey to Srinagar to be pleasant, but I felt well (not carsick), much to my surprise. There was one bit when I felt very queer, but fortunately the driver stopped at the right moment and we walked along the road and he caught us up, which just served the situation as far as I was concerned. He was the most marvellous driver, the best I think I have ever driven with. He obviously knew the route well, and the way he took the corners and the hairpin bends filled me with admiration because he kept up a very good average speed, and yet always gave an impression of safety [...]

The luggage arrived last night and today we have more or less unpacked much to the interest of the boys. We are staying in the guest house, which is the White House set further back from the main entrance.[19] We set up the dining room, which looked absolutely charming and was greatly welcomed by the boys. The boys are sweetness itself. They are ridiculously like RCK in one way or another. They couldn't be more friendly, very touching in so many little ways. For example, one of them put up curtains in our bedroom. They have also been teaching me how to tie a sari—five and a half yards of material wound round me [...]

Well, RCK has been installed as secretary to HH [Maharaja Hari Singh], and government, general and political federation is under him. He is immediately under the prime minister and is not under any of the others. He works in the same office as the prime minister, who is Dewan Bahadur Sir GopalaSwami Iyengar [*sic*], a Madurai Brahmin, with a firm hand for both Hindus and Muhammadans. There has recently been some trouble in Jammu over the killing of a cow, but he put down the trouble with a firm hand.

---

[19]Notably, the Red House, built to 'remind' Mummy of England, with a bit of mock Tudor exterior, was called the cottage.

RCK is really pleased with his job and looks forward to being really interested in his work again, which he was not at Customs. I am particularly glad that he has federation under him. He thinks things have fallen out happily. He says people will say, 'He has an auspicious wife! He marries and returns from England and gets a promotion. What a lucky fellow!'

The family comes visiting in full force, and I think they enjoy it because they stay for hours. The fact that they are coming from the family house is a sign of hope. A couple of the young ones are tremendous favourites of the grandfather and would never do anything to upset him. Last year, I scarcely saw anything of them! The difficulty for me with these large parties is the lack of conversation. But my photograph albums create great interest. Also, when I was sewing name tapes on my linen, all the girls wanted to help, and I hope I've been able to teach them something! I find they have scarcely any idea of sewing, but they want to learn. By the end, I usually feel completely exhausted, partly by being so unnatural sitting with half a smile on my face whether I understand the conversation or not! It is such a relief to get RCK to myself alone. But I find myself much more occupied than last time and am falling into a routine [...]

Yesterday we went to Gulmarg for the first time. The boys went up the hill where they had ponies, while RCK and I walked up the Ferozepur nullah. It was lovely! We just took an envelope of fruit and some hard-boiled eggs, and it was the first time we've ever been on our own in the Kashmir countryside. We went to the bridge where the valley narrows into a ravine and then walked up into the pine forest, which stretches right up to the mountains. There was a glorious hot smell of resin.

On Friday night, Brija took me to the exhibition ground. My first public appearance in Kashmir and I should say very public. I didn't go in a sari because we both felt that until I

> have learnt to walk, it is better to stick to clothes in which I have some self-confidence. I'm wearing saris all the time at home and find them very comfortable [...]
>
> [We had] lunch at the palace and tea with the chief justice. I went in a white georgette sari with a blue and yellow border and embroidery. [We] met several people both English and Indian. RCK hates tea parties, but I find them interesting even though they are not much in my line either. Nawab Khusru Jung told RCK that we are to be invited to lunch with HH at the end of the month. He also asked RCK whom he would like me to meet, 'We must arrange something for her here.' I hope I shall have the strength to rise to such heights!

Below is a very interesting excerpt from a letter from my maternal grandfather to Mummy. It reveals how difficult the decision must have been, even for him, to support her wholeheartedly and what her aunts felt about their niece's decision. Her letters obviously reassured Tantes and Grandaddy that she was satisfied and supremely happy in her new home, as he mentioned in this extract.

> My dear Margaret,
>
> It was a great joy to have your letter with the copious details of your experiences. It is great news about the secretaryship. My very hearty congratulations to Ramji. I feel quite proud to be the father-in-law to such a big noise! It is gratifying to know that the clan is beginning to get around you. No doubt the old people will come in time, but it is difficult for the old to consent to great innovations, especially when mixed with religious ideas! I wonder whether the aunts here are still grieving over your being 'unequally yoked'. I think we must send your letter to them but I must read it again before deciding!

By this time, it appeared that the tensions with Bhaigash were also easing, albeit gradually. As Bended wrote:

> I think the atmosphere in the other house continues to soften. The other morning someone brought to Bhaigash two baskets of grapes. He told someone to bring one basket to us immediately... RCK called in the other night to see his mother on the way home from office. She asked him to stay and have a cup of tea but he said no he must go. She pressed him but he still refused. Then she smiled and said to him, 'Who has brought you up so far, I or she?'

While Mummy came from an upper middle-class family, they had never hobnobbed with maharajas and nawabs! As a result, the pomp and circumstance she was exposed to in the first ten years of her life in India fascinated her immensely.

> The highlight of Tuesday was I was invited to view the *darbar* from the gallery with state visitors and other distinguished persons. RCK set off at 5.00 p.m., magnificent in white jodhpurs, an achkan made of gold brocade, a strawberry-coloured turban, an arrangement around his waist like an apron put on back to front blue of gold Benaras silk—a gilt belt, sword with a gilt pommel, and blue velvet scabbard. The result must be seen to be believed!
>
> I arrived at the private entrance of the palace in a beautiful sari with a very fine embroidered border. The Nawab looked resplendent, and in his turban he wore a jewel. He's a great nobleman and he certainly looked it. As always, he was particularly nice to me.
>
> This verandah is glorious. Beyond the river are picturesque, though ramshackle, Kashmiri houses half hidden by acacias and chinars. Behind the city, towers the fort of Hari Parbat on its conical hill, and behind the fort, dwarfing it to the dimensions of a molehill, rise the mountains. Gulab Bhawan, the new palace, may be pleasant as a home, but as a palace it is not to be compared with the Rajgarh. The darbar is at the end of this verandah. I passed by the entrance in order to reach the staircase to the gallery, and I caught

> a glimpse of hundreds of turbans, all strawberry-pink. The bodyguards were just about to file to the places behind the throne. I was met by a family friend and immediately taken to a window with two chairs. At the top end of the gallery, above the throne is the purdah gallery, where the Maharani [Tara Devi] sat, and the *zenana* members of the ruling house sat immured. Corresponding to this at the other end of the hall was another big window with two rows of chairs. Here sat the Resident, in monocle and gold lace, the English minister, English officials of the state and any visitors who have been honoured with an invitation[...]
>
> No one can leave the shows until His Highness [HH] does. For the Europeans, rosy with wine and dancing, this is not so bad, but the Indian section wilts [...] We finally got away at about 2.15 a.m. Very cold, but for all that, I thoroughly enjoyed it. The river looked beautiful, flooded in honour of the birthday and the effects from the verandah were lovely.

Mummy's detailed observations shed a vivid light on life in India, especially in Kashmir over seven decades ago. She was fortunate to be privy to people from a vast spectrum of social backgrounds, all of whom she respected and found fascinating. Right from maharajas and viceroys to family and a vast cross section of working class helpers from different regions of India.

> Mrs Wattal and the Begum both asked me what I did with myself all day, so did Sir Abdul Samad. I told them I didn't exactly know but that the days went very quickly with reading, sewing, writing and the children and the boys coming in and out. I think they rather wonder at me, lying so low, but I'm sure it is the best in the end. For one thing, in a place like this, where one always meets more or less the same set of people, I think it's just as well in order to avoid boredom and not to embark on a ceaseless round of social functions. Sir Abdul also commented on my having

come out to Kashmir last year and said, 'Very nice! One ought to see the country in which one is going to make one's home before one finally decides.' I think or we think that the sari and the fact of my lying so low, and also of my having come out previously has, to a great extent, already drawn the line between the unfortunate examples already experienced in Kashmir, and our case. And whatever may or may not happen in future, I put it on record that we are very happy now. 'Give yourself a pat on the back and say to yourself here's jolly good health we've had a good day today!'

All the boys are very thoughtful companions. The sitting room looks nicer than ever, with a wood fire burning. The whole family and I had tea on the floor by the fire. RCK got home 6.00 p.m. and played solitaire while I played draughts with the boys. The room seemed very cosy and home-like. After dinner, I made coffee for everyone. The women may be elusive, but the men are so completely friendly that one can't help feeling that it's merely a question of time for the women to come in also. RCK complains that I kiss him to an embarrassing extent at what he calls opportune moments, and Soshil (a niece) is getting the habit rapidly, so he has two of us to contend with! She does it to me too and clings around my skirt [...]

On Sunday, we went for a walk on the marshes much further than we could manage in the evenings. It is lovely. There are little canals and brooks here, there and everywhere. I've never seen so many kingfishers before. They are lovely. In Kashmir, they are called *koll toonch*, which means 'spirit of the stream'. Another Kashmiri word I like is *sangamal*, which is the special word for horizon, which literally means the necklace of peaks that surround the valley.

My mother's intense interest in the surroundings, the flora and fauna, language and the people, all added to her love of the country and made her adjustment so natural. She was a romantic and saw beauty in so many things. I experienced this part of her first-hand when she used to point out the smallest observations to me from my earliest days. I have imbibed this power of observation and curiosity from my mother and have found it brings joy and delight in noticing and enjoying these details wherever one goes. A constant feeling of wonder!

In October 1940, my mother wrote about meeting with Viceroy and Lady Linlithgow during their visit to Kashmir. She also refers to a visit with Lady Clutterbuck to check out the viceregal suite in the palace:

> On Wednesday, Lady Clutterbuck and I went around the Viceregal Suite with RCK etc. to see if we could make any suggestions or criticisms. Some of the things are lovely, most beautiful carpets everywhere and furniture and wonderful tile bathrooms. In fact, everything is the best that money can buy, in good taste, and, of course, from the chief rooms the most ravishing view of green lawns and terraces sloping to the Dal Lake and the mountains beyond. A certain Mrs Sutherland acted as decorator and furnisher of the whole palace. She was successful and clever and didn't spare expense, but there is something lacking. The general effect is of a very super fine international hotel. Then again there's no attempt anywhere to treat a room as a shrine for one perfect thing. There are far too many lovely things in every room. And the things are too English for my taste. I feel an Indian prince's palace should be a treasure house of the most beautiful Indian things of which there are so many. I'll give you an example here. In Kashmir, they make the most lovely embroidered bedspreads, some of which are perfect in both colour and design. But the viceregal bedspread is very fine silk, divided by rows of veining into squares. Very elegant, expensive and comely but insipid. Lady Clutterbuck and I were naturally very interested and wanted to stay on and explore a little more, but RCK, after two hours, began to feel

we had served our turn and unobtrusively and courteously pushed us out [...]

RCK rang up this morning and seemed very pleased with himself. He sat next to the Viceroy at dinner last night. He's having all his meals with the house party. Today, they went to the Shalimar Garden for lunch, and then for tea, and again, he was in attendance. I think it may be interesting for him. He is bound to have opportunities of talking to the Viceroy and to the private secretary and so, in the meantime, his humble wife sits at home and does her knitting!

Tomorrow is a great day. We are to be at the club at 10.30 a.m. and back at 2.00 p.m. in time for Her Excellency's [Lady Linlithgow] arrival at 3.45 p.m.

RCK sat next to Lady Linlithgow that night at dinner, and she told him that she had met his wife and said I was '[...] very charming and efficient. I didn't realise before that she was English. I don't really usually approve of mixed marriages, but this one seems all right!' So we have the Viceregal approval [...]

I find I say '*Acha*' instead of 'yes', even to English people! I feel my outlook and manners have changed in these years. I went to the shrine of Kheer Bhawani and I now feel more certain that all things are essentially one. We are made by the same potter, and the clay is one. We sat cross-legged in front of the shrine, where the Devi was draped with bright silk and tinsel. We bought flowers for worship and for a long time, there was silence—just birds in the trees, singing, and children shouting and running in the outer reaches, and many priests chanting the scriptures, which every morning must be sung. That atmosphere seemed very familiar. Any cathedral gives it, but here there is no building, but the sky and the trees.

Figure 9: Bhaiji and Bended in the social whirl of Kashmir with Lord and Lady Linlithgow, 1937

Illustration credit: Kashmira Tembulkar

While Bhaiji and Bended lived in Bagh Sundar, the joint family continued to reside in the ancestral home at Zaldragar. While my mother did not yet accompany my father each evening to sit in with the family around Bhaigash, she began getting invites to other family functions. Bended wrote:

> This week, I went to the house where RCK was born and brought up. It is right in the heart of the city, overlooking the river. The nephew of Wagri, my mother-in-law, now lives there. He was holding the sacred thread ceremony of his three sons and had invited me to attend. This is the first time I have gone to a family function and Wagri was in rather a flutter about it, but the nephew insisted and told her that he would not otherwise recognise his brother's wife (for here, everybody are brothers in the family). Anyhow, I went with BNK, and they were all very nice to me, and I think very interested. I loved seeing the house. The rooms were low and reminded me of old-fashioned rooms in England,

with moulded plaster walls and latticed windows, that have rather crazy-looking wooden balconies overlooking the river, along with an outer staircase leading up to the top of the house—wooden, very steep, and also rather creaky. The rooms seemed to be built without any plans. You see, what happens here is the family settles on a piece of land. Then, as the years go on and the daughters-in-law and their children arrive, the conglomeration grows and they build on to every available corner to increase the accommodation. In the city there's no hope of acquiring more land so the process goes on until the site is chock-a-block, when the family, if financially able to, migrates, as in our case, within a stone's throw, almost within arm's length of the house where I went. I loved hearing about who lived in which room. We sat in the room where RCK's grandfather, to whom he was very attached, used to sleep.

∽

I shudder to think what might have happened if the experiment to invite Bended to Kashmir had failed.[20] It had been an immensely risky decision. Even while the house was being built, minds could have changed. What then would have happened to the house, visible as a symbol of foolhardiness? What would have been my grandfather's status in his own family, having squandered the family wealth on a whim, exhibiting an overweening vanity in imagining that affections, notoriously unstable in Western relationships, would somehow stand the test of time? What gave him confidence—as a simple son of the soil, several years senior to this charming white woman he was wooing—that he had the qualities to sustain Bended's affection?

I believe the answer lies more with Bended than with Bhaiji. She was determined to make a go at it. So, she adjusted to Bhaiji's family, both immediate and extended, and bonded with them. She learnt the local language and connected with her adopted

[20]This section of the chapter has been narrated by Siddharth Kak.

land. She learnt to cook the Kashmiri cuisine her husband loved. She learnt to love saris and all things Indian. She persevered in appreciating the taciturn, proud man with whom she had decided to share the rest of her life. It was an adventure on a scale that neither of them could have really imagined, with consequences which ran far deeper than they had ever expected. While having an English wife may have helped Bhaiji to blend in with the 'high society' of Kashmir, it took half a decade for Bended to win over her father-in-law, during which time her own parents hesitated to visit their daughter in Kashmir and multiplying her joy. By the time Bhaigash and Bended truly bonded, he had already been overtaken by the illness which was to take his life.

Margaret Mary Kak was an unusual bahu. For years, when Bhaigash refused to speak to her, she bore the hostility and isolation with fortitude. She and Bhaiji would come and sit with him in his room, along with the rest of the family, in the evening after Bhaiji returned from office, as was the ritual. Wagri would call Bended to her side, but Bhaigash would not even respond to her namaste!

Bhaiji remembered that once, Bended had fallen seriously ill with jaundice and had been absent from the evening gatherings for six weeks. During this time, Bhaigash would quietly enquire about how she had been faring with Bhaiji's sons, who would visit her every day. He had asked Wagri one day, 'What should we do if she should die when things are just beginning to settle down again?'

Wagri had replied pertly, 'Oh ho! You don't even look at her, what is this? What is it to you if she dies?!'

∽

Bended had three miscarriages and lost two sons soon after birth; whether through hospital mismanagement or due to the difficulties of adjusting to the new life will never be known. One of the sons was buried in the flower garden of the hospital. During her labour, Bhaiji had been busy, so, Bended had been left with just a chowkidar and a nurse to attend to her as she had screamed in pain. Meanwhile, Balakrishna was born to Uma, Bhaiji's adopted daughter, in 1940 and Shyamsundar to Narendra Nath and Kamala, Bhaiji's eldest son and his wife, respectively, in 1941. So, their mothers were constantly in and out of the house.

In the spring of 1942, Uma was very upset when she found another child was on the way for her because she had married Bansilal Jalali and birthed Balakrishna when she had only been 18 and her husband was still unsettled in life.

Bended recalled, 'With babies so much in evidence, it was difficult to reconcile oneself to the loss of one's own particular baby. Therefore, the solution seemed to be to adopt the one whose advent was looked forward to with misgiving [Uma's second child].'

It was talked over and agreed to in advance by both families and when, on 9 August 1942, Lila (Billy) was born, Wagri took the baby Lila and laid her on Bended's lap. So, Billy became the second generation to be adopted within the Kak family. She brought with her great comfort and recuperative influence, not the least in forming a sort of bridge in the relationship between Bhaigash and Wagri and Margaret Mary, the daughter-in-law whose coming they had dreaded and resisted for so long!

In September 1942, Bended reported Bhaigash softening when it came to accepting her as a part of the family, nearly five years after she had married Bhaiji.

> At long last, five years after my arrival in Srinagar, it being Bab's birthday, his wife came over in the morning to ask whether RCK and I would go over in the evening and have our food there. Bhaigash, his father, had said that I was to go, so I went and found an old gentleman with a sloping dome of very polished bald head. He had fiery eyes, and a nose very much like RCK's. He seemed to me to look like an old-fashioned miniature of one of the Mughal emperors. I consider he has an extraordinary head, and I should imagine RCK gets most of his push and fire from him.

> He didn't of course say anything to me, but he threw some very searching glances in my direction. We sat in his room, where he reclined on bedding spread in one corner. There is no furniture but lots of mats and carpeting, so that it is comfortable to sit wherever one chooses. I don't know how often I am expected to go there now. I'm glad to think that I have been, and I think RCK will be happier now in that direction.

According to Bhaiji, Bhaigash eventually came around for two major reasons. For one, the children, including Uma, were being looked after very well by Bended and secondly, Bended's adoption of Billy became an emotional turning point.

Adoption within families was very common in Kashmir back then and very little was made of it. Hence, though perhaps aware of it as a fact in the back of her mind, Billy has never thought of herself as anything other than Bended and Bhaiji's child and nor did anyone in the family—neither Billy's Kashmiri half nor her English half.

Figure 10: Bhaigash reconciles with Bended after six years, in 1942

Illustration credit: Kashmira Tembulkar

Bended, finally in charge after marriage, successfully carried out a formal split from the joint family's division of assets and liabilities, with Wagri's help, now that she had to wholly look after Bagh Sundar and Bhaiji.

Though Bhaiji got himself a large Dodge car and a lorry for transporting goods to the Kak Sarai residence, as PM, he travelled largely by tonga or bus while he was in the administration. When Bended came to Srinagar, he hired a special tonga with a driver for their permanent service. This was a good thing, as Bended recalled Bhaiji being a very determined driver, to say the least. He would maintain his position in the centre of the road, gripping the steering wheel firmly and pushing on towards his destination until the opposite driver, realising that the large oncoming car was unlikely to change direction, would often veer off the road and sometimes into a ditch. Bended's memories of Bhaiji driving her to Srinagar on her first visit to India are equally hair-raising, with him swooping the car across mountain turns without reducing his speed.

The way Bhaiji drove, I believe, was a reflection of his determined personality, which not only caused his triumphs but also his greatest tribulations. It landed him in conflict with the Maharaja of Kashmir, whom he served loyally for 33 years, with grave consequences for the state and himself as he assumed greater responsibility in Kashmir for the moody Maharaja!

10

The Moody Maharaja

When my grandfather became the PM of Kashmir on 30 June 1945, it would have been difficult to find two more contrasting personalities heading the state. The Maharaja was the ultimate head of the state, from whom all power and authority flowed. Bhaiji was his executive arm. The former was whimsical, authoritarian and pleasure-loving while the latter was disciplined, intellectual and austere. The former was proud but mistrustful, the latter was loyal but mindful. The former was disconnected from the people while the latter was connected with the people. The former was born in wealth while the latter strove for it.

Despite these differences, in some convoluted manner, their personalities complemented each other, bringing some kind of balance to the governance of the state, albeit in fits and starts. One was hasty, the other was cautious. One revelled in duck and boar shoots, the other never attended one in his life. One was fond of puffing on foreign smokes and quaffing 'doubles', the other was a teetotaller and non-smoker all his life. One was suspicious and manipulative, the other was straightforward to the point of self-abasement!

Dr Karan Singh, the suave and articulate son of the Maharaja, who replaced his father as regent of Kashmir at the tender age of 21, wrote, in his expressive autobiography *Heir Apparent*:

> Quite clearly, my father was much happier racing than administering the state, which chore he left largely to his

carefully chosen PM and a small Council of Ministers, mostly from outside Jammu and Kashmir. In fact, although he enjoyed absolute power, he conducted himself rather like a constitutional monarch and hardly ever interfered with the administration of his Council of Ministers. In this regard he was far in advance of most of his princely contemporaries in India.[21]

Figure 11: The Maharaja's favourite pastime was duck shooting in the wetlands of Kashmir in the 1940s

Illustration credit: Kashmira Tembulkar

He added:

> In fact he often said to his friends that he was only waiting for me to be 21, so that he could hand over the State responsibilities and then do the things he loved—shoot, fish, cook, race and build. It is a strange irony that 21 was in fact the age at which I took over from him what remained of his

[21]Singh, Karan, *Heir Apparent: An Autobiography*, Oxford University Press, Delhi, 1983.

> authority, but under circumstances that could not have been even remotely imagined at the time.[22]

For the Maharaja, a good PM was a prerequisite, enabling him to devote time to the activities he loved, leaving the matters of state and their constant complications to his PM and the Council of Ministers. He was always on the lookout for a capable man to lead the state, largely from his non-local Jammu clansmen or Punjabi and British administrators working in India.

This desire was counterbalanced by his constant insecurity. Dr Singh observed:

> This highlighted a strange tendency in my father, that was ultimately to prove his political undoing—his inability to trust anyone for any length of time. He selected his Prime Ministers with great care, but no sooner had he appointed one, then he would begin cultivating someone else as a sort of counterbalance. With the exception of N. Gopalaswami Ayyangar, who was Prime Minister of the State for six years from 1934 to 1939, this happened with all the succeeding incumbents—Raja Maharaj Singh; BN Rau; Colonel KN Haksar; Pandit Ram Chandra Kak and General Janak Singh—right down to the crisis of 1947.[23]

The Maharaja was a whimsical man of many moods and working with him was always a complicated balancing act. It is surprising that his eye fell on Bhaiji, who perhaps had all the wrong qualifications. For one, he was a Kashmiri Pandit, who are obedient and capable but unlikely to have the appetite to manage the leadership of the unruly masses! For another, he was engaged in the archaeology department, which was as far removed from the Maharaja's interest as astronomy is from a duck in the sky!

I surmised that the Maharaja may first have heard about Bhaiji from the British head of the ASI, the distinguished archaeologist

---

[22]Ibid. 30.
[23]Ibid. 12.

Sir John Marshall. From a lowly start in 1913 as an intern at the excavation site in Gandhara and Takshashila, Bhaiji rose rapidly up the ranks under Sir John's watchful eye to the position of superintendent of Archaeology of Kashmir within a decade. Normally, such a post is achieved only after about two or more decades of dedicated service.

Even while working in the archaeology department, Bhaiji was enlisted by the political wing of the state to help organise various ceremonies, largely functional arrangements for visiting dignitaries, viceroys or princes, and the elaborate banqueting facilities required. Of course, the menus were something that the Maharaja and Maharani personally decided, as this was an aspect they enjoyed. Bhaiji had earned a reputation as a no-nonsense, disciplined administrator. Although he often got on the wrong side of the Maharaja's numerous courtiers and favourites while executing these arrangements, it is possible that Bhaiji gave the Maharaja the impression of a dependable and strong personality.

Bhaiji's first meeting with the Maharaja took place in 1920 in Delhi because Bhaiji did not want their meeting to become common knowledge, which would have happened had they met in the palace in Srinagar. During this fateful visit, the Maharaja asked what Bhaiji was doing, to which he proudly replied that he was the superintendent of archaeology of the state.

The Maharaja abruptly asked 'What is archaeology?'

Bhaiji was taken aback. Composing himself, he replied, 'Archaeology is a study of the past.'

The Maharaja shot back, 'What is the use of studying the past?.'

Bhaiji was disconcerted. It seemed quite clear to him that the Maharaja had no use for archaeology or history. Nonetheless, Bhaiji explained patiently, 'If one has an upset stomach as a result of things eaten the previous day and one does not know what one has eaten that has caused the problem, it can occur again and again!'

The Maharaja was not impressed by this explanation. Perhaps, at that time, Bhaiji thought nothing of it and left. But the Maharaja's disdain for the study of archaeology was to have a profound impact on Bhaiji's growing archaeological career.

As the Maharaja was absolute centre of power, courtiers jostled for his attention and trust, betraying each other in the process. This was a chaotic state that the Maharaja himself encouraged, as he deeply distrusted everyone. This was also why he kept changing his PMs frequently, lest they would become too powerful. Added to this, his wife, with whom he was often at loggerheads, and her brother, Nichint Chand, created their own power centre, eventually bringing in Swami Sant Dev, who sold the fantasy of a Greater Dogra Empire to the Maharaja, which eventually led to his downfall.

The Maharaja's whimsies encouraged intrigue. People knew he was prone to believe gossip. He was also a sore loser, which created disaffection. An incident recounted by Bhaiji bore out this trait. Once, Bhaiji happened to visit the home of Ranjit Singh, the ADC to the Maharaja, for some work. At the gate, he was informed by the chowkidar that Ranjit Singh had incurred the wrath of the Maharaja for some omission and had been ordered out of his government accommodation as punishment at 2.00 a.m. The Maharaja was so angry with Ranjit Singh that he did not allow the latter to even take his official car to transport his bags. He had to call for a tonga at the dead of night to transport his baggage along with his wife, who had just given birth to their first child. Bhaiji was disconcerted by this story, but he happened to run into Ranjit Singh a few days later. When he asked about the incident, Ranjit Singh, a plump and jovial fellow, merely giggled! Perhaps, he was aware of his master's temper tantrums and was waiting for the mood to pass. Sure enough, a few days later, he was restored to the Maharaja's service.

One night, Bhaiji received a call from the Maharani at about 10.00 p.m., saying the Maharaja had put out all the lights and was sulking in the darkness. He was refusing to eat any food unless it came from Bhaiji's house. The reason for this was not very clear, except that, perhaps, Bhaiji was in his good books at that particular moment as the minister-in-waiting. However, Bhaiji was having vegetarian guests over at this time—the prominent Gujarati businessman K.T. Shah and his family, who had taken care of Bended in Mumbai when she first arrived from England to meet Bhaiji in India.

Bhaiji told the Maharani that there was only vegetarian food in the house, which he would immediately send by car. If the Maharaja preferred non-vegetarian food, a butcher would have to be woken, a sheep slaughtered and cooked, which would take some hours. The Maharani left the phone to confer with the Maharaja and returned to say what the Maharaja said: 'Drop the idea.' It is not clear when or how the Maharaja's volatile mood ended and if he had his food that night. It would suffice to say that there were many fears and insecurities of the principal actors at the palace that could be whipped up or manipulated by those angling for favours. Bhaiji was fortunate in as much that he was the guardian minister to Dr Singh at a time when the relations between the Maharaja and the Maharani were at their most harmonious.

My father, Surakak, who was in the army at this time, remembered a strange trait of the Maharaja. He loved planning for banquets, deciding menus and hosting state guests. Despite his position and wealth, he had a tendency to be somewhat tight-fisted. Though in those days, English cigarettes were available quite cheaply (two annas a packet), my father recalled that the Maharaja would only serve cheap Indian cigarettes during banquets. My father knew this because he would go into another room to smoke with an ADC, since he didn't smoke in front of Bhaiji.

Once, while wandering around a banquet hall with a drink in his hand, my father had to hurriedly conceal the drink behind his back when he had bumped into Bhaiji. Two minutes after Bhaiji left, the Maharaja came up to him and boomed jovially, 'And where is your drink young man? I saw you hiding it behind your back. Drink up, don't worry!'

Bhaiji remained at the fringes of both royal entertainment and intrigues, but he did confide in me about an incident. Both he and his elder brother, Bab, used to initially respect the spiritual leader

Swami Sant Dev, who came to have a deep hold over the Maharaja and Maharani in the years before Partition, at a time when their marital relations were most cordial. They considered him to have some unusual powers. Sant Dev lived at Kud, near Patnitop, in summer and had his winter quarters in Lahore. Bhaiji recalls that he and Bab saw the Swami first at Haridwar in 1913. At that time, he had snow-white hair, a very fair complexion and was possibly 50- or 60-years-old. He wore silks, and his rotund body was always being scrubbed and perfumed by several attendants.

The story goes that when, in Srinagar, he lived in the Governor's Bungalow at Chashme Shahi, high on the mountainside overlooking the Dal Lake, he was one day bitten by a poisonous adder. Without expressing any distress, the Swami calmly obtained a particular herb from the hillside, applied a poultice on his swollen foot and miraculously was perfectly alright the next morning! This added to the legend surrounding his powers.

The Maharaja believed him to be about 250-year-old, but Bhaiji told me that he could not possibly have been more than 90-year-old in 1945. He narrated to me the story of how he had invited the Swami and the Maharaja to Bagh Sundar for a vegetarian meal, and the Maharaja had placed a present of ₹5,000 before the Swami, which he had brushed aside contemptuously, saying, 'What do I need money for? I have no daughters to marry off!'

While agreeing that this was perhaps a calculated gesture, Bhaiji reiterates that the Swami could not have reached this status without some real evidence of greatness at some stage. The Swami was one critical inflexion point in the triangle of intrigue between the Maharani, in association with her brother Nichint Chand, and the Maharaja and his favourites. Bhaiji, initially, made the mistake of trying to use the Swami as a lever with the Maharaja, but soon got caught in the intrigues of the Congress party, the Maharani and the Swami himself, from which he was never fully able to extricate himself.

Bhaiji told me that when the raiders entered Kashmir in October 1947, the Maharaja requisitioned the available Kashmir military transport trucks, loaded all his bags and baggage in the dead of night and left for Jammu. On the way, the Swami was dropped off at Kud. Thereafter, having perhaps lost his importance and power, there was little or no contact between the Maharaja and the Swami, who died a few years later, probably in Delhi.

There was no direct contact between the Maharaja and Bhaiji either, except once when Bhaiji was in exile in Bombay. In 1950, when Vallabhbhai Patel, commonly known as Sardar Patel, passed away, Bhaiji visited Birla House on Mount Pleasant Road to pay his respects. Coming out, he passed by the Maharaja in his car, who, upon seeing him, turned around and passed by after exchanging greetings, without saying anything of consequence. Two days later, his ADC came to see Bhaiji, saying, 'Now that you and the Maharaja are friends again...'

Bhaiji cut him short and responded, 'I have never been his enemy.'

'But won't you be seeing him?' asked the ADC.

'I really see no occasion for it,' replied Bhaiji.

In 1959, upon returning to Kashmir after a decade of exile, Bhaiji said that at the great insistence of the Maharani, he did go across for a meal to Chashme Shahi. Life had come full circle. There was no virtue in holding onto the regrets and resentments from a lifetime ago. Dr Singh was there and the occasion was marked by restrained cordiality. A semblance of the relationship that Bhaiji had with the Maharaja for more than 30 years was seemingly restored. However, the Maharaja, who had settled in Bombay, was already ailing by this time and passed away without a throne in 1961.

∽

Bhaiji, as we have seen, had a relationship with the Maharaja for more than 30 years. During this time, the two of them came to know each other well. Not only did Bhaiji rise steadily through the hierarchy, from a humble librarian to the director of the department of archaeology to the foreign and political secretary to the inspector general of customs to the chief secretary to army minister and the minister-in-waiting, he was also the guardian minister to the young Dr Singh, and as part of his duties for this role, he lived with Bended in the Talai Manzil, within the Maharaja's palace.

The Maharaja had indicated to Bhaiji that he had won his confidence over the years and that he now intended to make Bhaiji the PM of Kashmir. To that end, he appointed him as the minister-in-waiting from the army minister in 1943. This post is probably similar to that of a minister without portfolio in an elected government. But, in this case, it may be considered a peculiar perquisite of feudal governance, where the minister is only waiting to become PM!

I wonder what the job description of a minister-in-waiting in such circumstances would be—perhaps minister without a job? In a feudal setup, a job description is unpredictable. There is unlikely to be any organised form of internship, authority or transition. It can be quite frustrating for the incumbent, if carried on for too long. Perhaps, the minister-in-waiting would be called in for the meetings of the Maharaja and his PM to advise or perhaps, he would grow into an alternate centre of power. If Bended is to be believed, even as minister-in-waiting, Bhaiji, through the force of his personality, wielded considerable power.

Bhaiji was minister-in-waiting for two years during which time the Maharaja continued to dither. Eventually, Bhaiji became tired of waiting and threatened to resign. In order to avoid this possibility, the Maharaja asked the Maharani to intervene with Bhaiji, making him an offer he could not refuse. This, in the Maharaja's book, was an increase in salary, equivalent to that of the PM, but without the post. Perhaps they had not counted on Bhaiji's mettle or his resolve. He politely but firmly told the Maharani that he was motivated by duty and not by pecuniary gain. He also acknowledged that it was the prerogative of the Maharaja to appoint whomsoever he wished as the PM of Kashmir. But if the new incumbent were to be less experienced than himself, he would have no alternative but to resign. Bhaiji knew that the ever fluctuating choice of the Maharaja was now on a person with no experience or contact with Kashmir. As such, he compared unfavourably against Bhaiji's own experience of handling matters in Kashmir. It was now or never!

Both the Maharani and the Maharaja were shocked by this unexpected response. After some deliberation, finally, the Maharani called Bhaiji and told him that the Maharaja had agreed and had asked him to come over and meet him to discuss the details.

Bhaiji dutifully visited him the next day. The Maharaja, without preamble, simply asked him, 'When will you join?'

Bhaiji replied, equally simply, 'Whenever you wish.'

The Maharaja said, 'You have worked hard and deserve a rest. Take leave and resume office as the Prime Minister of Kashmir.'

It was a historic moment—the first time a Kashmiri Pandit had risen from the ranks to become the PM of Kashmir.

Bhaiji and Bended decided to take a holiday in the picturesque forest reserve of Dachigam, not far from Srinagar and home to the magnificent *barasingha* or *hangul* and the rare red bear.

Fate, it seems, has a way of intervening, when life is coming up roses. It had been an idyllic summer for Bhaiji and Bended. They were happy with each other. Bended had been accepted into the family. Bhaiji was soon to be the PM of Kashmir. His sons were well settled, the eldest in a firm in Bombay, the middle two in the army and the youngest, Khemendra Kak, a dashing pilot in the Royal Indian Air Force, already mentioned in dispatches and winner of the Distinguished Flying Cross (DFC) during World War II at the young age of 22. And, of course, their daughter, Lila, was three years old!

A perfect life, it seemed, lay ahead as they set out for a walk deep into the lovely forest that beautiful sunny morning on 4 June 1945. The Dachigam stream was overflowing, its waters sparkling in the sunshine. A soft breeze was playing. The air was full of the sound of birds, dense with the flight of butterflies and insects. Nature, it seemed, had arranged a spectacular display for the two of them! Bhaiji's heart overflowed. Normally a taciturn man, he exclaimed to Bended, 'If we could live like this, we could live forever!'

At that moment, they were interrupted by a breathless messenger requesting them to return to the rest house for an important message. When they returned, the officer deputed to deliver the message was unable to speak. Suddenly, the house phone rang. With a deep sense of foreboding, Bhaiji picked up the phone. It was a trunk call from the Royal Indian Air Force base at Risalpur, informing him that Khemendra Kak's plane had gone sickeningly out of control while describing a victory loop and crashed while landing and that he had died instantly. They were asking how the funeral should be held.

Ashen-faced, Bhaiji put down the phone and simply said, 'Khema Kak. Finished!'

They rushed back to Srinagar. Grief-stricken, Bhaiji never stepped out for 12 days, never saw or spoke to anyone.

Khema Kak, as he was affectionately known, was Bhaiji's youngest, handsomest and most accomplished son. Mentioned for his bravery in dispatches, with a trunk full of cups and medals for cricket, football, boxing and athletics, his was an unbearable loss. Bhaiji could not bear to read his letters, which, ironically, reached after his death. On 10 February 1948, the Air Ministry finally forwarded Khema Kak's DFC to Bhaiji, expressing profound regret that his son did not live to receive this recognition of his services. Bhaiji was unable to bring himself to read the letter or look at the DFC, a recognition which later Khema Kak's good friend in the Air Force Anand 'Nifty' Pandit, who went on to become an Air Marshal, also received.

The Maharaja, worried about Bhaiji's health, and out of sympathy and kindness suggested that he take over sooner as PM, to help distract his mind from the tragedy. It was a wise decision. In the midst of great tragedy, with his world having crashed around him, Bhaiji assumed the post of the PM of Kashmir on 30 June 1945.

11

Becoming the Prime Minister of Jammu and Kashmir

In his assessment of the problems and possibilities facing Kashmir in 1945, Bhaiji logically outlined the immediate issues he faced as he assumed the onerous responsibilities of the prime ministership. His elaborate analysis was typical of his diligent and systematic approach, which gave Kashmir a chance to not only attain stability but also development. Interestingly, Bhaiji also wrote about his self-assessment, which was never published or highlighted, after he stepped down as the PM two years later.

Bhaiji's observations about the immediate issues he faced were an eyewitness account of an important period in the history of India. When compared with the hasty judgements passed in the aftermath of the political upheaval of 1947, his understanding of the issues of the day and the way he tackled them merit a new assessment of his role as, perhaps, the most effective PM of Kashmir under the Maharaja's rule. This assessment was later borne out by Dr Karan Singh in his book *Heir Apparent*. Bhaiji was Dr Singh's guardian, and the latter acknowledged some important lessons learnt from Bhaiji before succeeding his father.

The following chapters quote extensively from Bhaiji's own words. In these detailed notes, he outlined the opposing political pulls and pressures in Kashmir, represented by the Jammu & Kashmir National Conference (National Conference), under Sheikh Abdullah; the All Jammu and Kashmir Muslim Conference

(Muslim Conference), founded by Chaudhri Ghulam Abbas; the Indian National Congress (Congress) party, led by Mahatma Gandhi and Jawaharlal Nehru; and the Pakistan Muslim League, led by Mohammad Ali Jinnah. At that time, political parties were working against the State from within, inciting strikes and violence even when entrusted with settling confrontations. Hoping to take advantage of the Independence-induced chaos, the Maharaja dreamt of an enlarged and independent Kashmir, including Kangra, under his rule, with Lahore as the capital. And all of this was happening in a Muslim majority electorate chafing under an undemocratic Hindu rule. That a PM could bring peace and development under such adverse conditions, until he was brought down by extraneous circumstances, is itself the stuff of history.

I believe Bhaiji's observations are, perhaps, the first and only assessment of the state written by a PM of Kashmir before assuming office. Fortunately, the original typewritten but unpublished memoirs about Kashmir written by both Bhaiji and Bended between 1945 and 1950 are indeed eyewitness accounts of an important part of our social, cultural and political history, and are being seen here for the first time.

When Bhaiji finally took over as the PM of Kashmir, he was 52-year-old and had been serving the Government of Kashmir for more than 30 years, first in the Department of Archaeology and subsequently in administrative and, finally, political capacities.

Over the years, Bhaiji was often asked by successive administrations and even by the Maharaja to write historical, geographical and political analyses for visiting viceroys and heads of state. On being appointed as the PM of Kashmir, he compiled and updated a comprehensive assessment, which was a valuable indication of the sensitive and vulnerable situation in which the state of Kashmir existed. He wrote:

Figure 12: Bhaiji's first day in office as the PM of Kashmir at the age of 52 on 30 June 1945

Illustration credit: Kashmira Tembulkar

Hari Singh succeeded his uncle, Pratap Singh, in 1925. No two persons could be more unlike each other. The uncle—old and mellowed by the struggles and disappointment of a lifetime—had, towards the end of his life, carved out a niche for himself in the affections of his people. He was accessible to rich and poor alike, whether at the palace or in the open country, under the shade of a spreading chinar, people would cluster round him, sitting on the ground, as he himself sat, and exchanging news and views regarding matters, public or private, which interested them [...]

The difference in the character of the two men was soon reflected in the attitude of the people towards the successor. Maharaja Pratap Singh looked with disfavour on any change, political or social. There was no question during his regime of any drastic statutory measures for the upliftment of

> depressed classes, prevention of infant marriages, relief from indebtedness for the peasantry at the expense of moneyed interests, still less of the creation of democratic institutions. Nevertheless, by his amiability and personal goodwill, he kept the people fairly contented. There was in any case no outward manifestation of serious discontent during his regime[...]
>
> Hari Singh, on his succession, made a clean sweep of all the dependants, protégés and employees of his uncle. As these were many, the new regime, at its very start and by its own action, found itself faced by many critics, who, in due course, became the nuclei of discontent. This was followed by ill-conceived and hasty action in implementing measures for the relief of the peasantry from indebtedness. Relief was sorely needed, but the method of granting it should have been conceived carefully after consultation with both the interests concerned, lenders as well as borrowers.

But, as Bhaiji narrated, once an idea entered his head, the new Maharaja proceeded to implement it at breakneck speed, brushing aside all dissident opinion as deliberately mischievous. This sometimes led to a farcical interpretation of democracy.

> Even to this day, he [the Maharaja] is fond of relating how he got his ministers to agree to his proposals on the subject of agricultural relief, as it was called. He was on tour at Uri, a small town about 70 miles from Srinagar, where he was living in a dak bungalow. He thought that the ministers were taking a long time in discussing the matter. They felt that the measures proposed practically implied the cancellation of transactions that involved millions of rupees and would vitally affect, for good or evil, the entire economic life of the country. They therefore tried to take into consideration all points of view. The Maharaja lost patience and locked them up in a small room of the bungalow, telling them that the door would be opened only when they gave him the

information that the discussion had been concluded and unanimous agreement arrived at in regard to what he desired. The door did not remain shut for long, but the trust which had taken generations to build up—sometime it must be admitted in ways not altogether upright—was destroyed. By these measures, the Maharaja alienated the capitalist and landowning classes who now came to the conclusion that here was a man whom there was no checking once he had started on his headstrong course. Contrary to expectation, however, the peasantry who were the beneficiaries of his largesse showed no real gratitude, after the first flush of emancipation from the moneylender because while they were glad to be rid of their previous burden, their avenues for obtaining credit for the future were closed. Moreover, the village moneylender, exacting as he was at times, was an acquaintance of long standing and could be cajoled, whereas the government-sponsored and controlled Co-operative Credit Department was more impersonal and its officers, in their own way, not less exacting. Nevertheless, the benefit to the peasantry was substantial and their goodwill to the Maharaja would have stood him in good stead, but for certain things he did in other directions, which caused bitter resentment among all classes of his subject except his own clansmen.

For one, in honour of his accession, Hari Singh granted a large number of *jagirs*. All but one of them were granted to residents of Jammu and all but two of them to members or retainers of his own clan. Most of the grantees selected villages in Kashmir for their jagirs, some of them the choicest spots in respect of beauty and fertility, such as areas in the Pahalgam valley. Simultaneously, a Jagir Committee was appointed to investigate the condition of the past and present jagirs, and the financial position of jagirdars and to propose measures to improve it. The committee made some extraordinary proposals, which were sanctioned by the

> Maharaja. The truth was that the proposals were made after he had approved them. Among these, the most objectionable was that if a junior member of a Jagirdar's family, who held a jagir in one of the two provinces, Jammu or Kashmir, would surrender his share of the jagir in favour of the parent branch of the jagir family, he would be entitled to get a jagir of double the value of what he had surrendered in the other province. In effect, this meant that younger branches of Jammu Rajput families could, in lieu of their meagre allowances from their parental jagirs, get substantial jagirs of their own in Kashmir. No one from Kashmir would or did take advantage of this new dispensation for the reason that for them, there was no advantage in going to an insalubrious climate. Besides this concession, the jagirdars were to be granted further concessions, example, (1) ownership of forests within their villages, though so far as agricultural lands in these villages were concerned, they had no powers of interference, since they were only entitled to the land revenue, which was usually paid to them either directly by the headman and indirectly through the tehsil treasury, (2) areas for setting up a home farm and certain rights over the wasterlands. The object was obvious. Whereas on the one hand the Maharaja had no objection to weakening the capitalist class—mainly Hindus other than Rajputs—and freeing the peasants—mainly Muslims—from the moneylenders' hold, he endeavoured to set up a landed aristocracy mainly derived from his own community who would function as the props and pillars of his *gaddi* in all parts of the state.

The logic was simple. Since they owed their present position and importance to the Maharaja, their allegiance to him would be undivided. In order that they might acquire local influence, the Maharaja provided by rule that they should build a house in the jagir and reside in it for a specified minimum period in the year. In short, he hoped to reproduce in Kashmir what Bhaiji called a squirearchy, more or less based on the English model. Unfortunately, as Bhaiji noted, a squirearchy takes generations to take root and cannot be created overnight by an 'order of the day', particularly if that squire is an alien planted among the people, whose language he cannot speak, who differ from him in religion, manners and customs, and who is, in most cases, no more than an absentee landlord. Such a person cannot influence local opinion, and this ill-judged act was exploited by political agitators in later years, costing the Maharaja all the goodwill he had acquired among the peasantry due to the economic relief he had offered them.

Furthermore, by excluding all boys not belonging to the Rajput community from the school founded in memory of Maharaja Pratap Singh, Bhaiji observed that the Maharaja rudely shocked the sensibilities of all classes of people. They felt that the Maharaja wished to secure his own community's dominant position in the civil services, besides reserving for them the greatest proportion of military employment.

Bhaiji's detailed analysis also covered the historical, cultural and political contexts that needed to be understood if the state had to be governed effectively despite its fault lines and contradictions. He provided three broad contexts for governance. The first context was geographical.

> The valley of Kashmir is the homeland of the main body of Kashmiri-speaking people, distinct in language and character from all the other communities which inhabit the state. High mountain walls have through the centuries presented a barrier which only the ardours and dangers of a long journey over difficult passes could overcome. This coupled with the fertility of the soil and a superb climate induced in the inhabitants a firm faith in the superiority of their own land and climate and themselves as its inhabitants. They [Kashmiris] are an intelligent people, but generally speaking, their isolation has prevented them from attaining

> breadth of outlook. They have looked to their horizon, which they call [...] sangamal, the garland of peaks, and they have tended to discount all that lay beyond. They have an ancient and an honourable history, now represented by a unique collection of architectural monuments as well as by literary and philosophical texts, revealing a high standard of culture and achievement in the past. The present population is mostly Muslim, who retain their Hindu ancestors' talent for artistic execution to which the mosques and other buildings of the present day Srinagar bear a living testimony. The minute minority who still retain their ancient culture and tradition unimpaired are now known by the name 'Kashmiri Pandits'. They are the descendants of the few families of Brahmins who refused to be converted and survived when the rest of the population was forced to accept Islam. Throughout the generations, they have occupied a position in some ways disproportionate to their numbers. By virtue of their inherited aptitude for intellectual pursuits, they have always been at the forefront of those who were suitable for administrative employment and since literacy is more or less universal in the community, classes have found it profitable to leave administrative work, particularly the minor jobs, in the hands of people who, even though the emoluments were meagre, preferred clerical to manual labour. In recent years, however, with the spread of education among the masses, members of other communities have joined the scramble for government employment in the hope of securing political prestige and power which, under an autocratic government, naturally devolved on the bureaucracy.

The second context for governance, related to his assumption of prime ministership in 1945, was economic, to which Bhaiji brought a seasoned insight.

> As the principal divisions of the state differed from one another in climate and the character of their population,

> so they differed in their economic conditions. Ladakh and Gilgit have always been deficit areas. The former has some minerals, but it is difficult to work the mines owing to the lack of communications and rigours of the climate.
>
> Jammu has considerable forests and is able to export large quantities of timber along with forest products such as resin and drugs. It also exports *ghee* in large quantities.
>
> The bulk of the revenue of the state, however, is derived from Kashmir, which has a well-developed tourist industry and produces a great variety of articles of high artistic beauty and value. Among these are the famous Kashmiri shawls, papier mâché and lacquer work, carved walnut wood, silverware, embroideries of all kinds and ornaments made of semi-precious stones such as turquoise, carnelian, jade, lapis lazuli, aquamarine, etc. In addition, Kashmir exports vast quantities of fruit and timber. It has a flourishing silk industry which is one of the four main props of state finance, the other three being forests, customs and land revenue. The fertility of its soil and abundance of water enable it to be self-supporting in food in normal times.

The economic diversity of Kashmir needed more effective communication to bridge the distances, both roads and, perhaps, more so, air services in the short term. Bhaiji was acutely aware of this deficiency for which long-term funds and planning were sorely required.

The only effective cure for Kashmir's lack of communications was establishing air traffic, but no step was taken towards this until 1946. Though landing grounds of sorts had been constructed some years before, they were available only for the Maharaja's aircraft. Finally, at the beginning of 1947, a regular air service started to function between Srinagar and New Delhi, bringing an ever-increasing number of the more well-to-do tourists into the city. But it ceased to operate directly [when] Kashmir became a battleground for India and Pakistan. Afterwards, planes commissioned by the Government of India used the Kashmir landing grounds to evacuate refugees and dispatch troops and munitions.

The third and perhaps most important context in effectively governing Kashmir was religious and cultural coexistence. Here, as Bhaiji observed, existed the widest gap that needed to be bridged in order to ensure peace and longevity of rule.

> It will be clear from what has been stated above that the population of the state was composed of such diverse elements that a sense of homogeneity could have been produced among them only if a deliberate and persistent attempt had been made towards that end. In point of fact, no such attempt was ever made. On the contrary, the endeavour of the rulers and their advisers has usually been so to devise and act that the differences between the various groups might be accentuated rather than that they should be obliterated. To give an example, discrimination was made against the Kashmiri speaking people with regard to recruitment of the state forces. In spite of a lapse of a century, the Dogra refused to look upon himself as anything but the conqueror and the ruler. He was, therefore, regarded by all classes with distrust, and often with active dislike. In the provinces, local patriotism was strong and, except in rare cases, there was in no part of the state any enthusiasm for a common citizenship other than in respect of securing government employment. A certain bond of kinship did exist between Kashmiri and Kashmiri, Dogra and Dogra and so on; and where religious matters were involved, between people of one persuasion in contradistinction to people of another persuasion. But it did not go further. The lack of a feeling of close kinship between the different communities living in the state was bound to react unfavourably on its integrity the moment a crisis arose which demanded any great sacrifice on their part. Thus, anybody possessed of an adequate knowledge

> of the state and a mind not warped by political prejudice could have foreseen the result when Kashmir received the shock of India's partition and was faced with the choice of accession to either dominion: a truncated India or a newly arisen Pakistan.

Bhaiji felt there was another influential group that the Maharaja antagonised since his ascension to the throne in 1925—the British residents of Kashmir and the British officers of the Government of India. This group had, after retirement, made Kashmir their home because of its salubrious climate and comparatively peaceful conditions or because they were entrusted with administrative responsibilities, including a few being appointed as the prime ministers of the state. This group had become accustomed to the old world courtesy and lavish hospitality of the late Maharaja Pratap Singh, which the Maharaja somewhat churlishly refused to show them.

Had the Maharaja contented himself with a refusal to show them undue deference but treated them with friendliness and courtesy, they would have understood the position as being natural in a young man brought up in modern ways and not being resentful. But he made a practice of deliberately offending them through inconsiderate behaviour and slighting remarks. He thought he was justified in his deep dislike of the British because a British officer had gotten him involved in the humiliating affair known as the 'Mr A Case'[24], in which he had cut a very sorry figure.

> To some extent his feelings on the subject were understandable, but it is only fair to say that the British community generally had sympathised with him on the occasion and the British he came in contact with and to

[24]'Mr A' was a fictitious name given by the India Office, London, to the Maharaja to protect the his identity white setting a court case of blackmail. The then Maharaja-to-be had been trapped by a British conman having an affair with a local lady of leisure in London. He had to pay £300,000 in 1921, who had found out that the Maharaja was (approximately £13,100,000 in today's value) as settlement.

> whom he behaved grudgingly felt that he was behaving unreasonably. Because one Englishman had behaved abominably, and it was universally conceded that he had done so, they held that there was no reason for the Maharaja to entertain a violent dislike for the British nation, and that at the very least, he should in his own interests behave to them with common decency in public.

Bhaiji remarked that the Maharaja withdrew all the small concessions the British community had enjoyed previously. The sting was not in the cancellation, which most people thought was inevitable in the changed conditions, but the manner in which it was affected, causing maximum friction and inconvenience, to say nothing of the humiliation the concerned persons faced. In a few years, the intemperate actions of the Maharaja, even in gestures of a liberal nature to appease the majority population, backfired and rapidly dissipated his goodwill.

> The position towards the end of the 1920s was that a band of young men was ready to take up the banner of revolt against the autocratic administration of the Maharaja. Notwithstanding what he had done to relieve the peasantry, particularly in regard to their indebtedness, he was much less popular than his predecessor who had done nothing so spectacular. The reason was that while his intentions were ostensibly the best, it was felt that he was not actuated so much by unselfish motives and a desire to relieve suffering humanity. The motive force behind all his philanthropy was what he himself could get out of these measures in the shape of popularity among the masses, however detrimental his acts might be to certain classes. Where his own personal interests were concerned, he never yielded anything except for a definite and visible quid pro quo. Secondly, it was soon obvious that whatever in the way of patronage was available, the recipients were almost always his clansmen whether individually or as a class.

> Though a sense of bitterness and frustration was generally prevalent, Hindus as such were averse to taking any action which would weaken the hands of the government, however aggrieved they might feel against the Maharaja personally and his clan. Muslims received encouragement and financial assistance from Indian political and religious organisations, many of whose important members were Kashmiri in origin. An All-India Kashmir Committee was set up in Lahore with the objective of advocating the cause of Kashmiri Muslims. The Muslim notables of the state, even those occupying high government office, had affiliations with these organisations, since, even apart from natural sympathy with anybody whose avowed object was the uplift of Muslims, connection with influential political organisations opened out a welcome prospect of advancement and promotion for themselves.

Bhaiji's study and understanding of the historical factors underlying the Kashmir problem are of great significance. Even more important is the ability of one man to encompass such a breadth of knowledge and bring it to bear on the conduct of his administration. I do not believe any other prospective PM of Kashmir had compiled similarly comprehensive cultural, historical and administrative perspectives before or since, which went on to offer insights and influence policy and governance decisions. These insights, in fact, helped preserve peace in the Valley even when the rest of India was aflame with political and religious turmoil. Nonetheless, Bhaiji had a premonition of things to come.

12

The Strongman of Kashmir

More than 50 years ago, Bhaiji spoke to me about his work and legacy as the PM of Kashmir. I was an immature youth with neither any great understanding of the issues he faced nor the magnitude of the problems that he tackled on several fronts simultaneously. My preoccupation at that time was to document his words for posterity. So, I would religiously note down my conversations with him and transcribe them diligently by hand into paper files. I am astonished that the original handwritten papers are still intact, if a little worse for wear but still legible.

Figure 13: Bhaiji, as the PM, directly talking to peasants regarding their problems in 1945

Illustration credit: Kashmira Tembulkar

What followed was a unique, if unexpected, self-assessment by a PM of his work in office, an assessment necessitated by the fact that the political circumstances in his state and country were unlikely to give him a fair trial. Bhaiji began with the situation that confronted him in his very first few days in office in July 1945:

> Directly after I assumed office, I discovered that the financial and the political situation needed immediate attention. Financially, things had gone wrong badly. The financial adviser had been submitting report after report that the reserves were depleted to a dangerous extent and that, in effect, the state was verging on bankruptcy. The budget was a deficit one and current expenditure had to be met by a loan from the Jammu & Kashmir [J&K] Bank. In addition, liabilities were mounting, as there was a demand from the services for enhanced pay, owing to the higher cost of living and from government departments for expansion involving heavy expenditure. During the period of the war, many of the states and provincial governments profiting from larger revenues due to war requirements production, had built up considerable reserves, but Kashmir was not one of these. It had, on the contrary, consumed a large proportion of the previously accumulated reserves by drawing on them for what was called capital expenditure. As works involving a cost of ₹50,000 and over were designated capital works and as few of them yielded any profit and further as the dwindling reserves could not be replenished, since the government budgeted its expenditure to the limit of its revenue, the financial position went on worsening from year to year until, in 1945, ordinary expenditure had to be met by borrowing, and minor items of development, example, opening some primary schools and raising some secondary schools to the standard of high schools had to be held up.
>
> What was therefore urgently called for was the exercise of vigilance to reduce day-to-day expenditure, and strict

> scrutiny of proposals involving fresh outlay, as well as the improvement of existing sources of revenue. The efforts made in this behalf brought about the satisfactory result that in the following year's budget, which was the first of my prime ministership, I was able to earmark ₹70 lakhs and the first instalment for a post-war development fund, besides showing a surplus of over ₹7 lakhs after meeting all the demands from the departments and paying off the loan taken in my predecessor's time.

In the following excerpt, Bhaiji made an interesting observation, considering we are referring to the educational facilities in the mid-1940s in Kashmir. Bhaiji's visionary new ideas regarding an education policy for Kashmir could be considered a precursor to contemporary skill development policies, countering the deeply entrenched academic education system, which were not broached in India till nearly a century later.

> As in the rest of India, the chief trouble with the prevailing educational policy is that while it provides a number of people with useful qualifications, the scope of employment for such people is limited. Whatever the value of a university degree, this country, proportionately, has more degree holders than can be absorbed in the professions or the public service. In Kashmir, this is peculiarly so, as while the demand is very restricted, the supply is very large, since one of the communities has always been distinguished for its high educational attainments, and has, in relation to its total numeral strength, produced a larger number of persons of high educational qualifications than the sister communities. With the spread of education, which enabled other classes of people also to enter the competition for employment in the public services and professions, the field for employment of those who had, by heredity and inclination, been confining their hopes and ambitions to employment in the government services and the learnt professions became more and more

restricted and unemployment among them increased with accompanying distress and discontent, which soon spread to other communities also, since the ambition of every so-called educated young person was to get a job in a government office. Incidentally, the acquisition of university education was not a difficult job in Kashmir.

College fees were nominal and the expenditure involved in pursuing studies to the university standard negligible. Indeed, because openings for employment were so few and the cost of college education so small, the harassed heads of families often decided to send their offspring to college, as that would, in any case, keep them out of mischief for a few hours in the day.

Whatever the reason, the fact remained that there were a large number of educated unemployed throughout the country who had no avenue open to them, which would enable them to earn a living, except manual labour. To this, they did not take kindly.

Even those young men who belonged to working class families—whose parents worked, for example, as dhobis—yearned for clerical jobs at ₹20–25 per month, though they could earn three or four times that amount if they went into their family business. Their objection arose out of the feeling that having passed the matriculation examination, it would be derogatory for them to engage in mere manual work [...]

What, therefore, the country needed, was a new orientation of the educational policy, the basic idea of which was to relieve the pressure on higher education and yet ensure that the country would have at its disposal all the resources needed for its development in both higher and lower standards of education.

It seemed that the simplest way to achieve this objective would be to make all education free but so regulate recruitment to the various standards that instead of becoming a social misfit, each individual would fit into his place in society and do the job he was most suitable for. The proposal was that primary education should be made compulsory up to the age of 11 or 12 for all children. Thereafter, 10 per cent of the best among the children should be selected on the basis of a competitive examination, allowance being made for special circumstances in particular cases, and this 10 per cent should be admitted to high schools, where they would—side-by-side with the ordinary academic education—be taught trades and crafts, and the simplest types of technical work, like craftsmanship, mechanical engineering, electrical repair work, farming, weaving, etc. Out of this lot, one-tenth would be selected on the basis of merit, for what would be equivalent to college education. In other words, not more than 1 per cent of the total school-going population of the country would normally reach the college stage. This 1 per cent would, on the completion of their education, provide the lawyers, engineers, doctors, civil servants etc., whose services are essential to modern society.

Though education would be free, there would be no wastage of good money on bad material, since selection would ensure that only those would be eligible for higher education who possessed the requisite ability.

There, however, are some individuals who do not shine in examinations. It was contemplated to permit such persons to continue education if they paid a prescribed fee, which normally would not be pitched too low—this to discourage indiscriminate advantage being taken of the departure from the rule.

The utility of the scheme was obvious in that it would serve the purpose of providing opportunities to everybody to learn some trade or profession, and it would automatically act as a brake in the swelling multitude of young people, who were possessed of university degrees and diplomas, but unable to or unwilling to turn their hand to practical use.

Bhaiji went on to write of a unique problem he faced at a sheep breeding farm in Banihal:

> It is often difficult to persuade an expert that his aim, though laudable, might be difficult of achievement, that though a whole loaf is a very desirable thing, one might perhaps, on occasion, do well to be content with half a loaf.
>
> I was confronted with this problem at the sheep breeding farm at Banihal. This farm had been established some years before with the advice and cooperation of the Imperial Council of Agricultural Research, which contributed a majority of the expenditure on the experiment. A number of Merino rams had been imported from Australia and, since Kashmir is a wool growing country, it was thought that if the Merino was crossed with and ultimately replaced the indigenous sheep, the wool industry would receive a great fillip. Years went by and though reports used to be received indicating how many rams had been bred and distributed and what flocks raised, so far as the naked eye could see, nothing very much seemed to be happening.
>
> When I discussed the situation with the expert, he said that he had not yet been able to issue the breeding stock to owners of flocks. He explained that he had tried the experiment but found that in the third generation, the imported strain seemed to disappear and the animal showed little trace of Merino in him. At this rate, improvement was hardly likely to be rapid. So, I suggested that since the number of the male lambs born at the farm was, and would in all likelihood always be, in excess of requirements, it would be possible to issue fresh rams for breeding before the strain became too diluted, we could go on doing so until the new strain stabilised. In any case, by continuing extensive issues of breeding stock, we could achieve some improvement in the general standard without, in any way, interfering with the expert efforts to stabilise the strain at the farm. Stabilised breeding stock could be issued later.

This was one reform that needed more time. There is still a sheep breeding farm in Banihal, but its overall success is still doubtful. However, one of Bhaiji's legacies that has survived more than half a century was his afforestation drive from 1945. It led to, among other things, the Shankaracharya Hill facing the Dal Lake acquiring a wooded cover that can be seen even today. Bhaiji's scheme was to enlist the common population in planting trees and allowing them to use the wood for domestic use, which was enthusiastically taken up and has been mentioned by Bended in her letters. Lakhs of trees were planted in Anantnag and Baramulla and, indeed, on any available wasteland, through a visionary public private partnership.

If one were to read between the lines of Bhaiji's memoir, one can assume that the austerity programme that he referred to brought about improved governance and, no doubt, successfully plugged loopholes exploited by a corrupt system for existing and future projects. It is astonishing that Bhaiji not only earmarked a substantial sum (in those days) of ₹70 lakh within eight months for the following year's Budget for a post-war development fund but also generated a surplus of ₹7 lakh, even after providing for and repaying ₹22 lakh to the J&K Bank, the amount being borrowed by the government for paying staff salaries and for day-to-day administration. The austerity measures amounted to about ₹1 crore being saved in less than one financial year. Thus, the extent of profligacy and misappropriation prevalent in the previous administration can be imagined, not to speak of lack of foresight. Bhaiji did not rest on his laurels but immediately launched the state on a path of industrial and economic recovery.

> The fact that a state which had repeatedly been declared to be on the verge of insolvency by administrators and financial experts of distinction [...] was found not only thoroughly solvent to undertake considerable expenditure without resort to fresh taxation or borrowing, had far-reaching influence in unexpected directions.

For instance, in relation to industrialists, round about 1940, the state had started discussions with Tatas for the establishment of a drug industry, since the Kashmir forests had a great abundance of drugs and herbs, large quantities which were exported in a raw state to India and overseas. The intention was that the state should in conjunction with Tatas, who would provide the capital and industrial organisation, start an industry in its own territory and export the finished product instead of the raw material.

Already for some years, a pilot plant had been functioning, in which experiments were being done. It was proposed that Tatas should take this over as the state's contribution towards the industry. The discussions which had been initiated in 1940 between Tatas' representatives and the state had dragged on for five years during which the prime ministership had changed hands four times. But no final conclusion had been arrived at. Latterly, the position had been complicated further by the presence in the state cabinet of Mr Afzal Beg, who was opposed to any idea of an alliance with Tatas. He wanted the industry to be run in consonance with the ideals of 'New Kashmir'—without recourse to capitalists and big business and only as a co-operative peasant enterprise. As in the state, there was a lack of finances and technical knowledge as well as of the incentive resulting from industrial experience, obviously such an alternative was not practicable. The industry was expected to start with a capital initially of a crore of rupees, of which Tatas had agreed to provide 51 per cent. The state and its people were invited to provide up to 49 per cent in case they so desired. Failing their ability to do so within a given period, Tatas were prepared to take up the balance of the shares. Tatas did not expect that the state would be able to provide anything more than what it had already invested on the pilot plant which was about 7 or 8 lakh rupees. Nor did they expect that many private individuals in an area so industrially backward would come forward to purchase any considerable number of shares. In this they were not mistaken, for notwithstanding the many attempts made by several prime ministers, there was hardly any public response for purchase of shares of the projected company.

When, therefore, in the cold weather of 1946, the Tata representatives came to Jammu to conclude the arrangements, which they were anxious to do, it was a surprise to them when I said that the state would underwrite 49 per cent of the share capital. To the question whether the government would buy this 49 per cent of shares or whether the people of the state would do so and, if so, to what extent, I replied that so far as Tatas were concerned, the Kashmir government would buy all the shares. It would be open to them to pass on as many as they might like to the people immediately or later. I thought of utilising 49 lakh out of 70 lakh which I knew I would be crediting to the post war reconstruction fund. It was my strong view, being that the state, when it started its first major industry, in conjunction with a firm like Tatas, should not be relegated to the state of a poor relation.

The great problem of Kashmir, apart from food and clothing, was the increasing scarcity of fuel. This sounds strange considering the fact that Kashmir possessed forest areas extending over 10,000 square miles in the aggregate. The trouble however was not the scarcity of fuel itself but the high cost of transporting it from the forest to the consumer. This ultimately amounted to several times the cost of extraction. The forests nearer the towns and cities had long been exploited. Firewood had now to be brought over long distances on backs of ponies and by cart and truck. This added heavily to the cost. Things ultimately came to such a pass, that to provide the people with fire-wood, valuable timber, which would normally have been used for constructional purposes, was cut for use as fuel.

This state of affairs was forcibly brought to my attention during my tours in the countryside. I accordingly decided to induce the peasants to utilise the waste lands and the village lands for plantation... I found the peasants enthusiastically receptive to the ideas, particularly when I told them that the trees they planted in the village lands, would be wholly their property and those that they planted on Government land, they would share equally with the Government.

The response was so great indeed that in March/April 1946, 30 lakh trees were planted in the two districts of Anantnag and Baramulla, on the waste lands and hill sides, along roads and canal banks. In fact, wherever plantation could be affected, it was carried out. The Government did not pay a single penny for these operations, which were voluntary and remunerative.

These and other measures which were really to the nature of exploratory experiments, the aim of which was as far as possible to bring Government activity into line with the life and requirements of the mass of the people and to enlist the co-operation of the latter in a general endeavour to raise their social and economic level had two definite results. The first was that the mass of people started to look upon the Administrative agency not as a necessary evil which had at the best only to be tolerated, but which was usually execrated. Now they began to view it as something of a foster mother, who might be stern at times, but whose motives were unquestionably friendly and actions based on genuine sympathy. The immediate outcome was that the peasantry whose uplift engaged most of the attention of the Administration tended to by-pass the political leaders whose trump cards had been that they could get things done by the Government for them. When the peasants realised that the Government themselves were anxious to co-operate with and help them, the role of politicians in a primitive society which was not moved by political theories and ideals

> but only by the daily needs of individuals and their families ceased to be important.
>
> The other result was to me startling and unexpected. The endeavour to harness the forces latent in the people and yoke them with the administrative agency for the common purpose of building up the life of the country necessarily brought me into constant and intimate thought with people of all classes, in all parts of the state. The new direction given to the thoughts and hopes of the people of all classes strengthened the government and gave confidence to those who were entrusted with the task of carrying on the administration whether at the headquarters or in the districts and villages. Surprisingly, however, I began to discover that the Ruler viewed this development with misgiving. Satisfied though he was with the suppression of political agitation, he seemed to have thought that the rise in the stock of the government among the people of the state was too much of a good thing so far as he himself was concerned, as it automatically brought into relief his failure to achieve anything similar in the preceding 21 years of his regime. It is very doubtful whether the people as a whole ever entertained any idea of this kind, but his own inherently suspicious nature, coupled with the constant reinforcement received through hints dropped by his immediate entourage, seem to have caused him considerable disquiet, particularly, as, on certain occasions, I could not see my way to fall in with his wishes, even in matters which he thought would be gratifying to me personally.

Bhaiji here is referring to the Nehru confrontation and arrest a year later, in June 1946, which attracted global attention for its David and Goliath overtones. In this confrontation, my grandfather, backed by the Maharaja of Kashmir, was David and Nehru, backed by Mahatma Gandhi and the Congress, was Goliath. The grateful Maharaja wished to reward his loyal PM in the only way he knew, but given the inflexible values of his PM, it spawned an unexpected result.

> Soon after the Nehru episode, I was told by the Maharani that it was the Maharaja's intention to grant me a hereditary jagir. While asking her to convey to him my thanks for his intended kindness, I signified my inability to accept the grant, not realising that the refusal might be liable to be misunderstood. My reasons for the refusal were entirely practical ones, example firstly, in the new social order being born, jagirs were an anachronism, and secondly, I felt that the proper time for recognition of my services to the state would be when I retired and not at the moment when such recognition was sure to be interpreted in the context of the events immediately preceding. It appears that my refusal was construed as an ungracious act on my part, and as indicative of my feeling that I was unwilling to accept a favour from the Ruler.
>
> Nevertheless the year 1946 passed off without any visible sign of the Maharaja's discontent and when, in January 1947, he left for Bombay, he gave no signs of entertaining any feeling other than satisfaction as regards how things were developing!

This was one aspect of Bhaiji's assessment of the Maharaja where unfortunately he proved to be entirely wrong, with disastrous consequences eventually, not only for himself but also for the state and the nation.

It was unfortunate that circumstances conspired against his vision of state pride, a participative democracy and financial discipline for Kashmir, which might have been transformative if he had been more diplomatic in surviving the vagaries of the political dispensations of that time. Had he done so, he may have qualified for an assessment as one of the most practical and efficient PM of a self-sufficient Kashmir.

Unfortunately, maintaining the well-being of the golden goose of Kashmir was not the uppermost in the minds of the main political actors of that time, including the Maharaja. The political game of chess for dominance being played out in full view in Kashmir was more important to them. The political situation was extremely fluid. The only thing that seemed certain, as mentioned earlier, was that there was no group favourably inclined towards the government. It only needed a spark to start a conflagration. That spark was provided by the Silk Mill Strike engineered by the National Conference within days of Bhaiji assuming prime ministership, when he was at his most vulnerable. Meanwhile, the Muslim Conference of Jammu, affiliated to the All-India Muslim League, passed a vote of no confidence against Bhaiji on the day he assumed office.

> The Muslim Conference was furious because they felt cheated by [...] the fact, among other things, that Sheikh Abdullah's nominee, Afzal Beg, had been appointed a minister, though the Muslim Conference group in the Assembly was the more numerous. They were intensely critical of the government and called a conference at Rawalkot in Poonch to frame a fresh scheme of active opposition.
>
> The National Conference was intransigent, as Sheikh Abdullah started feeling that his nominee did not have all the power he ought to have.
>
> Sheikh Abdullah wanted to eat his cake and have it too. By having one of his principal lieutenants as a minister, his object was to utilise all the authority and prestige of the government for the benefit of his party and of the members thereof. At the same time, he wanted to carry on untrammelled his propaganda against the government, which he characterised as irresponsible, bureaucratic and inefficient.
>
> In fact, Afzal Beg expected and asked that he should have the freedom to exercise his vote as he thought fit in the Assembly and not necessarily with his colleagues in the government. This proposition could obviously not be

accepted. Sir B.N. Rau proposed to solve the dilemma by providing that the so-called 'popular' ministers should not have a vote in the Assembly. This raised other problems for which there was no obvious solution, and the Maharaja declined to accept the suggestion. The National Conference thereupon set about the business of making administration as difficult as they could. As a first step, they stirred the operatives of the Silk Weaving Mill to make unreasonable demands, then failing to get satisfaction, to bringing about a strike. Moreover, a session of the National Conference was scheduled to take place in the beginning of August 1945 at which, among others, Mr Nehru and certain other leaders of the Congress were to be present.

The Hindus were exasperated because whether the Muslim Conference got the upper hand or the National Conference, they still stood to lose. They showed their discontent in various ways. The Sikhs, for example, laid claim to certain buildings at the Hindu shrine at Anantnag, which had never really belonged to them, though generations before, when Sikhs were treated merely as a reformist sect of Hindus and not as a separate community, the Hindus had permitted them to keep a copy of the Granth Sahib in one of the rooms. The custodian on behalf of the Hindu community was the Dharmarth Trust, of which the Maharaja was the head. The dispute was between the Sikh community and the Dharmarth Trust; and two years previously, the government had undertaken to devise a settlement, but had in fact failed to do anything. So the Sikhs served what was tantamount to an ultimatum to the government, threatening direct action unless the building was handed over to them by the Dharmarth Trust by a specified date.

Transcending all these local causes of disquiet, there was the general feeling of unsettlement at the end of the war and the expectation of a revolutionary new order being inaugurated soon. In India, the main political interests, the

> Congress and the [Muslim] League, were busy marshalling their respective forces, and the leaders were jockeying for position in the coming struggle, as it was deemed certain that should Labour come into power in Great Britain as a result of the impending general election, the British would transfer power in India to Indian hands.

Thus, the scene was set for a showdown on multiple fronts as soon as my grandfather took the stage as the PM of Kashmir. How Bhaiji defused the situation and resolved the multiple confrontational deadlines, both within the state and without, in his first year of office, is the Chanakya-like story of the next chapter, which gave Bhaiji a doubtful reputation as the strongman of Kashmir.

13

A Political Game of Chess

From the harmless administrative board games of his previous tenure, Bhaiji was suddenly catapulted into the thick of the political endgame being played out in Kashmir, between the rulers and the ruled, between the Centre and the states, among political parties, between British Paramountcy and state authority and, indeed, even between India and its neighbouring countries, where Kashmir was seen as an important pawn. Bhaiji had to quickly adapt to a lethal cocktail of power politics and religious counter currents, which called upon him to exercise his best judgement instantly or bear the consequences. Bhaiji was aided by his connection with the people as a Kashmiri himself, his reputation for integrity and his genuine desire to help people. In the process, he had to develop Chanakya-like qualities to stay afloat in this political maelstrom. In this, as his unpublished memoir attests, he was not particularly adept.

> Recalling the main incidents of my regime as prime minister, I felt that I certainly could not have acted otherwise than I did. I assumed office on 30th June 1945. Until then, I had for nearly four years been army minister and minister-in-waiting. This latter was a glorified designation for an office combining the functions of the private secretary and the military secretary to the Maharaja. Before that I had been chief secretary for over four years and among the other public offices I had filled during my official career were those of

Figure 14: Sheikh Abdullah and Mirza Afzal Beg negotiating the arrangements with Bhaiji in his PM office for the National Conference's river procession held in August 1945

Illustration credit: Kashmira Tembulkar

inspector general of customs and excise, political and foreign secretary, director of archaeology and research, etc. Thus, I had a fairly comprehensive knowledge of the working of the administration, so far, in any case, as the state of Jammu and Kashmir was concerned. I had travelled extensively and knew the state and its people intimately. As chief secretary, I had to deal with the various political movements and leaders and was aware of their background, motives, methods and capability as well as the nature and extent of influence they would be capable of exercising in given circumstances.

The state of Jammu and Kashmir comprises of four principal provinces, each of which has a character of its own and is occupied by people who are easily distinguishable from the rest, in feature, clothing, language and general hearing.

Of the four provinces, Kashmir is the most advanced and politically most conscious. For this, the reasons were that the Kashmiris proper have a high standard of intelligence and both Hindus and Muslims have produced men who have achieved great eminence in India and elsewhere. These latter—more particularly the Muslims—naturally took an interest in their kin in Kashmir and devoted both time and money and the considerable influence they had with the then rulers of India to put pressure on the Kashmir administration to bring about the upliftment of their kinsmen. Though signs were not wanting before 1925 that the awakening of the masses of Kashmir, who were mostly Muslim by faith, was at hand, it was only after that that the movement gathered a new impetus. This was largely due to the fact that the Maharaja, having newly succeeded, wanted to mark his accession to rulership by [...] revising the laws with the object of affording reliefs to the peasantry from agricultural indebtedness. His intentions in this behalf were good in themselves, but the methods followed in carrying them into effect produced bitter animosity between the lending classes—mostly Hindus—and the borrowing class—mostly Muslims—of which the political agitators were not slow to take advantage. Moreover, the peasant himself soon found out that the relief he had secured from the demands of the moneylender was illusory as the Co-operative credit societies which were set up to provide rural credit, were dominated by officials and their satellites who were as grasping as the old moneylender in some respects and less amenable to human appeal. Consequently, so far as the Maharaja was concerned, he had only succeeded in disrupting the economy of the state as a whole and incurring the hatred of a large section of people without gaining anything more than the verbal applause and expressions of loyalty from those whom he sought to benefit and who had actually benefitted in the sense that the burden of debt had been removed from their shoulders.

At this juncture appeared on the scene Sheikh Abdullah, who was a schoolmaster and Chaudhri Ghulam Abbas, who was a budding lawyer—the former as leader of the Muslims of Kashmir and the latter as leader of the Muslims of Jammu.

An incident very trivial in itself supplied the occasion for the rising of the Muslims throughout the state in 1931, in which there was considerable loss of life and property, and in which Muslims from Punjab participated by sending Jathas to join the insurgents. Punjab eventually declared the dispatch of Jathas to Kashmir unlawful, and the persons composing these Jathas were arrested. At one time, there were as many as 27,000 people in jail in Punjab on this account. The agitation was ultimately suppressed but as a concession to Muslim demands. Two commissions were appointed, both presided over by high British officers for investigating: (1) the general grievances of Muslims against the state administration and (2) for the allegations of police and military excesses during the insurrection.

At this time, Sheikh Abdullah and Chaudhri Ghulam Abbas were leaders of the organisation known as the All Jammu & Kashmir Muslim Conference. As a result of the recommendations of the first named commission, known popularly as the Glancy Commission because the Chairman was Mr B.J. Glancy (later Sir Bertrand Glancy) of the Indian Political Department, a legislative assembly was set up comprising official and non-official members. This assembly started functioning in 1934. In 1939, the constitution of the assembly was modified in the direction of: (1) providing a majority of non-official members and; (2) giving it the power to vote on the Budget. In 1944, a further accession to the assembly's power came in the shape of the privilege to elect two ministers from among its own members for the state council. For this last step, I was primarily responsible, being then minister-in-waiting of the Maharaja and, therefore, having the opportunity of conveying to him the feelings of the people on important matters. Incidentally, I was also responsible for the election of the two particular individuals, Wazir Ganga Ram and Mr Afzal Beg, as ministers, as I happened to possess some influence with the members of the assembly, though I was myself neither in the assembly nor a member of the government as such.

This last measure which was a considerable step towards the achievement of full responsible government and was highly applauded by Sheikh Abdullah, who had some years before [he] parted company with Chaudhri Ghulam Abbas and the Muslim Conference. The parting of the ways between them was mainly due to their rivalry for power and its perquisites, each claiming to be the best-trusted leader of the people. In fact, however, though there was a section of Muslims in Kashmir who adhered to the policies and the creed of the Muslim Conference, particularly among the wealthier classes, there were very few Muslims in Jammu who accepted Sheikh Abdullah as their leader. Nevertheless, for the reason that Sheikh Abdullah had now aligned himself with the Indian National Congress, and, therefore, had the bulk of the Indian press behind him and for the reason that the majority of the Muslims in the state were Kashmiris, Sheikh Abdullah acquired greater prestige and had more funds at his disposal. He could, therefore, make his weight felt, particularly in the administration inside the state.

On my taking over the prime ministership of the state in June 1945, the bosses of all political parties instinctively sensed that the policy which had paid them dividends so far was not likely to do so in future. Therefore, all of them decided to make things difficult for me before I had time to make a direct approach to the masses. Seeing which way the wind was likely to blow, I also decided in my mind that if I waited for time to consolidate my standing with the people, I might have to wait forever.

Curiously, my first encounter was with the prominent non-Muslim communities, namely Kashmiri Pandits and Sikhs. There was a dispute between these two communities regarding the possession of a building located in the premises of a Hindu shrine. For some reason, the government had, two years before, taken on itself the task of adjudicating on the clashing claims of the two communities, instead of letting them establish their respective rights in a court of law. But the government had done nothing to implement their promise and, just before my assumption of office, the Sikhs had challenged the government to pronounce the award by a specified date, failing which they [had] threatened to take the law in their own hands. I came to know three or four days after I assumed office that the Sikhs had taken possession of the building. As Kashmiri Pandits were determined on offering Satyagraha, there was imminent danger of a breach of the peace. The Muslim Conference, which was in session at Poonch on the day I assumed office, forthwith passed a resolution expressing its lack of confidence in me. The National Conference officially welcomed the appointment but, within a week, engineered a strike of the operatives of the government silk weaving mill for the redress of certain alleged grievances. No notice was given to me of any intention to strike and the first I heard of it was when public demonstrations were held after the strike had been declared.

These were manoeuvres by different parties to measure their strength with the government before the prime minister had actually settled and with the deliberate intention of preventing him from setting himself in the saddle. The moves were in accordance with their previous practice, the procedure being to start an agitation and then to offer mediation between the agitators and the government. If government accepted mediation at the hands of the leaders, it placed itself immediately under their thumb—they could bring about a settlement on the particular issue if the government accepted and paid the price demanded. Soon after, the same people would start another agitation on another pretext and with the same result. Each time the government would be forced back and the leader–mediator would emerge with his prestige enhanced.

While the silk weaving mill strike was still in progress, Pandit Jawaharlal Nehru paid a visit to Kashmir. He stayed for a month during which arrangements were made for his various engagements and activities by the National Conference. During this period, the most important function that he attended was the session of the National Conference at Sopore, which incidentally was attended by other Congress leaders, including Khan Abdul Ghaffar Khan. At this conference, strong speeches condemnatory of the state government were made, particularly by Sheikh Abdullah.

In connection with this function, the National Congress decided to take out a river procession in which the Congress leaders as well as Sheikh Abdullah and his colleagues of the National Conference were rowed up the river through the heart of the city. At that time, certain parts of the city, particularly those below the fourth bridge and on the right bank of the river were strongly pro-Muslim Conference, which was the rival Muslim political organisation in the state and affiliated with the Muslim League as the National Conference was with the Congress.

Sheikh Abdullah came to see me in this connection and suggested that, as there was danger of a clash between the rival groups and as certain Muslim police officers posted in the city were in sympathy with the Muslim Conference, I should remove these officers and replace them with others—presumably those having National Conference sympathies. This was such an extraordinary suggestion that, without any hesitation, I turned it down. Acceptance would have made the position of the government impossible, as other political bodies would certainly have put forward similar demands with respect to officers they did not like and each time, we would have to post forces to suit the inclinations or, more correctly, the prejudices of particular political leaders. I told Sheikh Abdullah that government was responsible for the maintenance of the public peace and it was their job to see how that peace could be maintained—that public servants were expected to be non-political in their views so far as the discharge of their public duty was concerned and had to discharge their public functions without fear and without favour in relation to all political parties. Finally, I assured him that, though I did not approve of the route of the procession and would much rather that the river procession avoided the parts of the city which were known to be hostile to the National Conference, I would see that nothing untoward happened.

In giving this assurance, I was, however, counting without my host. For while I directed the police to ensure that no hostile group took the opportunity to cause trouble, I did not anticipate that the National Conference themselves would take the initiative in doing so. On the morning of the day on which the procession was to be taken out, the operatives of the silk factory, between 2,000 and 3,000 strong, marched in a column to the areas which were known to be out of sympathy with the National Conference. In these areas, people had made no preparations to dress up the riverfront for the occasion, not being at all enthusiastic about the function. The silk factory operatives—who, being the biggest single group of organised workers in Srinagar, have always functioned as the storm troops of the National Conference—used force majeure in an endeavour to compel the inhabitants to be less apathetic. This naturally made the victims furious and the revenge they eventually took was characteristic. When the procession passed through those areas, they made obscene demonstrations and stoned the boats. This in turn incited further violence. When the

Vol. 1.

Margaret N. Kak.

Margaret N. Allcock.

Left Srinagar for Delhi – Sept. 22 1947.
Left Delhi for Bombay – Sept. 29.
Left Bombay for Tilbury. Oct. 17.
Arrived Tilbury. Nov. 3.
" Belton. Nov. 5.

Top: A young Bended in England, 1930s
Bottom: Bended's diary detailing her and Billy's escape from Kashmir shortly after Independence, 1947

Top left: Bended with Billy, 1944
Top right: Bended's father Edward Allcock and Aunt Tantes, 1932
Bottom: Bended (centre) with her siblings, Nancy, Dick and Gerard, c. 1915

Top: Bended at Bagh Sundar soon after her marriage to Bhaiji, 1937
Bottom left: Caricature of Bhaiji, London, 1932
Bottom right: Bhaiji at Bagh Sundar soon after his marriage to Bended, 1937

Top left: Bhaiji's youngest son, Khemendra Kak, DFC posthumous, 1945
Top right: Bended when she took up secretarial work, shortly before meeting Bhaiji, 1930s
Bottom: Bhaiji and Bended gathered round the spring at Dara with Siddharth's mother Sarla and sister Sumita, 1960s

MAN FROM KASHMIR MOWS THE LAWN

A FRENCH window, a clump of rhubarb, a spade . . . suburban scene at Hampstead. The man with the lawn-mower? It is Pandit Ramchandra Kak, who 20 months ago controlled 4,000,000 people as Prime Minister of Kashmir.

Now he is exiled. And every morning, in lounge suit and cloth cap, he leaves his home in the Garden Suburb to take his six-year-old daughter to school.

Often he will collect the family rations in a string bag on his way back. And when neighbouring mothers are out shopping he doesn't mind looking after their children when they come to play in the tiny garden with his own.

In 1946 this man caused a world sensation by arresting Pandit Nehru when he went to the state to support Sheik Abdullah's demand that the Hindu Maharajah, Sir Hari Singh, should quit and hand over his country to the Muslim majority. Abdullah was tried and gaoled for subversive activities.

Premier Kak's policy was to maintain the independence of Kashmir. In 1947 he resigned. The Maharajah released Abdullah and made him Premier instead. A few weeks later Pandit Kak was in gaol himself on charges of using his office for personal ends. Last November he was released unconditionally but exiled. A few weeks ago he joined his English wife and daughter Lila in London. He is now reflecting on Sheik Abdullah's recent statement that "independence guaranteed by the U.N. may be the only solution" for war-torn Kashmir and wondering if he may be allowed to return. —News Chronicle picture.

Pay moves to keep school dentists

Some local authorities are raising the pay of school and other dentists they employ, pending negotiations for new salary scales, to stop the drift to higher-paid work outside.

Mr. Bevan, Health Minister, told the Commons yesterday he was pleased that this was taking place.

He was ready to help negotiations by forming a dental Whitley Council. Dental organisations which previously refused were now willing to come in, with certain reservations; the Local Authorities Association had not yet agreed.

ONE-MINUTE SERMON

The word of God is not bound.
2 TIMOTHY 2.9

PAUL was in bonds. His Master had known bonds

Top: An English newspaper report on Bhaiji after release from Kashmir in 1948

Bottom: Bhaiji mowing the lawn with Billy in Hampstead Garden. This had become his treasured activity during exile, 1949.

Top: Bhaiji and Bended with Billy after her day at school, 1950
Bottom: Bhaiji and Bended outside the Red House, 1970s

Top: Bhaiji discussing village matters with the local community, with his retainer Lassa in attendance, 1960s
Bottom: The waterfall at the bottom of the garden from the Dara spring, which was used for bathing, frolicking and washing clothes

Top left: Bended in the late 1970s
Top right: Bhaiji on one of his meditative walks, 1970s
Bottom: The Kak family houses in Zaldragar in the 1940s. They are typical constructions with a *dab* or balcony on the second floor.

procession reached the fourth bridge, there was a clash between the two parties as a result of which one man was killed and 20 police, including a magistrate, injured. A 100 arrests were subsequently made. Curiously enough, both sides claimed the dead man as belonging to their party.

After this, it was no wonder that Sheikh Abdullah inveighed so violently at Sopore against the government.

The next item of Mr Nehru's programme was a trek in the mountains, starting from Shopian, where incidentally he was to address a public meeting. Being now more conversant with the methods of the National Conference, there was no doubt in my mind that such a public meeting would not pass without incident. The district magistrate banned public meetings and processions in various parts of the Valley, including Shopian. As soon as Mr Nehru came to know of these orders, he told the people assembled to meet him at Shopian that no meeting could be held and that the orders passed by competent authority must be respected.

The next major attempt on the part of the National Conference to try conclusions with the government was also in connection with the silk factory operatives. Towards the end of September, in the State Assembly, which was in session, the leader of the National Conference Group moved a resolution recommending that 90 per cent of the profits of the silk factory should be made over to the labourers. The factory, it must be remembered, is owned by the government and its profits are credited to the public treasury, which also bears its losses, should there be any. As the revenue from sericulture was one of the major sources of the state's income, the recommendation, if accepted, would have caused serious financial embarrassment. But, of course, with the National Conference, the main consideration was to embarrass the government and simultaneously to gain credit with the labourers as their champions against a heartless government. To fortify the resolution, the [National]

Conference decided to march the silk factory operatives to the courtyard of the Assembly at the time the resolution came up for discussion. As the demonstration was intended simply to intimidate the members and the government, I warned all concerned that no demonstrations in the vicinity of the Assembly would be permitted. On this, Afzal Beg, who was one of the leaders of the [National] Conference as well as a minister in the government, came to me and said that in case the demonstration was not permitted, the situation would become uncontrollable and the consequences would be serious. I told him that whatever the consequences, it was not possible for me to agree to the Assembly being subjected to this sort of intimidation from outside and that under no circumstances would I agree to such a demonstration being held. I added that orders had already been given to the magistrate and the police to see that this decision was carried into effect, as also ensuring that nothing untoward was allowed to happen.

Nothing untoward happened. The operatives and other leaders of the National Conference, finding that their attempted intimidation had no effect, subsided and quietly dispersed. In the Assembly, I declared on behalf of the government that while it was obviously impossible for the government to accept the resolutions, we would examine the position and would do everything in our power to improve the earning capacity of the operatives. This, I subsequently did, and did in consultation with the operatives themselves without the intervention of the National Conference leaders.

These and similar incidents in the course of the three months during which I had held the office of prime minister, served the purpose of convincing the National Conference which, in effect, meant Sheikh Abdullah and two or three of his colleagues, that agitation and indirect intimidation as a means of coercing the government were no longer likely to pay dividends and that a direct trial of strength had become inevitable.

ᔕ

Lord Wavell, then viceroy, visited Kashmir in the middle of October 1945. In those days, the so-called Jammu and Kashmir State Exhibition had become a seasonal fixture. The exhibition remained for the greater part of the summer. This being the tourist season, the exhibition became a sort of central market for the sale and purchase of Kashmiri goods, like carpets, shawls, papier mâché, woodwork, etc. During the viceregal visit, Lady Wavell and the Maharani of Kashmir paid a shopping visit to the exhibition. While they were there, an incident took place, which is interesting as being indicative of how 'incidents' can be created. The President of the Exhibition Committee Mr Mehkri, who was the minister of development, had borrowed from a friend some ancient pictures. These pictures had been exhibited on several occasions before on these very premises and he thought that, as they were rather exceptional, they might prove an added attraction during the viceregal visit. One of these pictures represented Prophet Muhammad.

When Lady Wavell and the Maharani were in the nearby stalls, suddenly shouts and yells were heard that blasphemy had been committed and Islam insulted (by the exhibition of the picture of the Prophet). In the commotion that followed, the whole lot of pictures disappeared. They have not since been found.

Mr Mehkri came to me naturally somewhat agitated and reported the incident. Sheikh Abdullah on this occasion publicly attempted to pacify the vociferous crowd of Muslims who had scented the insult to their religion. How the insult had been caused or intended, it is difficult to see. The pictures were two or three hundred years old and had been exhibited on this very spot in previous years. On this particular occasion, the person who had secured them on loan from their owner was a most devout Muslim himself and, therefore, the last person who could be accused of deliberately insulting Islam. When the matter came to the ears of the Viceroy, I was asked whether any special precautions or change in the viceregal programme would be necessary as a result of the unexpected development. I replied so far as the question of maintenance of peace was concerned, there need be no misgivings. Peace would be maintained. No change in the programme took place.

Later, Afzal Beg expatiated on the assistance which Sheikh Abdullah and the National Conference had given the government and myself on this occasion in pacifying the infuriated Muslim mob, who would otherwise have caused tremendous trouble. He observed that but for Sheikh Abdullah's intervention, the house of the owner of the pictures would have been pulled down 'brick by brick'. I asked him whether it had occurred to him to try and surmise what I, as head of the government responsible for affording protection to law-abiding citizens against disruptive and anti-social elements, would be doing while a raging mob was pulling down the house of the unfortunate person who had been persuaded to lend his property to a minister of the government, who incidentally being himself a staunch Muslim, could scarcely be accused of being unmindful of Muslim sentiment. Afzal Beg gave no reply.

As, however, the occasion of the talk was with reference to certain demands made by him, the acceptance of which would enable him to exercise overriding authority over the government of which he was a member and a freedom of action in public—even in opposition to the government—which was denied to other ministers, it was obvious that Afzal Beg's mention of the exhibition incident and the helpful attitude evinced by Sheikh Abdullah, for whatever reason of his own, was by way of charging a price for services supposed to have been rendered. I was not greatly impressed by the argument.

My object was, I strove every nerve to establish direct relations with the masses to win their confidence and not to allow them or myself to become tools for the aggrandisement of political groups who professed to function in the name of the masses that they exploited in every possible way. Such groups were naturally exasperated by my policy of direct approach and of speaking to the peasants as well as to the factory workers face-to-face and man-to-man.

My contacts were generally of an informal character. There were no set speeches and no reading of addresses. Mainly, it was a cause of question and answer in which any member of the public was free to take part. This method immediately put me on a par with my interlocutors and was effective in eliciting individual opinion and views. A few examples will suffice:

The silk factory in Srinagar is or was reputedly the largest single silk-reeling plant in the world. In its heyday, it used to employ 4,000–5,000 workers, but in 1945 the strength of labour employed was about 2,000. The labourers were discontented, as their earnings were very small. Enquiry indicated that the rate of wages was not low as compared with the prevalent rates for skilled and unskilled labour. The total earning of the silk factory worker was, however, considerably lower, as on the average he worked only 12 days in a month.

This was a surprising state of affairs, but it was sanctified by past practice, as 12-days-a-month work had been in vogue in the factory for several years past. Naturally, labour was disgruntled and willingly lent its ears to people who held out promises of improvement. The reason why this practice prevailed was that production had to be kept within a certain maximum. In order to do that, the factory was unable to give full employment to its operatives. To the obvious objection that in the circumstances, the reasonable course would be to reduce the strength of labour and employ only as many as could be given full employment, the reply I received from the factory directorate, was that the political bosses had been objecting to reduction in labour and, therefore, the government, which owned the factory, had decided to keep the number employed when production was high and reduce the working days, with the result that everybody in the factory was underpaid. Not only was this so, the officers responsible for running the factory had gone one better in that, over a period of years, they had kept up the same strength, regularly replenishing the ranks depleted by death or desertion. The reason given was that labour themselves demanded that the vacancies should be filled up, generally by the dependents of the previous incumbents.

I put it to the leaders of the operatives that they had reduced the administration of the factory to a farce. My view was that labour should be retrenched by half, in which case those that remained would, allowing for Sundays and holidays, have a full month's work. It was agreed that this would be the best and most sensible course but fear of incurring odium made them reluctant to following such an obvious course. As an alternative, they suggested that if certain modifications in the process of production were made, it would be possible without government losing any money to increase the monthly working days by five. The sericulture authorities were sceptical and advised against the acceptance of the suggestion but I felt that, in the circumstances, even if the government lost some money in making a trial, it would be well worth doing so because, in case the suggestion proved effective, the labourers would get an advantage without the government suffering undue loss. In case, however, the directorate expected, it proved infructuous, the monetary loss would be counterbalanced by the advantage of a demonstration to the operatives that their suggestion had been accepted but had been found fruitless.

A week's trial showed that the operatives were not wrong in their anticipation and the director of sericulture agreed to introduce the new system throughout the factory, much to the gratification of the labourers and the discomfiture of the professional agitators who had been all along insisting that the government really did not mean to do anything and were only putting the labour off with specious promises.

Thereafter, throughout the period I functioned as prime minister, whenever the silk factory operatives wanted anything done, they came straight to me or to the concerned authority without the intervention of any intermediary.

∽

Sheikh Abdullah was in an especially advantageous position during this period, since besides the publicity he received and the prestige he enjoyed in India as a result of the patronage extended to him by important personalities in the Indian National Congress, he had one of his chief lieutenants Afzal Beg in the strategic position of a minister in the Kashmir government. This enabled him to have an influential voice in the deliberations and policies of the Kashmir government, through Afzal Beg, while he himself was free to criticise the government and all its works in the press and on the platform. This he had been doing always, and the appointment of Afzal Beg as minister made no difference. In fact, during the time of my predecessor Sir B.N. Rau, Afzal Beg had already gone to the length of putting forward the demand that he should be permitted the freedom to vote in the state assembly against the government while continuing as a minister of the government. Sir B.N. Rau proposed to meet the situation by suggesting that ministers who were elected from among the members of the Assembly should not participate in the voting. Before, however, any decision could be taken on this proposal, Sir B.N. Rau relinquished office as prime minister.

Towards the end of 1945, Afzal Beg renewed the demand and coupled with it certain other matters, the purpose of which was to give him a freer hand and more powers in the administration of the departments in his portfolio than the regulations permitted. Among these was an extensive amendment of the Municipal Act. Another of his demands was the creation of a separate secretariat for his portfolio to be wholly answerable to and dependent on him.

These demands were, by way clearing the decks, to precipitate a crisis which would force a fight on the government. The National Conference like other similar organisations had lost much of its backing in the country in the preceding months, since the people found it easier to approach and deal with the government directly instead of invoking the good offices of political leaders and parties—a situation naturally galling to them.

Afzal Beg, with an eye to the future, instead of mentioning to me personally and discussing with me as he did other things in the almost daily meetings we had on various matters pertaining to the administration, sent me a formal letter dealing at length with the disabilities he felt he was suffering under both politically and administratively and virtually presenting an ultimatum to the effect that unless his wishes were acceded to, he would be compelled to resign, I sent him a written reply explaining the position as I conceived it.

As regards the contention that he should be permitted the freedom of vote in the Assembly and freedom of speech against the government of which he was a member, condemning the policy in the framing of which he had been a party, though possibly a dissenting one, and also publicly censuring the government, the answer was plain.

Acceptance of such a demand, I argued, was wholly outside practical politics. Further, I explained, if he were given the privilege he sought then the same privilege would have to be extended to our other colleague who like him was an elected member of the Assembly. This would create a very curious position. Of the five ministers who composed the council, three non-elected ones, including the prime minister, would vote one way and each of the two elected ministers could vote differently, so that the five colleagues who had jointly been responsible for framing the policy might cast their vote in three different directions. Further, since it was intended to increase the elected element in the council, when the number of the elected ministers was increased and each minister had the option to vote as he chose, the resultant situation would be farcical.

As regards the amendment of the Municipal Act, I expressed myself willing to meet his wishes to the utmost extent possible and, in fact, accepted practically all the amendments he had proposed. These amendments subsequently—after he had resigned—became law.

As regards the separate and exclusive secretariat, I realised that a certain discrepancy did exist between him and the other ministers. This was by reason of the fact that before his appointment, there were only four ministers. Their portfolios were spread over four secretariats. Though each minister had to deal with more than one secretariat, the majority of a minister's work was dealt with in one secretariat. Subject to and in accordance with the provisions of the delegation orders, he controlled the staff of that secretariat. Since the secretariats were only four and the ministers, with the appointment of Afzal Beg, five, he didn't have a special secretariat exclusively under his control though he had a small personal office of his own.

The portfolio being a new one, the staff dealing with it was scattered. Afzal Beg did not, therefore, exercise

> any power of appointment and dismissal over the clerical establishment who were dealing with his work. Originally, in Kashmir, secretariats were planned and organised as departmental offices. Each minister had his own secretary and clerical establishment, dealing with the departments in his portfolio. The secretary was not 'secretary to the government' but 'secretary to minister', and he had nothing whatever to do with any other ministers. During the prime ministership of Sir Gopalaswami Ayyangar, the system was revised though the controlling authority so far as enforcement of discipline and appointments were concerned remained with the Maharaja.

So long as the political chess moves were confined to Kashmir, it was possible to contain their fallout and obtain broad concurrence from the Maharaja, who was the sole authority. However, the consequences became truly explosive when the conflict escalated to the national stage, where Nehru forcibly attempted to enter Kashmir in support of his jailed friend Sheikh Abdullah in the summer of 1946 and was detained at the border. This incident was considered brave, foolhardy or principled, depending on one's vantage point. However, Bhaiji's succinct description of the incident in the next chapter will, hopefully, end much speculation regarding this incident, which has assumed importance far beyond its actual significance.

We must remember, Bhaji was not an independent player. He was PM to the Maharaja of Kashmir and his decisions necessarily were only made with the knowledge and sanction of the Maharaja, who was the sole and overriding authority in Kashmir.

While his support was forthcoming during both Sheikh Abdullah's and Nehru's detentions, the behind-the-scenes intrigues, the Maharaja's territorial ambitions and his weakening resolve to support firm actions to preserve peace in Kashmir undermined the authority of Bhaiji's actions, which were taken with his consent. Considered the strongman of Kashmir, Bhaiji's position was weakened to the point where his resignation was accepted and chaos was let loose in Kashmir. Had Bhaiji remained PM during that difficult period, it is possible that the Maharaja may not have had to, in effect, abdicate and flee Kashmir, leading to his continued role in the peaceful accession of the state to India.

14

Pandit vs Pandit

Bhaiji's first year as the PM ended with an event in June 1946 which has become notorious as the clash of two most unequal forces, when the pygmy PM of a princely state dared to defy a colossus of the Congress and the future PM of India. Ironically, both were Brahmin Pandits of Kashmir. The dispute was not religious but ideological. It could have ended only in one way and it did. But while it lasted, it remained the single most publicised event of a long-drawn-out confrontation between the Congress government and the princely state of Kashmir before Partition was announced by the British Crown for India.

At a simplistic level, the confrontation was between a democratic nation's approach to governance as opposed to a princely state's privileged approach to rule. At a less obvious level, however, the subtext was the anxiety of a Hindu-ruled minority state—which, despite a majority Muslim population, had effectively maintained peaceful conditions in its domain—to maintain the status quo at a critical moment in its history; as compared to a Hindu-majority nation that was already aflame with sectarian turmoil as the trauma of Partition approached. There were both ideological and practical elements to the confrontation, with much at stake on both sides.

There are, of course, numerous lurid accounts of the detention of Nehru on 21 June 1946, which made for sensational headlines in the papers. It was a David and Goliath confrontation in which, at least temporarily, David won the first round. At the core of this confrontation was Nehru's support of a person who was proving to be a thorn in the side of the Maharaja, calling for him to 'Quit Kashmir', on the lines of the Congress agitation against the British to Quit India. This call was illegal, as it went far beyond calling for democratic rule in Kashmir, and Sheikh Abdullah was sentenced by a court and imprisoned. Nehru, however, was insistent on meeting Sheikh Abdullah in jail, which the Kashmir administration resisted due to the disruption it was likely to cause at a sensitive time.

This chapter contains Bhaiji's first-person account of the actual events of 21 June 1946 and how they unfolded with see-sawing fortunes until finally Nehru was officially detained at the rest house at Kohala, inside the Kashmir border. He graciously accepted a book of plays to pass the time from a flustered district magistrate, who had successfully detained him. To Nehru's credit, once he was served with the official orders, he complied with them implicitly and did not attempt any violent protest or outcry against the imposition. This was in keeping with his democratic values, which he had displayed even earlier, when he had visited Shopian the previous year. However, he made visiting Sheikh Abdullah in Kashmir a mission or point of honour, ensuring that the agitation was pursued by his party colleagues and by the headlines that dominated the newspapers.

Among the many dramatic stories that circulated, one was that Nehru had been bayoneted by a soldier detaining him, and had sustained a neck injury. Bhaiji, in his memoirs, denied any such incident. Nehru himself said nothing. Regardless, at the time, both sides dealt with the situation with honour and dignity. Every facility was kept at Nehru's disposal, including a car and a plane. Nehru occupied himself in reading or telephonic consultations for which he had to travel some distance from the rest house. Bhaiji wrote in his unpublished memoir:

> The position [Sheikh] Abdullah had acquired in Kashmir politics and the immunity he had so long enjoyed, made it

certain that any attempt to arrest him would be followed by widespread disturbances in the Valley. This had happened before when he had been arrested in 1931 and 1937. My aim was to nip disturbances in the bud and not to let them gather momentum. The plan we evolved to deal with anticipated civil disturbances hinged on our preventing large assemblies at any point. Traffic had to be kept on the move, since it is easier to do that than to disperse a multitude once it has gathered and is massed. The forces at the disposal of the state government are necessarily limited and, in the last resort, dispersal has to be accomplished by troops opening fire. Once that happens, a wave of resentment against the authorities rises in the public mind. However right the government may have been considered initially, and though it may have been recognised that their action though drastic had most likely saved the state from something much worse, public sympathies, on such occasions, are more often than not against the authorities.

When I learnt that Sheikh Abdullah had consulted neither the working committee of the National Conference, nor even the All India States People's Conference of which he was at the time president when he launched the Quit Kashmir movement, I realised that a head-on collision with him had become inevitable. I was informed that though both the National Conference and the All India States Peoples' Conference were in favour of popular representative government, neither approved of the Quit Kashmir movement. The all-India body particularly could scarcely be expected to approve of such a movement in one state without approving of similar movements in other states. Sheikh Abdullah had obviously taken the bit between his teeth and was bent on bringing about a crisis as a result of which he hoped to present all concerned, including his friends in India, with a fait accompli. This was to me a very understandable line of action on his part.

[...] Having launched the movement, Sheikh Abdullah announced that he would be going to Delhi to see Mr Nehru. It was obvious that his idea, having given the initial push, was to keep himself at a distance outside the state and direct the movement from there. In view of this, and the fact that he had already made speeches which rendered him liable to prosecution under law, it was decided to arrest him and put him up for trial.

Accordingly, Sheikh Abdullah was arrested when he was on his way to Rawalpindi. Simultaneously, the police and troops marched into Srinagar and took positions at all important crossroads and traffic centres. Before noon, all actual organised agitation in the city had died down, since the disposition of the forces in the city was such that no crowds could collect at any point.

But while agitation on a large scale was thus forestalled, disturbances in certain sections of the city and some district towns and villages continued for some days. These disturbances were characterised by blocking of traffic, for example, by digging up roads or putting loose stones across or removal of planks from bridges, cutting of telephone and telegraph wires, burning of government property, etc. In connection with these disturbances, eight deaths took place, including one woman. This last incident happened at Anantnag, where the National Conference stalwarts had organised a procession the day the Maharaja and the Maharani were expected to pass near the town on their way from Jammu to Srinagar. Prudently, considering that discretion was the better part of valour, they placed a number of women at the head of the procession. When required to disperse by the magistrate, the women, deeming themselves invulnerable by reason of their sex, and their menfolk, by reason sheltering behind the infallible shield provided by the women, became defiant and attacked the magistrate, the police and the troops, who thereupon opened fire. They fired first in the air, but one bullet ricocheted from the wall and hit one unfortunate woman, who succumbed to the injury in the hospital.

But except for the Friday gathering at Hazratbal, where the Muslims of the city and of the neighbouring villages gathered in large numbers to offer their Jumma prayers, and the meetings which took place at the Khanqah Mualla [Khanqah Mohalla], where a few persons delivered inflammatory speeches and thereafter offered themselves for arrest, the state was completely quiet, in strange contrast to the lurid pictures painted from time-to-time in the Indian press and despite the powerful support, which the National Conference received from the Indian National Congress.

A number of National Conference leaders, including Bakhshi Ghulam Mohammed, Mr G.M. Sadiq and others, had left Kashmir before Sheikh Abdullah's arrest. They were in close contact with Pandit Jawaharlal Nehru and the Congress leaders, into whose ears they repeatedly dinned that innumerable atrocities had been and were being committed on the people of Kashmir by the government. On the basis of these stories, Pandit Jawaharlal Nehru issued a number of strongly worded statements that were very inaccurate as regards their content. In reply to one of these statements, I issued a statement in which I, inter alia, suggested Mr Nehru should come to Kashmir and see for himself how far removed from the truth his information was.

Meanwhile, Mr Nehru had sent a telegram to the Maharaja calling on him to release Sheikh Abdullah forthwith, set up a committee to advise on constitutional reforms in the state, transfer power to Sheikh Abdullah, and offering his own assistance in framing the future constitution of the state. To this, the Maharaja replied that so far as the form of government in the state was concerned, Kashmir was in advance of most states in India, and as regards Sheikh Abdullah, he was accused of certain activities, which made him liable to action under the law and he would, therefore, be put up for trial before the competent court.

Mr Nehru sent another telegram, this time to me, asking that proceedings regarding Sheikh Abdullah's trial be held in abeyance, until arrangements had been made by him, i.e., Mr Nehru, for the defence.

Curiously, my suggestion that he should come to Kashmir to see for himself to what extent the tales he had been told by interested parties regarding the events in Kashmir, were even approximately correct, upset Mr Nehru and he came out with an exceedingly vituperative statement, in which he made the most fantastic allegations, besides making a direct personal attack on me, calling on me to submit to a trial by an impartial tribunal for my alleged numerous misdeeds of omission and commission in connection to the suppression of the National Conference agitation. Among the allegations he made were that mosques had been destroyed, that dead bodies of Muslims had been soaked in petrol and burnt, etc. The allegations, singly and collectively, were utterly false and I lost no time in issuing a reply to his statement which also received wide publicity contradicting each allegation separately. Mr Nehru never questioned the truth of my reply, as, in fact, it could not be questioned. The fact of the matter seems to have been that, as so often happened, the protagonists of the National Conference, who had sought refuge and received encouragement in India, had filled Mr Nehru's ears with fantastic tales, which he had uncritically and unquestioningly absorbed and become saturated with. He produced these stories with his usual missionary fervour, but when their truth was questioned, he chose to remain silent rather than admit that he had acted on wrong information.

After this, it appeared obvious that Mr Nehru was on the war path so far as Kashmir was concerned and that he was unwilling to see any side but the side which was presented

> to him by the National Conference. He telegraphed to the Maharaja intimating that he would be coming, with lawyers elected by him, to defend Sheikh Abdullah. The Maharaja replied that while there would be no objection to any lawyer being sent by him to defend Sheikh Abdullah, it would be highly inadvisable for him to come himself until things had quietened down to some extent. Partly due to the commotion created by the Quit Kashmir movement, but much more [due] to the unwarranted and baseless accusations Mr Nehru had made against the government, the atmosphere in the state became very inflammable and critical of Mr Nehru for the unwarranted and unfounded aspersions he had cast on the state administration. The people in the state knew the truth, though Mr Nehru might not have. An eruption by him—accompanied as it would no doubt be with public gatherings, processions and speeches—was certain to exacerbate public feelings; hence, the Maharaja's advice to him to postpone his visit until a more opportune time.

Would it be accurate to say that Nehru's visit had the potential to escalate the impact of what was perceived as a local state administrative action into a Hindu–Muslim conflict? Would it be true to believe that while the letters to the Indian government were doubtless drafted by Bhaiji, the Maharaja signed the letters in full agreement, not in the least because Bhaiji's stern response to the Quit Kashmir movement had kept the state peaceful even while India burned?

Even in 1946, the British Paramountcy—as part of its 'divide and rule' policy in India—continued to offer the princely states a choice to remain neutral and not accede to either Pakistan or India during the impending Partition and remain under British Paramountcy till a new constitution for India or Pakistan was declared. This gave a lease of independent life to the Maharaja in a new order.

Bhaiji knew that any decision based on religion would ignite violence, as both Hindu and Muslim communities lived side-by-side and coexisted more or less peacefully in the state, so long as their religious identities were not threatened. Sheikh Abdullah's call to Quit Kashmir, supported by the Congress, was a grave threat to the constitutional rule of the Dogra over Kashmir for more than a century.

Nehru supporting Sheikh Abdullah and asking the Maharaja to hand over Kashmir to the Muslim majority agitated not only the state administration but even more so the local Hindu and Pandit population, who were left at the mercy of the National Conference agitators. It certainly was the flashpoint for a major confrontation in the state. Bhaiji's desire to remain neutral stemmed from precisely this fear.

> We had no illusions as regards Mr Nehru's willingness to accept our advice. I, however, thought that perhaps Mahatma Gandhi might act as a brake on Mr Nehru and accordingly sent him a letter describing the chain of events ultimately leading to the arrest of Sheikh Abdullah. I finally suggested that he might take steps to dissuade Mr Nehru from issuing provocative statements with regard to Kashmir. This letter was sent by hand of Professor K.T. Shah to Mussoori, where the Mahatma was at the time. At Mahatma Gandhi's instance, Professor Shah met Maulana Azad who undertook to speak to Mr Nehru and also advised Professor Shah to see him. Professor Shah met Mr Nehru and explained the situation as he knew it, since he had been in Srinagar when Sheikh Abdullah was arrested and had come straight from the scene of action. Nothing, however, came of this attempt to settle the matter peacefully, as Mr Nehru strongly disapproved of the proposed telegram to me, which Professor Shah had drafted after his talk with him, considering that it implied he had changed his opinion with regard to the Kashmir events. The telegram was, therefore, never sent.
>
> When it became clear that Mr Nehru was not prepared to change his attitude, I, for my part, made it clear that

> we did not approve of Mr Nehru's projected incursion and would not, should the necessity arise, hesitate to stop him from entering the state territory.

Note here, Bhaiji's subtle change of grammar from 'I' to 'we', indicating the reality that Bhaiji was not acting alone but at the will of the Maharaja. It would be unrealistic to assume that Bhaiji's personal intention to arrest Nehru would have been sufficient for that action to be carried out unilaterally in Kashmir under the Maharaja, given the implications of such drastic action. Meanwhile, political events were moving to an inexorable climax. A British Act of Parliament had proposed June 1948 as the deadline for the transfer of power.

> All this time, the Cabinet Mission was sitting in Delhi, discussing the future of India. The Viceroy Lord Wavell knew our views on the matter and tried to dissuade Mr Nehru from precipitating a crisis with regard to an issue which, but for the attitude Mr Nehru had taken up with regard to it, was a very minor one when compared with the problems for solution of which the Cabinet Mission had come to India. On the morning of the day preceding the date of Mr Nehru's intended visit to Srinagar, Dwarkanath Kachru, who claimed to be his [Nehru's] secretary, arrived at my house with an envelope addressed to the Maharaja, containing a letter from Mr Nehru. He wanted me to take delivery of it and give him a reply. I told him that the envelope was not intended for me and the obvious thing for him to do was to go to the palace, deliver it there and ask for a reply.
>
> About 10.00 p.m. the same day, the British Assistant Resident Mr Daubeny rang me up and said that he had an urgent message to communicate to me. He added that the Resident was out of town and, as the message was a clear-the-line telegram emanating from the Viceroy's house, he wanted to come immediately and deliver it. He came and read out to me a decoded telegram from Lord Wavell to the

Resident stating that, despite all persuasion, Mr Nehru had refused to be dissuaded from proceeding to Kashmir and would in fact be flying to Rawalpindi the following evening, whence he proposed to go by car to Srinagar. The Viceroy hoped that nothing untoward would happen (or something in that sense). Daubeny asked me what reply was to be sent to the telegram, as an immediate reply was necessary.

I explained to him that my position was very clear and definite. I was responsible for the security of the state and for the maintenance of law and order in it. It was my business and responsibility to judge what was the right thing to do in a given situation and to act accordingly. No one else could take that burden off my shoulders, nor take a share of the blame if things went wrong. My opinion was that if Mr Nehru came under the circumstances [...] it would be impossible for the government to discharge its elementary responsibility of maintaining the peace and ensuring the security of life and property of its citizens; that the people who had suffered at the hands of the National Conference, and by its high handedness and the lawless manner in which its members conducted themselves to those who held opinions other than their own, looked upon the government to protect them; that a government which failed to offer its people the protection they were due, was worthless as a government; that it was a wholly unacceptable proposition for one authority, whether it was the Indian National Congress or the Government of India, to dictate the policy while another authority, in this case the Kashmir government, should have to bear the brunt of the implementation of that policy. If, therefore, Lord Wavell thought that Mr Nehru should be allowed to proceed on his course without let or hindrance and should have complete freedom to do whatever he liked in the state, it was open to him to arrange with the Maharaja to have a new prime minister to carry out that policy. So far as I was concerned, orders had been passed already to stop Mr Nehru

> at the border if he persisted on entering the state territory. Convinced as I was that his entry would lead to disorder of a serious nature, it would be impossible for me to agree to the modification of the orders already passed. As a matter of fact, the district magistrate was already at the border to carry these orders into effect, should the occasion arise. Before, however, the reply could be sent, I suggested to Daubeny that the Maharaja should be informed of the contents of the Viceroy's telegram in case he might want to send a different reply. For my part, the reply was that if the Government of India insisted on intervening in this matter, I would forthwith resign [from] my office of prime minister rather than lend myself to be used contrary to my convictions.

This was a critical inflection point for Bhaiji in determining the real feelings of the Maharaja and his determination to express them to the Government of India. It was a time of stress and uncertainty. Daubeny and Bhaiji may have met the Maharaja at the palace close to midnight on 20 June. The events thereafter, though, gave Bhaiji confidence that he had the Maharaja's firm support.

> Daubeny and I went to the palace, Daubeny read the Viceroy's telegram to the Maharaja, as also my proposed reply. The Maharaja observed that he approved of the reply but that he wanted it to be added that if the Government of India persisted in dictating to the state a course of action which the state did not consider right, he himself might be forced to abdicate rather than follow the direction of the Viceroy.
>
> The telegram was accordingly sent to the Viceroy by the Resident. Next day, Mr Nehru arrived at Kohala and refused to turn back when the district magistrate showed him a copy of the order prohibiting his entry into state territory. He insisted on being put under arrest if he was not allowed to proceed. The district magistrate complied with his wishes and escorted him to the Domel dak bungalow, where he stayed for some days.

Since Mr Nehru's arrest created a great sensation at the time, it is necessary to narrate what actually happened and how the arrest was affected. According to the report furnished by the district magistrate, Mr Nehru and his party, including Mr Asaf Ali, Dewan Chamanlal and others of their party, arrived on the Indian side of Kohala and went to the dak bungalow where they had their meal. After this, Mr Nehru crossed over to the Kashmir side, where he was met by the district magistrate at the Customs' post near the bridge-head. A number of people had collected on both sides. The district magistrate told him that he could not permit him to proceed to Srinagar, whereupon Mr Nehru took a seat at the customs' post and asked him if he could give him a book. The district magistrate happened to possess a volume of plays, which he presented to Mr Nehru. Until the evening, nothing of note happened—Mr Nehru would not go back and the district magistrate would not let him go forward.

Altogether there were about 40 armed police at Kohala, they had instructions under no circumstances to resort to firing. As a matter of fact, it was not expected that any occasion for violence could arise, since Mr Nehru, accepting the Congress creed, could not be expected to be anything but non-violent. We, however, were not adept in the tactics of non-violence and did not then know that it is possible to be non-violently violent.

In the afternoon, people from the Indian side, mostly residents of the North-West Frontier Province, then ruled by the Congress government of Dr Khan Sahib, crossed over in twos and threes to the state side until they grew into a crowd of 1,000 or 1,500. The district magistrate and the police thought that they were mere spectators and did not try to prevent their crossing into the state territory. Having attained this strength, they took Mr Nehru in their midst and began to march in a solid mass, shouldering their way but without lifting their hands or making any show of violence to the police. The latter, having strict orders not to fire and being only 40 in number, automatically found themselves shouldered aside. Meanwhile, the National Conference, no doubt by previous arrangement, had sent cars from Srinagar. The moment, therefore, the police were shoved out of the way, Mr Nehru entered a car and drove on, with the district magistrate following him and his party to Muzafarrabad. Having achieved their purpose of pushing Mr Nehru into the state, the crowd melted and disappeared across the bridge.

Upon arrival at Muzaffarrabad, the district magistrate—now more confident, as he was well inside the state territory and sure that there could be no possibility of a clash with a mob from outside the state—told Mr Nehru that he would definitely not permit Mr Nehru to proceed further, on which Mr Nehru observed that unless the district magistrate put him under arrest, he would proceed. Thereupon, the district magistrate informed him that he should consider himself under arrest.

The same evening, a report was broadcast on the radio that Mr Nehru had been bayonetted at Kohala and next morning, newspapers published the report in page-wide headlines. In point of fact, this was wholly untrue. Mr Nehru, when eventually he left the state after a week or so, himself categorically denied it, though two days after Mr Nehru's arrest, Dewan Chamanlal, who had accompanied Mr Nehru, came to Srinagar from Muzaffarrabad and—as I was told—held a press conference at which, in reply to the question whether Mr Nehru had received any personal injury, he confirmed that not only had Mr Nehru been injured as reported but that he himself had been injured too. Asked to show his injury, he put his finger on one cheek but, since on examination the cheek was found entire, he added it must be elsewhere.

From now on, we had no real trouble, since after

> Mr Nehru was told that he was under arrest, his behaviour was exemplary.

Figure 15: Nehru being stopped at Kohala border by the district magistrate on Bhaiji's orders in June 1946

Illustration credit: Kashmira Tembulkar

In 1945, too, when Nehru's programme had included a trek in the mountains starting from Shopian, where he was to address a public meeting before starting, once a ban had been issued by the district magistrate, he had cancelled the meeting, asserting that the orders passed by a competent authority and the rule of law should be respected. This code of mutual respect for each other and for the law was followed equally by the Kashmir authorities. Bhaiji further wrote:

> Being asked to describe the exact position by representatives of the press, I explained that Mr Nehru was, in fact, not under arrest in the ordinary sense of the term, as all we wanted was that he should not proceed on his journey to

Srinagar. He was free to go anywhere else he wanted, and the moment he expressed a wish in this behalf, the state government would provide all necessary facilities to enable him to reach his destination, the only condition being that that destination must not be Srinagar. This was published, broadcast and also communicated to the Government of India through the Resident.

The Cabinet Mission was, meanwhile, waiting at New Delhi for Mr Nehru to decide his course of action. Mr Nehru refused to come back. To inquiries from his Congress colleagues and Maulana Azad, the then president of the Congress, he replied that his honour was at stake, and he would not go back. For some days he stayed at the Domel dak bungalow, where a state car was in attendance to take him to Rawalpindi the moment he signified his pleasure to that effect.

Ultimately, a request was received from the Government of India that Mr Nehru might be brought to a place where he could himself have direct telephonic communication with Maulana Azad. He was accordingly brought to Uri, where a special telephone was installed to enable him to converse with the Congress President. After an interchange of views on telephone and the assurance given to him by Maulana Azad that the Congress deemed his honour as its own honour and would redeem it accordingly, Mr Nehru consented to return to Delhi. We were asked to arrange a plane for him. A service plane was sent by the Viceroy—to whom Mr Nehru's request was communicated—to Rawalpindi, where Mr Nehru travelled in a state car that was at his service.

Meanwhile, the lawyers selected by Mr Nehru and accompanying him for preparing the defence of Sheikh Abdullah started their work. It soon became evident that the defence would not be in respect of the actual events and incidents of the Quit Kashmir movement and Sheikh Abdullah's part in them. These were not denied, but the case

> that was sought to be made was in respect of the virtue of democracy over any other form of government and the claim that Sheikh Abdullah, being an advocate of a democratic form of government, did all that he did in pursuit of that end; was appropriate and laudable; and finally, Quit Kashmir really meant that the government should be democratic.
>
> Simultaneously, token agitation—which, however, had only nuisance value—was kept up. In the afternoon, a number of women collected at the Khanqah Mohalla, and after a preliminary canter of shouting slogans, which were not always polite, dispersed in groups until, in due course, the thought of hungry babies took them home. At Hazratbal, one or two people daily offered themselves for arrest after making objectionable harangues. The police duly took them into custody. They were let off either immediately or after a summary trial soon after. Apart from this, life in the country followed its even tenor and, on the whole, people were glad that an unruly element had been curbed, that there was no danger of their receiving an unexpected blow or of their turbans being snatched off their heads as they unsuspectingly went on their daily avocations. At long last, they felt that there was some semblance of security in the country.

This is a crucial piece of Bhaiji's memoirs, since there are many interpretations of this incident and also because this was a turning point in the relationship between the Government of Kashmir and the Government of India.

In retrospect, Bhaiji's sense of relief and, perhaps, that of a part of the local community about peace having finally descended was premature. A political whirlwind had begun to blow and the vortex arose from the arrest that shocked the world.

I can imagine that for Nehru, the defiance of another Pandit, who had no national stature, was really an irritation—an annoying fly that needed to be swatted. He had larger designs for Kashmir and on the Maharaja for his undemocratic rule, which no buzzing fly could sidestep. Though more important issues loomed in India, Nehru's ego and sense of honour were hurt at being thwarted by a flyweight. He then produced a giant democratic fly swatter, in the shape of Mahatma Gandhi and Sardar Vallabhbhai Patel, to swat away the buzzing fly.

Meanwhile, Bhaiji—secure, as he imagined, under the umbrella of British Paramountcy and the Maharaja's support of his actions—ignored the ominous brandishing of collective national power by Mahatma Gandhi, Sardar Patel and Nehru. My grandfather, sticking to his principles, naively believed that the Maharaja and even the common man would continue to rally behind him. This was not to be, particularly because, after a few months, the rules governing British Paramountcy in India were changed, removing British Protection for princely states and clearly advocating their accession to one or other dominion. In March 1947, Lord Albert Mountbatten arrived in New Delhi as the last viceroy of India and advanced the date of Partition to August 1947. He oversaw Partition and stayed on as the first governor-general of India till June 1948, which had been the original date fixed for the partition of India and Pakistan.

15

Reaping the Whirlwind

Bhaiji was summoned to meet Sardar Patel regarding the proposed future of Kashmir in Bombay in early July 1946. When Sardar Patel learnt during the conversation that Bhaiji's larger intention was to remain neutral and sign Standstill Agreement with both India and Pakistan, he was startled. He immediately arranged a meeting between Bhaiji and Mahatma Gandhi, which Bhaiji recorded in his unpublished memoir.

> Mahatma Gandhi opened the conversation by remarking that he had heard a great deal about me, that he remembered having seen me on-board ship, when he had gone to attend the round table conference. (I frequently attended the Mahatma's evening prayers on-board the *Rajputana* in 1931, when we were on our way to London to attend the second round table conference). His next remark was, '*Aap bare goonehgar hain* [You are a sinner].' Thinking this was intended as a joke, I replied that had I not been a *goonehgar*, I wouldn't have been hauled up before him to explain my conduct. It, however, soon became evident that far from being in a jocose mood, Mahatma Gandhi was in deadly earnest. He immediately adopted a minatory tone with reference to the acts of my administration, mainly connected with the events leading up to Sheikh Abdullah's and finally to Mr Nehru's arrests. He advised that Sheikh Abdullah should forthwith be released, and as required by Mr Nehru, a committee should

be appointed to frame a new constitution for the state on what he called democratic lines, meaning transfer of power to Sheikh Abdullah. Further, no hitch should be placed on Mr Nehru's visiting the state, which he intended to do almost immediately. He lightly brushed aside all I said with regard to Sheikh Abdullah's activities and the unrest caused by them in the state as also the reasons why the state government felt that it would be unwise for Mr Nehru to visit the state in immediate future. He insisted that Mr Nehru was bound to proceed to Kashmir immediately and had told him that on his way to Bombay, groups of people had met him at each railway station exhorting him to go and asking him to tell them the date so that they would be in readiness to accompany him. As regards Mr Nehru's anxiety to proceed to Kashmir, he said that Mr Nehru considered Sheikh Abdullah as his friend and brother and was prepared to lay down his life for him. To the objection that we were practically certain that if Mr Nehru went and interfered in the local affairs, there was bound to be deep discontent in the state, probably leading to bloodshed that could not be prevented except by resorting to suppression, which might lead to shooting, Mahatma Gandhi replied that being the head of the government, if I thought it was necessary for me to order shooting, obviously it would be my duty to do so. I gave the obvious reply that the question of shooting would arise only because of Mr Nehru proceeding to Kashmir and inciting activities which would lead to disturbances. Why not, therefore, follow the plain course of advising him not to proceed to Kashmir. On this, Mr Gandhi reiterated his previous statement, viz. that Mr Nehru was going to the state and considered the state as his native land and would not be dissuaded and should not be prevented from going to Kashmir.

Figure 16: Bhaiji, in his last days as the PM, with Mahatma Gandhi and Sardar Patel in Delhi in June 1947. He was summoned there by the Mahatma to discuss Nehru's visit to Kashmir.

Illustration credit: Kashmira Tembulkar

One may argue that personal feelings are rarely the ideal basis for a country's actions, particularly when they may result in bloodshed or religious turmoil. One can imagine the intense pressure on Bhaiji to capitulate to what he saw as petulance by the leader of the Congress in India being endorsed by the Mahatma. Essentially, the man with the highest moral authority in India, plainly showed his irritation with Bhaiji while berating him. Any lesser man would, recognising the vast forces arrayed against him, quietly accede or, at any rate, agree to carry this strong message to his boss, the Maharaja. Instead, Bhaiji remained defiant. However, his sophisticated arguments fell on deaf ears.

> On this, I told Mahatma Gandhi that I refused to accept a position where one authority, in this case the Congress and

its leaders, were to dictate the policy and another authority, in this case the Kashmir government of which I was the head, were to bear the consequences of that policy. Since we had to bear the consequences of that policy, we were definite in our refusal to agree with the view put forward by him. In point of fact, I had a letter in my pocket from the Maharaja, addressed to Mr Nehru, advising him not to come to Kashmir until a more opportune moment. I added that I was prepared to hand the letter over to him, if he so desired. He might hand it to Mr Nehru or open it himself, as he chose.

By this time, Mahatma Gandhi was thoroughly upset, particularly as, at one time, I had the temerity to quote the Gita in defence of my attitude, explaining to him that as he considered the discharge of his duty paramount, irrespective of the consequences, such discharge might entail on him, so did I consider the discharge of my duty paramount, notwithstanding the consequences to me personally. The only difference between him and me in this respect was that we had divergent conceptions of our duty. When he found that I refused to submit to admonition and insisted that I felt convinced that I was doing right in acting as I had done and proposed to do, he nearly lost his temper and said, 'After all you are only four million and on this side there are four hundred million. How do you think you will be able to withstand them?' I replied that the case was not of counting heads and hands, but of doing our duty. If, in the discharge of that duty, it was to be our fate that we should sink, we would sink, but all the world would see was that we had given as good an account of ourselves as we could.

Mr Gandhi opened the envelope which I handed to him, read the letter and handed it back to me. He said that this would not do at all and that we must agree to Mr Nehru proceeding to Kashmir. I pointed out to him that the letter was from the Maharaja, who had categorically stated that

> Mr Nehru should not come to Kashmir at the time proposed. So, there was no question of my being able to modify the letter. Mahatma Gandhi replied that he was not prepared to accept that position and that he knew quite well that, '*Riyasat Maharaj ki hai, raj aapka hai* [The kingdom is the Maharaja's, but you are ruling it].'

Mahatma Gandhi's quote that Bhaiji, acting in the name of the Maharaja, was the actual power behind the throne, puts a finger on precisely the perception that Nehru, Sardar Patel and the Mahatma had of the situation. That this was not wholly true and that the Maharaja was himself incensed by Sheikh Abdullah's conduct was glossed over. My grandfather could not have acted otherwise if the Maharaja had not been in agreement. It was also not taken into account that by strongly supporting the Maharaja's bête noire, Nehru was, it may be speculated, driving the Maharaja towards desperate measures, as was soon to become evident.

> The interview with Mahatma Gandhi lasted an hour and fifteen minutes, as he was careful to point out before he left the room. Before leaving, however, he said that I must see Maulana Azad, then president of the Congress. I replied that as I had arranged to leave at 6.00 the next morning, it would not be possible for me to do so but both he and Sardar Patel, who throughout the whole interview had scarcely uttered a word, insisted that I must see Maulana Azad next morning before leaving.
>
> Next morning, I saw Maulana Azad. Professor Shah was also present. Azad talked to me and at me for three quarters of an hour, during which I hardly spoke though Professor Shah succeeded in occasionally getting a few words in. My chief impression of this interview is primarily of the ornate Urdu spoken by Maulana Azad and of the strikingly dramatic gesture—a quick jerk of the hands with thumbs down—indicating how I should deal with the Muslim rivals of Sheikh Abdullah, in case they gave trouble.

I have no recollection of anything of substance having been said by Maulana Azad.

Incidentally, the only other person whom I met at Bombay on this occasion was the Maharaja of Bikaner, who sent his ADC post-haste to me. He said that the Maharaja wanted to see me. I told him I had no time, but he insisted on taking me along at that very moment to the Bikaner House. There, I found Mr Panikkar [K.M. Panikkar], prime minister of Bikaner, awaiting Mrs Sarojini Naidu, who was expected at any moment. I was taken straight to the Maharaja who, as soon as he saw me, made a great show of cordiality and effusively embraced me. He spoke admiringly of the firmness I had shown in a very difficult situation and how proud he felt of the way I had acquitted myself.

On arrival at Srinagar, I explained personally, besides sending a written note, to the Maharaja all that had transpired at Bombay in the interview I had with the various Congress dignitaries.

A revised letter was sent by the Maharaja to Mr Nehru, in which it was stated that though the moment was inopportune for his coming to Kashmir, there would be no objection to his doing so, but it must be remembered that orders were in force at the moment, under which political meetings and demonstrations etc. were prohibited and it was hoped that Mr Nehru would keep this in mind when he came. I sent copies of this letter to Mahatma Gandhi, Sardar Patel and Maulana Azad. The Maulana did not acknowledge my letter, Sardar Patel sent a telegram saying that he had received the letter and thought it would be all right. Mahatma Gandhi wrote acknowledging my letter and saying, among other things, with reference to the Maharaja's letter to Mr Nehru, '*Yeh aapki chaturaiya, sahanshilata aur dhairya pe nirbhar hai* [This will depend on your understanding, maturity and patience!]

Soon after Pandit Nehru's arrest in June 1946, the Maharaja had offered a jagir or gift of land to Bhaiji, in honour of his courageous services. Bhaiji, with his strong sense of integrity, refused the Maharaja's offer, despite the Maharani's appeals, leading to an unnecessary rift between the Maharaja and himself at a critical juncture of Kashmir politics, which only widened as the storm clouds gathered. Perhaps, the jagir was one way in which the Maharaja believed he would secure the obligation and loyalty of his subjects, but, in Bhaiji's book, it was tantamount to him becoming a toady to the Maharaja! His refusal meant that for the Maharaja, Bhaiji was far too independent and could not to be trusted to toe the line.

> Towards the end of 1946, Indian states, faced with the prospect of transfer of power to Indian hands, found it necessary to reorientate their outlook vis-à-vis India and the British Crown.
>
> The position of Kashmir had always been peculiar and in the new set-up, it was likely to become more so. The question of partition of India had not yet assumed any immediate significance. The interim government included the nominees of both the Congress and the Muslim League. All that was necessary for the states to decide was whether, on India being raised to the status of a dominion, they should accede to the dominion or stay out and face the consequences that isolation might entail.
>
> The Kashmir government decided to remain outside the dominion but continue to maintain friendly relations with it. This decision was communicated to the Government of India through the Resident in Kashmir.
>
> Soon after, the arrival in March 1947 of Lord Mountbatten as viceroy and governor-general of India, the decision was taken to partition India and to set up a second dominion, Pakistan. The states were now faced with the problem not only of accession or otherwise as such but also, should they

decide to accede, whether they would accede to India or to Pakistan...

Muslims constitute 76 per cent of the population of the state. Its western border wholly and its southern border for the most part runs contiguous to Western Pakistan. As against this, the affinities of important groups of the population in the state are largely with India. Moreover, in Kashmir are some of the holiest of Hindu places of worship, which attract votaries from all over India, and indeed form an integral part of the general Hindu religious corpus. These places are not man-made temples or shrines, but natural phenomena—lakes and springs and rivers, snow-clad peaks and glaciers—which have remained enshrined in the consciousness of the Aryan race since the time, in the dawn of history, they crossed the great barriers and gazed at their Promised Land—Aryavarta.

In the circumstances, if the state had decided on accession whether to India or to Pakistan, there was bound to be serious trouble from the side not chosen as well as from within. Therefore, the partition of India reinforced the state government's decision regarding non-accession. A formal communication to the Government of India reiterating its previous stand was again sent by the Kashmir government with the addition that the state would like to enter into Standstill Agreements with both dominions. The idea of Standstill Agreements between the dominions and the states was the Government of India's own, as the statute provided for states acceding to either dominion or not acceding at all. In the latter case, they could make Standstill Agreements with either or both dominions to keep their mutual administrative arrangements going until after full consideration and mutual discussion, they would be in a position to enter into permanent arrangements.

In June 1947, Lord Mountbatten who had visited Kashmir more than once before as supreme commander,

> South-East Asia, now paid a visit as viceroy of India. During his stay, he tried to impress on the Maharaja, and separately also on me, the advisability of accession and the benefits accruing therefrom, omitting however to name the dominion to which the state should accede. Since, however, the Kashmir government had already come to the conclusion that its safety lay in non-accession, these conversations did not lead to anything conclusive.

In July 1947, Lord Mountbatten invited the states to send representatives to a conference in New Delhi, which he was convening to resolve the doubts of such states as might still be unconvinced of the advantages of accession. Bhaiji went to Delhi in response to Lord Mountbatten's invitation to explain to him and all concerned the pros and cons of Kashmir's Standstill Agreements.

> First of all, I met Lord Mountbatten specially at his request. As before, he explained to me the advantages of accession; adding, with reference to any possible fears we might entertain regarding the future of the ruling family after accession, that rulers would continue as constitutional monarchs—that he was by birth, upbringing and conviction, a constitutional monarchist and that he could not, therefore, advise the rulers, some of whom were his personal friends, contrary to their interests. I replied that our policy was based, so far as I was concerned, on instinct because inherited knowledge of the country and the people as well as the experience of a lifetime was in favour of non-accession. Nevertheless, since he so strongly recommended accession, would he, I asked, please advise, which dominion Kashmir should accede to?
>
> Lord Mountbatten emphatically replied that that was a matter which we should decide for ourselves, keeping in mind our geographical position, our political situation and the composition of our population. My reply was that

> these certainly were important considerations but there were others also, which we could ignore only at our peril; and since the two sets of considerations militated against each other, the safety of Kashmir lay in adhering to the path it had chosen and not deviating from it by acceding to either Dominion.
>
> (The argument ebbed and flowed until finally Lord Mountbatten, seeing that I was maintaining my ground, suddenly asked whether I had met V.P. Menon. My reply being in the negative, he sent for Mr Menon and asked us to discuss the question of the accession of Kashmir. He also desired me to see Mahatma Gandhi and arranged an appointment for me with the Mahatma next day).

Meanwhile, Bhaiji also met with Sardar Patel, who told him that several moves were afoot to remove him as the PM of Kashmir not only by the National Conference of Sheikh Abdullah, who was in jail, and the Muslim Conference—whose head, Chowdhry Ghulam Abbas, had also been detained by the Kashmir administration—but also by the Maharaja's own palace courtiers as well those who had met him and floated different names for Sardar Patel's approval in the past few months. Sardar Patel had told the messengers acting in the Maharaja's name that he could not respond to such cavalier suggestions and that if the Maharaja indeed wished to obtain his advice, he should come to Delhi and meet him. Sardar Patel then point blank asked Bhaiji if his relations with the Maharaja were cordial. Bhaiji's response, in his own words, was:

> I replied that, I had no ground for believing that they were anything but friendly, though naturally, from time-to-time, matters arose in which my opinion did not coincide with the Maharaja's.
>
> Sardar Patel asked me what I thought of the situation.
>
> I replied that it seemed obvious that an intrigue was going on in the Kashmir palace circles, but I was not sure how far the Maharaja himself was a party to it. The Sardar

replied that he had been told that I would be put in prison when I went back from Delhi and suggested that I should not go back. I replied that the country was facing a most critical situation, and anyone who deserted his post at such a juncture for reasons of personal safety would not deserve the name of man; that the job was greater than the man and the country greater than the job. Moreover, if and when I left Kashmir, I would do so as a man and not like a thief in the night. Therefore, I would go back and face the consequences, whatever they might be...

Sardar Patel then said that I should tell the Maharaja on his behalf that it was most unwise and dangerous, during a period of crisis like the one the country was passing through at the moment, for a ruler not to see eye-to-eye with his prime minister. There was no reason, in case the Maharaja could not get on with the present prime minister, why he should not have another prime minister with whom he could get on. But so long as there was a prime minister in office, the Maharaja should uphold his authority and prestige and not undermine it by negotiating state arrangements behind his back and without his knowledge. If he persisted in carrying on as he had been doing, he would only succeed in destroying the state—a calamity in comparison with which any incidental damage to an individual, whether he was the prime minister or the ruler, would be a matter of trifling consequences.

Next day, I saw Mahatma Gandhi at the Bhangi Colony and explained the situation to him as I had to Lord Mountbatten and Mr Menon. Except for a few questions tending towards the elucidation of doubtful points in my argument, he offered no comment so far as the question of accession of the state was concerned. He was more worried about Mr Nehru's intended visit to Kashmir and the release of Sheikh Abdullah. He said that though repeatedly dissuaded both by himself and Lord Mountbatten, Nehru was bent

> upon visiting Kashmir and that he would forego everything else in order to have his wish.

So far as the state was concerned, there was no ban on Nehru coming to Kashmir, though the Maharaja did not like the idea. As we have seen, Nehru had visited Kashmir in July of the preceding year, only a few weeks after he had been stopped from proceeding to Srinagar. It could mean that Mahatma Gandhi's anxiety was perhaps more about securing Sheikh Abdullah's release, for which Pandit Nehru was insistent on visiting Kashmir again, even though Partition and the possibility of a holocaust loomed just a month away.

> ...After seeing the Mahatma, I lunched at the Viceroy's House. Lord Mountbatten asked me whether I intended to see any political leaders in New Delhi. I told him that I intended to see Sardar Patel (whom I had already seen once) and possibly Mr Jinnah. He said that it would be worth my while to see Liaqat Ali Khan also and offered to arrange for me to see him the same day, as Liaqat Ali Khan was lunching with Lord Hastings Ismay [Chief of Staff to Lord Mountbatten] in the Viceroy's House precincts. I replied that I felt that it would be enough if I had a talk with Mr Jinnah.
>
> Next day, I met Mr Jinnah at his house. He asked me what Kashmir intended to do now that India and Pakistan were being constituted as separate dominions. He said that if Kashmir acceded to Pakistan now, it was sure to get favourable terms which it would be not likely to get after Pakistan had become established and had consolidated its position. I replied that the situation, both internal and external, of Kashmir was such that any attempt on its part to align itself with either dominion was likely to prove disastrous not only to itself but perhaps even to the dominions, since the people of both dominions were so closely linked with the various aspects of the Kashmir problem that a quarrel would soon develop if Kashmir showed any preference.

> Consequently, I said, we had come to the conclusion that not only in our own interest but also in the interest of both India and Pakistan, it would be best for us to remain outside, though in [a] close and friendly relationship with both. We particularly felt that this was a course which would prove beneficial to the dominions in as much as Kashmir being a point of contact, the present embittered feelings between the two dominions might, through this channel, give place gradually to cordial and friendly relations. Mr Jinnah said that he would not object to Kashmir staying outside both India and Pakistan so long as he was assured that this was genuinely the policy of the state. He added that he had more than once publicly declared his opinion that the states were free, in terms of the statute granting dominion status to India and Pakistan, to accede to either dominion or to stay out. I assured him that the policy of the government of the state was one of non-accession coupled with the maintenance of the friendliest relations with both dominions.

Jinnah's no objection may have been a temporary agreement to prevent Kashmir from voluntarily falling to India. Bhaiji, meanwhile, may have wished to allow matters to settle to find an appropriate moment to align with India because of Kashmir's importance not only geopolitically but also, in terms of its key religious and philosophical position, historically, for India.

> Finally, I saw Pandit Jawaharlal Nehru. With him, my interview was very brief. He observed in general terms that events were marching rapidly and mediaeval ideas would not long prevail etc. As he had a dinner engagement at the Viceroy's house, I took leave, telling him that I would be coming again to Delhi in a fortnight's time and then, if he desired, would meet him again.

There were no further meetings, since these meetings happened at the end of July 1947. By then, fully aware of the rapidly shifting political developments and palace intrigues swirling around him, Bhaiji realised he was treading on shifting sands at a time when Kashmir and India's futures were at stake. He felt it was an opportune time to resign if he had lost the Maharaja's confidence. Given the events of the last six months, the answer was a foregone conclusion.

16

Oh What a Fall!

Across the nation, gurus and godmen have wielded disproportionate influence over the centres of power. Swami Sant Dev first appeared in Maharaja Pratap Singh's court in Kashmir as a spiritual guide and rose to the position of Rajguru or chief spiritual adviser to the Maharaja. After Pratap Singh's death in 1925, the Swami was banished from the court by the agnostic Hari Singh, though he continued his lifetime *mukarari* or fixed pension of ₹300 per month granted by Pratap Singh. Maharani Tara Devi, wife of Maharaja Hari Singh, who took over palace politics after Hari Singh's ascension, became a devout follower of the Swami, facilitating his access to palace affairs and the Maharaja's ear. The vacuum that the end of British Paramountcy created in India leding up to Partition likely enabled the Swami to convince the Maharaja that he was destined to become the ruler of a new kingdom till Lahore. The Swami so beguiled the Maharaja that he specially commissioned a new crown encrusted with diamonds and emeralds for his coronation as the ruler of this new kingdom, to be called 'Dogristan'.

Increasingly aware of the Maharaja's growing allegiance to the Swami's beguiling vision of an extended empire of Dogristan, excluding the state government from any knowledge of it, Bhaiji felt it was now impossible for him to continue as the PM. He was surprised, though, at the Maharaja's reaction when he brought the matter of his replacement, as Sardar Patel had suggested, to his attention. Bhaiji wrote in his unpublished memoir:

Figure 17: Swami Sant Dev with the Maharaja and Maharani sitting before him at a havan for Dogristan at the Chashme Shahi guesthouse lawn in Kashmir, worshipping the crowns of Dogristan, in May or June 1947
Illustration credit: Kashmira Tembulkar

I returned to Srinagar on 27th July, and saw the Maharaja on the 28th. I narrated to him all that I had learnt in Delhi, particularly what Sardar Patel had told me with regard to the attempts made in the Maharaja's name to secure a new prime minister. The Maharaja's reaction was one of undisguised astonishment. He repeatedly exclaimed, 'Honestly I don't know what to say.' I conveyed to him Sardar Patel's message, viz. that in this very dangerous and critical time, it was essential that the ruler and his prime minister should pull together but if that seemed impossible, there was nothing to prevent the Maharaja [from] having a new prime minister. For my own part, I added, I entirely agreed with Sardar Patel and would be prepared to apply for retirement at any moment. The Maharaja said that I should let him have a note on the subject. On 30th July, I sent him a note, offering my analysis of the situation and my resignation, if he so desired.

The Maharaja did not reply immediately. In his note, Bhaiji did not mention that Sardar Patel had informed him about the intention to imprison him upon his return to Kashmir. A couple of days later, Mahatma Gandhi came to Srinagar. My grandfather met him twice and showed him his resignation note. Mahatma Gandhi read it and remarked that nobody could be expected to do more than what Bhaiji had done. Perhaps, the Mahatma was relieved that Bhaiji was stepping down. Regardless, he patiently heard Bhaiji's views on the future of Kashmir.

> During Mahatma Gandhi's stay at Srinagar, I had two long talks with him, each lasting more than an hour. The talks were on Kashmir's past, present and future. I again explained to him how dangerous it would be for Kashmir to accede to either dominion. His last question was whether I thought I would be able to resist the pressure that was likely to be brought to bear on the state from various quarters once the dominions were set up and the security provided by the exercise of paramountcy of the Crown had vanished with the cessation of the British authority from India. My reply was that while no one could, in a rapidly changing world, indefinitely guarantee the continuance of any particular state of affairs, it was my belief that, by working on the sentiment of local patriotism and appealing to the common background of the different classes of people in the state, I stood a good chance of succeeding. Further, during the period that I had been prime minister, I had succeeded, without the use of any force worth the name, in maintaining law and order in the country among all classes of people to a degree not achieved before, and in face of far graver provocation from outside and inside the state had experienced at any time previously. While Punjab and the North-West Frontier Provinces, not to mention other parts of India more remote from Kashmir, had been going through a bloodbath since the autumn of 1946, in the state, not a breach had stirred to disturb its

tranquillity. I stressed that the chances of maintaining such a satisfactory state of affairs would be few indeed if occasion arose for people to make a choice with regard to accession to a dominion because then considerations which were dormant now would become active and people's passions and prejudices would rise to sway their judgements and direct their actions. So long as a man was not called upon to take a positive decision, he was likely to take the line of least resistance. But confronted with the duty of making a choice particularly in a matter where the choice was bound to be interwoven with religious considerations, it was most unlikely that in the present stage of Indian society, anybody—whatever his religious persuasion, except the very few among the most enlightened—would decide otherwise than in accordance with his religious prejudices. This applied equally to all communities. It would be futile to argue that in a matter of this kind, religion would play no part in face of the fact that the division of India, however one may try to explain it now, was in fact based on religious considerations. And not only does this apply to India as a whole but also to the provinces. For example, Punjab and Bengal were divided, the Muslim majority areas going to one side and the Hindu majority ones going to the other side. So were districts divided on the same principle, example, Gurdaspur and Sylhet.

Again, the North-West Frontier Province had for years been ruled by a Congress government. Pro-Congress redshirts had been a very powerful political force. Yet the people voted solidly for Pakistan when required to decide whether they would join India or Pakistan. Incidentally, the fact that the North-West Frontier Province was represented in the Indian Constituent Assembly so long as the Congress government remained in power in the province had no effect. Once the people of the province were asked to decide where they would like to accede, of the votes cast, hardly 1 per cent was for accession to India. The arguments that the pro-India

> elements deliberately stayed away from the elections is scarcely tenable in a sober appraisement of the result.
>
> On the conclusion of my second talk with Mahatma Gandhi, I was asked by the representatives of APT [Associated Press Trust] and UPT [United Press Trust], who were in the Mahatma's entourage, what I thought would be the future of the state. I replied that I thought the state should remain on terms of friendship and goodwill with both dominions. This was duly published in the press at the time.
>
> The Mahatma had an interview with the Maharaja and the Maharani at which I was not present. I asked the Mahatma, who honoured me by calling at my house on his way back from the palace, whether he had a satisfactory talk. He replied, 'We only talked of this and that—*idhar udhar ki baatein hui*.' According to the report published in the papers after he left the state, he had advised the Maharaja and the Maharani to transfer power to the people, which, as it was Mahatma Gandhi who was advising, in effect meant to Sheikh Abdullah. The report added that Mahatma Gandhi had said the Maharaja and the Maharani had agreed. The Maharaja, when asked whether this was so, replied in the negative.

Bhaiji's historically reasoned recipe for keeping Kashmir peaceful was only possible if he was responsible for implementing it. He perhaps still remained trusting and hopeful as one can gather from his long conversations with Mahatma Gandhi. Nonetheless, the air was rife with speculation and dissemination of untruths.

For a few days after Bhaiji's letter of ultimatum, if not resignation from 5 August 1947, nothing happened. The Maharaja went away on yet another shooting expedition; ironic, considering another, far more serious actual shooting was looming just a few days away! It was the lull before the storm.

> On 11 August, I received a letter from the Maharaja stating that he had reluctantly accepted my request for retirement.

> He added that my services to the state were well-known and stood in need of no special mention. Only a few weeks before, he had insisted on recommending me to the Government of India for the conferment of an honour, KCSI [Knight Commander of the Order of the Star of India], KCIE [Knight Commander of the Most Eminent Order of the Indian Empire] or KBE [Knight Commander of the Most Excellent Order of the British Empire], in recognition of the services I had rendered as prime minister.

Once Bhaiji read the letter, he realised there was no time to lose. He was out of power and forces inimical to him would ensure that he would be unable to rise ever again. He picked up the phone and spoke to the auditor general to transfer the sum available in his provident fund account to his personal account immediately. The auditor general suggested he wait for a few days or else he would lose ₹40,000 to ₹50,000 interest—a very substantial sum in those days—due to premature withdrawal. Bhaiji insisted that, regardless, he wished for the amount to be transferred to his personal account immediately. Bhaiji's friend, who was the manager at the Lloyds Bank, where he had maintained an account for years, phoned him confirming the receipt of the amount within an hour. Bhaiji told me this story many years later, but, in his unpublished memoir, he simply wrote:

> Within a few minutes of my receiving the letter from the Maharaja, I handed over charge to the successor nominated—Major General Janak Singh, who had, nearly 20 years before, retired from the post of revenue minister and was now about 79 years of age. Next day, I left Srinagar for Gulmarg, where I intended to stay pending arrangements to secure passages for myself and family to go to England.

By the evening of 11 August, their bags were packed and next morning, at 7.00 a.m., the family left for Gulmarg to avoid the unpleasantness ahead. Bended recalled how they walked up to

Gulmarg from Tangmarg with their gunman walking behind. Anything could have happened at that time.

Crowds gathered around the Gulmarg cottage where they were staying, yelling abuse, till Bhaiji summoned the police officer and told him that they had a young girl (my aunt, Lila) with them, whom they had to put to sleep at 5.00 p.m., so she may not be frightened by the shouting that had started at 6.00 p.m. Bhaiji had a gun, and told the officer that if anyone came within 300 yards of the cottage, he could shoot them. The hours were fraught with danger.

It is a moot point that had Bhaiji been less trusting and dependent on the Maharaja's good sense in riding out the crisis in Kashmir, he may have, on return from Delhi on July 27, had time to discuss ways and means with his bank manager to save a substantial amount of interest on his personal income. At the last minute, he was not only forced to forego the benefit of a lifetime of saving but also a lifetime of service as he was soon to find out.

> I stayed in Gulmarg for a month. On my return to Srinagar, on 11 September, I wrote a letter to the Maharaja stating that I intended to leave for England and would like to say goodbye to him before leaving the state. This was in accordance with the established convention. I mentioned the date on which I was leaving. No reply came to this letter. But on 14th September, the Senior Superintendent of Police delivered to me an order signed by the Prime Minister intimating that certain complaints had been received by the Maharaja alleging irregularities committed by me during my tenure of office as prime minister, that a commission had been constituted to investigate the charges against me, and that I should present myself before the commission to answer the charges on 24th September.

Bhaiji, of course, refused to attend the proceedings of this commission based on what he knew were trumped up charges.

Many years later, journalist S.N. Pandita, in his extensive tribute to Bhaiji, wrote:

> R.C. Kak's political outlook may not have had many takers then and some may not even endorse it today. But opinions on either side can be worthy of respect. And this has to be considered in the light of the fact that the subcontinent in itself, and Kashmir in particular, was in for political changes of far-reaching consequences. No single person therefore can be faulted in absolute terms, particularly when history was in the making. By destiny R.C. Kak was one among the many who were in the vortex of it. Though shattered but never vanquished, he lived true to his salt and the values and ideals he believed in [...] no homage is sufficient for this man of steel, guts, impeccable integrity and intellectual sagacity. One day history will vindicate him.[25]

Bhaiji suffered the same fate as many other PMs. Furthermore, he had complicated matters not only by going directly to the people—raising suspicions of an alternate power centre, though, ironically, it was in favour of the Maharaja—but also by being strong-willed in opposing the Maharaja's whims and fancies. Besides, he dispensed with social niceties such as the evening durbars of the Maharaja with his friends and hangers-on that continued late into the night over drinks, dinner and gossip, which might have oiled the wheels. He did not even accept gifts and favours, which alienated both the Maharaja and Maharani when it might have cemented a sense of his personal obligation to them. Politics is the art of the possible. Failure to be diplomatic alienates the goodwill of even well-wishers. It was a catch-22 situation.

> One day, in July 1947, I was asked by the Maharaja to meet the rulers of Sirmur, Mandi and Jubbal, who had

---

[25] Pandita, S.N., 'Ram Chandra Kak: An Intellectual with Integrity', *Naad*, July 2007, https://tinyurl.com/583jbrmz. Accessed on 11 May 2023.

> been invited to Srinagar. In the course of the conversation, I learnt for the first time that there was a scheme afoot of setting up a new kingdom composed of the Himalayan states, including Kashmir, embracing the territory as far as Tehri Garhwal, with the Maharaja of Kashmir as suzerain. Asked to give my opinion, I pleaded for time to consider. Really, I wanted to discuss the matter separately with the Maharaja of Kashmir. This I did next morning, when I told him that the scheme was fantastic and unworkable if only for the reason that it was foolish to expect that the forces which had compelled the British to depart from India would not be strong enough to curb the ambitions of princelings, who dreamed of carving out new kingdoms out of the ruins of the British Empire. Further, assuming that such a confederation of princely states in western Himalayas did, in fact, come into being, so far as Kashmir was concerned, the other states, even if they survived as independent units which was most unlikely, would only be a liability, as they were small, weak and resourceless.
>
> I, therefore, wanted the Maharaja to exercise great caution in associating himself with a scheme which, on the face of it, was impractical and dangerous. All that would happen if he persisted would be that he would bring a hornet's nest round his ears. The Maharaja seemed, outwardly at least, to see my point. In any case, so far as I was concerned, that was the last I heard of the scheme. But [the] Maharaja's inner cabal—which included the Swami and the Maharani, who had conceived it and spent much money on missions to Shimla and other hill states—were unwilling to give it up.

It was politically innocent of my grandfather to assume that this would be the last he would hear of the scheme. Those who had invested both time and money in imagining this grand future of being reborn, phoenix-like, from the ashes of the British Empire, would not give up on such satisfying daydreams easily. After all, a new crown had been designed that would adorn the Maharaja's head on the climactic day. Belief is not something that lends itself to logical explanation, and belief accompanied by divine blessings seems supremely plausible. Bhaiji discovered this the hard way.

> In pouring cold water on the scheme I, in fact, trod on very influential toes. The Maharani and her brother had, for their own purposes, so worked on the superstitious nature of the Maharaja that he really believed it was his destiny to become, through the grace of the Swami, the emperor of northern India. Consequently, it was not difficult for them to go one step further and convince him that the only impediment between him and his high destiny was the unbelieving and headstrong prime minister.

This is pure speculation, of course, but perhaps one thought behind the grandiose plan for a greater Kashmir may well have been that the Maharaja felt it was the best way to counter Sheikh Abdullah by creating a constituency that was no longer just the Muslim-dominated Kashmir. This would deprive Sheikh Abdullah of his dominant support base. The Maharaja, governing from Lahore and including the Kangra valley along with Hindu-dominated Jammu in its fold, would become an imagined counterweight to the Muslim population of Kashmir. It was a fanciful thought, but then the whole idea of Dogristan was fanciful.

The Swami had beguiled the Maharaja to the extent that he sacrificed the very PM who had kept his throne secure in critical times, accepting his resignation on 11 August 1947 to fulfil this Quixotic dream of becoming an emperor. As warned by my grandfather, however, the Maharaja was forced, only two months later, to abandon this impractical mirage and sign the Instrument of Accession to India in the face of the approaching tribal groups from Pakistan in October 1947. At midnight, he fled with his family to the safety of Jammu, accompanied by the Swami, who got off at his ashram in Kud. Neither did the Swami and the Maharaja ever meet again nor was the Swami heard of again. He died a few years later, probably still drawing the mukarari, of ₹300 a month for life, gifted to him by the Maharaja after the death of his uncle Maharaja Pratap Singh in 1925.

In the process of designing a new crown, the Maharaja figuratively lost his own head. He handed his throne over to his son, Dr Karan Singh, who became prince regent after the Maharaja stepped down in exile in June 1949. His wife, Maharani Tara Devi, and he were separated in 1950, and she went back to live separately in Himachal Pradesh. The Maharaja's bête noire, Sheikh Abdullah, became prime minister, with Nehru's support, and in 1952, by a resolution, abolished the Dogra monarchy. The Maharaja's world came crashing down. He died a lonely man in Bombay in 1961. He lost everything in pursuit of a whim—a foolish dream that became a nightmare.

Bhaiji was sent to jail, accused of corruption—a crime farthest from his characteristic, uncompromising integrity. Eventually, he was released into exile, since no evidence was found to convict him. Ironically, though acquitted of all charges, no retrospective compensation was ever given to Bhaiji for the 12 years he spent fighting the state to which he had dedicated 33 years of his life. He was offered exemption from exile if he officially requested the state to be allowed to stay. As Lila recalls, her proud father once told her, 'I was born in Kashmir, grew up here, love it and served it with all my heart. I am not going to ask for permission to go to where I belong!' While this was happening, Bended was in England and would hear terrifying rumours that her husband might be assassinated any time.

Regardless, it was typical of Bhaiji to stick to his principles even in moments of greatest adversity. This was the man who had been recommended by the Maharaja for a title for his distinguished services, only to be forced to face a court of enquiry by the same Maharaja a few months later. Politics and ambition can make a person behave irrationally.

As William Shakespeare famously wrote in his play, *Julius Caesar*:

> 'O, what a fall was there, my countrymen!
> Then I, and you, and all of us fell down,
> Whilst bloody treason flourished over us.'

17

Escape from Kashmir[26]

In 1947, in the midst of the turmoil in India and, more specifically, Kashmir, my father decided, after his resignation had been accepted, that we should leave Kashmir and go to stay with my mother's family in England. Though he was prevented from leaving with us, he insisted that my mother and I continue the journey, as he believed it would be much easier for him to manage the situation if it was just him on his own. Subsequently, he was put under house arrest at Bagh Sundar before being moved to the Central Jail, near Hari Parbat.

My mother's letters during this period are revealing of her courageous response to this dire situation. She unhesitatingly takes on the role of a protector. At the same time, she did not wish to worry her family, who, separated by thousands of miles, would imagine the worst and become distraught.

> 4 August 1947
>
> We have been living at high pressure, or rather RCK has, and I vicariously at one remove. He went to Delhi last weekend for three or four days and while he was there, he met all the big guns—the Viceroy, Gandhiji, Mr Jinnah, even Pandit Jawaharlal Nehru at long last! He felt satisfied with the contacts he made, and felt that he had made

[26]The first section of this chapter has been narrated by Lila Kak Bhan and the second by Siddharth Kak.

headway in putting across his point of view. He hoped that he had persuaded them enough to make them give up the project of visiting Kashmir. But apparently Pandit Jawaharlal Nehru is determined that either he should come [to Srinagar] or Gandhiji. RCK got home on Monday and on Friday, Gandhiji arrived. No one can say that, apart from his inherent qualities, which inevitably make him an embarrassing guest, he tried to make trouble. He stayed only two days and studiously said very little, but all the same, it has meant a very anxious time for RCK, as his presence here in support of one party of Muslims, Abdullah's lot, did crystallise the opposition of the other section that sympathises with the Muslim League and Pakistan. The two sections hate each other more than they love anybody else, but Gandhiji and the other Congress leaders are really pawns, which only mean anything in so far as they hope it will make them one up on the opposite section. The result was that Gandhiji's car was stoned on two or three occasions. Fortunately, no damage was done, and any major action by the police or military was avoided. But RCK says it will take very hard work, and about two months, to reduce the temperature of the countryside to normal again. However, now that the great man has been and gone, I hope and believe they will not do anymore for a while, but after all they can't send any bigger guns. RCK saw him twice and he seemed friendly and understanding. How much of that he will publicly admit remains to be seen.

He [Gandhi] came here to call yesterday morning and stayed for about ten minutes with us (the daughters-in-law, Kamla and Sarla, and the children Jalla, Shyam, Billy and me). I was astounded to see how robust he looks. His flesh looks smooth and firm! He talked only in Urdu. RCK says he speaks faultless English, and so I didn't follow much of what he said. People, I feel, are rather disapproving that I can't follow Urdu but, all the same, I can Kashmiri. Billy handed

> him fruit on a silver thal and was very interested and keeps asking why it is that he doesn't wear clothes on his top!

Though I was only five, Mahatma Gandhi's visit is clear in my mind. He sat at one corner on a divan-cum-sofa in our Munshi Bagh living room. I was wearing a pretty frock and carried a silver thal of fruit to offer him. My mother was close behind me, encouraging me and giving me the feeling of safety. I think he picked up a piece of fruit and the thal was then placed by me on a table near him. If there was some little conversation, I cannot recall it. But this event is very vividly etched in my mind.

My mother had the presence of mind to take note of the events unfolding around her and report them. Although, when Bhaiji's resignation was accepted, my mother made light of it, no doubt to assuage her family and not get them worried when they heard the news over the radio. This letter describes the events that led up to the resignation and my parents' decision to go to Gulmarg before leaving the Valley. Before leaving for Gulmarg, the large house we lived in during RCK's prime ministership, at Munshi Bagh, had to be packed and the goods removed to Bagh Sundar.

> August 14, 1947
>
> I don't know whether the news of RCK's retirement penetrated to the BBC. If it did, I do hope you didn't worry. I thought of sending a cable but then decided what little I could say in that wouldn't tell you much either one way or the other. It was a great surprise in the sense that it came at that particular moment, but not in the general sense, and I think you must have gathered even from the little I can say in my letters that there was the strain and that in the last resort he wasn't prepared to compromise.
>
> We went to Dara for the day on Tuesday, and came back for Gandhiji's visit on Wednesday morning. RCK saw His Highness, who said nothing about anything except that he also deserved a holiday and was going fishing until Sunday.

He came on Sunday afternoon, but didn't see RCK on the plea that he was tired.

On Monday morning, RCK went to the office and almost immediately received a letter telling him that, having thought over what RCK had said, HH had come to the conclusion that RCK [...] had lost confidence of various parties in the state and therefore he was to be permitted to retire and was to hand over charge that day to General Janak Singhji, 77, retired minister of state and a distant relative of His Highness.

RCK was back home at 10.30 a.m., and we set to work to pack up like furies because he felt that it was best to clear out as speedily as possible from Srinagar and remove himself from the arena. After RCK resigned from prime ministership, we left for Gulmarg at 9.00 a.m. on Tuesday—pretty good, with that huge house—to be moved down to Bagh Sundar. Actually, in the end we left the books and crockery for Kashinath to see to, as RCK was anxious to get away early and unexpectedly, to avoid demonstrations. You see, the National Conference people have come up with a bump—in fact, all the elements which have been kept down these two years to get a bit of peace. Actually, on the way up here [to Gulmarg], no one said a word, but there were red flags—the National Conference flag—on all the tongas and a good many of the shops. It was very lucky that our hut (the local term for chalets in Kashmir), this year, was without a tenant so that we could just walk in. It has, of course, caused a tremendous sensation and there is great uneasiness about the likelihood of outbreak of communal trouble here on the lines of that. Outside, fortunately they have, we hear, announced that they will for the present join neither dominion, but make terms with both. This was RCK's firm policy and the intriguing elements wanted them to join the Indian Union which would inevitably mean bloodshed. I don't quite know why they didn't; they may have lost nerve at the last moment. However, that now, as RCK says, is not his pigeon.

> Since we came here [to Gulmarg], that is last night, and the night before, about 30 people one day and 50 people another came and shouted rude remarks in unison: 'Ram Kak go back' et cetera for about five minutes and then galloped back again to the end of the *marg*, [from] where the bazaar is about a mile and a half away. We have got about seven men here, and the police and state officers are all very good and helpful, so there's really nothing to worry about and anyhow, RCK thinks even this will die down in a day or two, or rather they will have other things to think about than us. It's a bit eerie while it lasts.

The two nights of protesters sitting on a slope outside our hut in Gulmarg and shouting slogans against my father hugely impacted me. I clearly remember being on my mother's hip, while she, my father and I stood on our verandah. Outside, there was a cool drizzle. My father deemed it best to face the shouting group rather than remain indoors. It rained both the evenings the protesters arrived to shout, and for years after, if I was not home when it rained, I fretted to be with my mother. She fully understood!

We stayed for a few weeks on the beautiful alpine slopes of Gulmarg. Opposite our hut was Leopard's Valley, a sweep of green covered with flowers. The surroundings were idyllic, with a carpet of purple gentians, white pyrethrum daisies, swaying buttercups and forget-me-nots. The green meadows were dotted with ponies grazing at their will, against a backdrop of stately deodars and firs. I was enrolled, temporarily, in a lovely little school in one of the glades of Gulmarg near our hut. It was perhaps the calm before the storm.

Rather predictably, I would cry fearfully as soon as it began to drizzle or rain. To assuage my trepidation, Gaffara, our chowkidar, would stay close at hand with his horse and take me back home on the pony under the protection of a large black umbrella!

My mother was very dutiful about keeping her family regularly informed about us in great detail. She compared my fears with hers and was very empathetic as always. She has also described the beauty of the place and some day-to-day activities, like jam making, that helped maintain a semblance of normalcy during such turbulent times.

> Dearest Dad and Tantes,
>
> It's begun to rain again just now. I feel it will be an added anxiety to me until she [Billy] gets over it, since especially here in Gulmarg, being in the mountains, it rains five or six times in a day! I think myself that the rapid packing up, combined with chitchat she might have heard, has alarmed her. It's possible she feels that since we packed up so quickly that time, we might do it again while she is in school, and then where would she find us? But I must remember what a fearful soul I was and be patient. The school is right in the forest and I dare say when one of these dark, black storms comes over, it does look pretty gloomy.
>
> We've got a sweet little garden here with yellow daisies and dog daisies and lupines and cosmos and some very good white raspberries and black currants. We made some black currant jam which I hadn't tasted for years and find very good. Billy is very thrilled with the idea of coming there and one of my greatest joys is the thought of you seeing her. I suspect that she's the type of small girl that you'd like! The school report is very flattering, that she's distinctly above average in intelligence, and she was moved up into the second form last week. Have you a village school in Belton?

Later, writing from Bagh Sundar, Mummy explained the reason they didn't hasten out of Kashmir, but decided, instead, to go through the formality of taking the Maharaja's leave.

> We may have to be patient a little longer. I'm afraid of how things will turn out, and when or where—we just can't see! We came down from Gulmarg on Thursday September 11th, as we thought we would make a push and get out of the state

> as quickly as possible. Bhaiji didn't want to seem to slink away, and anyway it is usual to write to His Highness asking to pay respects on leaving the state after retirement. So he wrote the usual note to this effect, and that we intended to leave on the 17th by air. To this came no reply but later on, on the 14th evening, notice was served on him, calling for an inquiry under the Public Servants Enquiries Act that would be held on September 24th, to inquire into various complaints and affidavits made against him. We had known for a fortnight or so that they were going through everything with a tooth comb to see if they could make up anything. Every bit of land ever bought, all the brothers-in-law's affairs, etc., with a view to proving corruption influenced by others. They've got 11 charges, which arrived today, all of the most flimsy character. In actual fact, there is nothing, and that is that. He has put in far more work than any profit ever taken out, and the salary is the only profit. This time last year His Highness offered him a jagir, which he refused. This year, in June, His Highness recommended him for KCSI on HH's birthday list. However, to go on with the story, RCK replied to the present prime minister that he would not participate in the proceedings which he considered likely to prejudice the interests of the state and the prestige of the ruler that he had served for five years as minister-in-waiting, and over two years as prime minister, and received many marks of His Highness' appreciation, especially during the last two years, and no complaints.

The strain of living in a hostile environment was compounded in Srinagar and the vagaries of our departure increased, but my mother continued to faithfully report the day-to-day situation in her letters. On 19 September 1947, she wrote, 'Various attempts to leave Srinagar failed for one reason or another, some of which seemed engineered! Finally, one of the flights, scheduled a day earlier, that had turned back earlier, eventually got off, indicating that the weather had improved.'

Then, we were not allowed to leave Srinagar. Our plane was stopped, as Mummy narrated in her letter:

> [...] The three of us, arriving at the airport, were told the crew arrived late, the flight was cancelled, so we couldn't fly. Then, the weather turned bad and that night came an order for detention on the grounds that RCK's going out of the state, 'Would be prejudicial to the relations of the state with other governments.'
>
> On Wednesday, the plane came back to Srinagar because of bad weather. RCK was detained again by government orders, no one seems exactly to know why, but we are led to believe that none of our family, at least for the moment, are allowed to leave! A plane left, at long last, at 1.30 p.m. today. The air company's furious at the detention and all the passengers [are] bursting with indignation. They must have reached Delhi today. Now, the question is will any air company risk sending up more aircraft? Meanwhile, the land route is far from safe, and, in any case, it looks as if even Billy and I won't be allowed to leave. RCK is very keen that we should go at the first opportunity.

As is amply evident, preventing Bhaiji from leaving the state was the goal of the administration. He was eager and determined to get my mother and me to safety outside Kashmir. It must have been very hard for my parents, not knowing how, when or even if they would meet again and where. Bhaiji was the most affectionate of men, but quiet in his outward demonstrations. As we departed, leaving him behind in Bagh Sundar, I am sure he stroked me behind my neck as he would do while making me sit on his lap and reading to me. It was a special gesture full of affection that Siddharth and I recognised and would ask for a, 'tickle and scratch', if he ever forgot! He must have held, squeezed and stroked my mother's hand and patted her shoulders, being discreet because Kashinath and the other helpers, who were at Bagh Sundar then, had come to bid us adieu and were looking on. Our baggage was also searched, but sheepishly.

On Monday, 22 September 1947, we finally left Kashmir. Even as she and I flew out, my mother's attachment to and love for the Valley was manifest as she gazed down, probably trying to distract herself, through the small window of the Dakota at the familiar landmarks she was leaving behind—landmarks that had become so much a part of her. This next excerpt was written after we finally got out of Srinagar. General Scott [Sir Henry Scott] proved to be a very loyal friend and did his best to make our departure as smooth as possible, but he was unable to see us off at the airport the final time. My father was, by then, under house arrest.

In Delhi, my mother set to work immediately and met various influential people whom she wrote about in the following letter. How she sallied forth on this difficult mission stuns me and makes her more extraordinary, determined and admirable than ever; more so because she was far from being a pushy woman. She was, however, upright and determined, and these qualities gave her amazing courage.

> The last letter I wrote to England was from Srinagar, just after we had been prevented from leaving. I expected not to be able to leave, but on Sunday morning, the 21st, General Scott rang up to say that he had been authorised to say that the detention applied only to RCK and not to any other member of the family. I don't know how he managed it, and he must have had a row with the authorities, because he sent a one-word message, that there were 'sufficient reasons' that he was not able to come and see me off himself and he was, at his own request, being released on November 23rd, 1947 or earlier, if he could get a passage [out of Kashmir]. RCK reiterated that he was definite that Billy and I should get out. He says he will join us as soon as he's able to, and, in any case, he feels that he can manage to look after himself, but that all extras are a source of embarrassment. I didn't argue. I feel at the moment our affairs are all shrouded in mist.

My mother had developed an extensive network of contacts in the last decade, both in England and in India, due to her active participation, with Bhaiji, in duties relating to the Maharaja and by virtue of her being an Englishwoman in a country under British Paramountcy. Hence, she was able arrange high-level meetings with key national leaders, like Sardar Patel, in her efforts to free Bhaiji from his detractors. She strained every sinew, but never made much of her efforts and was modest about her network of contacts too.

> Billy and I left on Monday the 22nd, [September 1947] with Kamji, Bab's 19-year-old son. We stayed in Delhi for a week. Both Nana Kak and Sura Kak (our sons) were there, so I was well looked after. While I was there, I had lunch with Sardar Patel, the deputy prime minister who is in charge of the state department, the successor of the political department. Miraben Patel came in and apologised for the Sardar being late. After some time, Raj Kumari Amrit Kaur arrived. She spoke impeccable English, but rather irritated me by assuming that if Ramji (RCK) had taken the side of the Congress, all would have been well, but otherwise she was sympathetic. The Sardar soon came and I told him the whole story from our side and showed him all the papers. He said he would, if he could, do something to help, but he had always told RCK he should get out of Kashmir. He was friendly and very kind and attentive. The present government (British) is negotiating with them and they do not want one side (India and Pakistan are the two) to get through. Now that object has failed anyhow, the state is running downhill with lightning speed. The price of rice shot up, in this very scarce time, there's no salt, no sugar and no petrol. Now I hear the Sheikh [Abdullah] is the last being released, but not anyone from the Muslim League, whose leaders were also in detention. So now there is bound to be trouble with Pakistan. Everyone feels very

> doubtful whether Kashmir will, in future, be capable of being a home for Hindus. I still hope and pray and believe and I think Ramji does too, but we don't know. I hate the thought of leaving Kashmir and Ramji does too because it does seem so very much our own land. However, we shan't be the first to have been driven into exile if we eventually are. At present or rather up to the time I left, there was no Hindu–Muslim animosity to speak of. But between mismanagement and irresponsibility rampant in the state, there's no knowing when it will break out. Meanwhile, in the west Punjab, many say openly that in the east Punjab, there is no government.

Separated by two continents, my father bore his fate in Kashmir in the stoic manner to which he was accustomed. He was prepared for it, having refused opportunities to leave Kashmir when he could have done so without any difficulty.

I was very young and secure with my mother besides me. I looked forward to exploring new places and visiting England for the very first time. My mother, meanwhile, embarked upon the most difficult period of her life, responsible for a young child in tow and making every effort alone to have her husband released and rejoin her in England. She had no way of knowing when this might happen, or even if it would ever happen, because detention and incarceration could often take years.

∽

These same incidents were recorded by Bhaiji in his unpublished memoir, which has been reproduced below.

> Since in my letter to the Maharaja, I had definitely stated that I intended to leave Srinagar for England on 17th September, the obvious intention of this order was to prevent me from leaving the state without the government having to own that my stay was anything but voluntary. I decided to ignore the order and wrote to the Prime Minister that

the complaints were frivolous and that in my opinion the appointment of a commission in regard to frivolous matters like those mentioned was likely to be fraught with serious consequences for the ruler and the state; that, therefore, I must decline to appear before the commission. The inquiry having been instituted under the Public Servants Inquiries Act—even assuming that the provisions of the Act would be taken to apply to the head of the government—the penalty provided by the Act, assuming that the guilt of the accused person were proved, is loss of pension. Since it was my conviction that everybody knew how absurd the complaints were and why in reality the commission had been appointed, the holding of an inquiry of this kind was inevitably bound to cause the deepest dissatisfaction among the people and resultant loss of prestige to the ruler and shattering of the peoples' confidence in him. I, therefore, preferred to take the risk of loss of pension which, after all, was only a personal risk to being an instrument in bringing about the almost certain downfall of the state and so [I] came to the conclusion that the appropriate course for me was not to lend myself for participation in the inquiry.

On learning that I was determined to leave the state, the Maharaja and his government were compelled to expose their hand completely and to prevent my leaving the state by ordering my detention.

I went to the airport to take off in the plane in which seats had been reserved for me and my family. Major General Sir Henry Scott, Chief of Staff, had come to see me off at the airport. Besides being prime minister, I had been army minister for six years and General Scott had been my right hand in regard to all army matters. Moreover, the airport was a charge of the army department, and no doubt, as chief of staff, General Scott felt it his duty to see me off—not knowing that the Maharaja had other views in the matter.

The plane was not allowed to take off. The commandant

of the airport gave one excuse after another. He even tried to persuade the pilot to say that the plane couldn't leave because of engine trouble. Having failed in this and running short of excuses which would convince the chief of staff, who after all was his superior officer, he finally said that the plane could not leave without the district magistrate's permission. General Scott telephoned the district magistrate, who said that he could do nothing without authority from the Deputy Prime Minister. The latter, on being rung up, said that the matter was within the district magistrate's jurisdiction and that he had nothing to do with it. Finally, at about 11 a.m., the plane having been scheduled to take off at 7.45 a.m., General Scott was told that the plane could not leave that day. We returned home as did all other passengers.

In the evening, the Superintendent of Police came to my house with an order from the district magistrate directing that I should not leave the state because, in his opinion, my leaving Kashmir would prejudice the state's relations with other governments. The order did not mention which governments were referred to nor did it state how the district magistrate had come to such a conclusion.

Next morning, I rang up General Scott and told him that though it might be within the competence of the Maharaja and his government to put me under detention, since I was a subject of the state, my wife was not a Kashmiri subject, and she and our little daughter would be leaving for England as arranged. If it was the intention to detain them, she would get in touch with the UK High Commissioner forthwith on the subject. I requested him to inform the authorities accordingly. General Scott telephoned on the following morning and told me that he had referred to the concerned authorities and had been told that there was no objection to any member of my family leaving the state if they chose to, except myself.

My wife left Kashmir on 22nd September. Incidentally,

the last call on my telephone was this one with General Scott. Thereafter, my telephone as also my brother's telephone was rendered inoperative though the instruments were left in situ until Sheikh Abdullah's assumption of power.

It would be absurd to conceive that the Maharaja genuinely believed in the allegations for investigation of which he had appointed a commission of inquiry. Indeed, it is demonstrable that these allegations were deliberately concocted to meet the exigencies of the situation that had arisen after I relinquished office. The Maharaja had to find an explanation to satisfy the vast number of people both within and without the state who were interested in and pressing him for his accession to India. Their argument was that except for my lack of enthusiasm for accession, I had been a good prime minister, that I had conducted the administration of the state as it had not been conducted for many years; that I had maintained law and order under the most difficult circumstances and in face of unprecedented difficulties, example, when Punjab and North-West Frontier Province were in flames and massacre and rapine formed the order of the day. My relinquishing office was, in their eyes, justifiable only as a necessary step precedent to the accession of the state to India, and they expected that now, as the main obstruction to the course approved and advocated by them had been removed, the Maharaja would lose no time in acceding to India.

When, however, nothing happened, people began to grow restive and they began to ask why, if the policy of the state still remained 'non-accession', had it come to pass that a person—who, except for one matter in which they did not see eye-to-eye with him, had been satisfactory in every way—had been compelled to relinquish office at a most critical juncture? Since the policy in regard to accession continued unchanged and the internal and external dangers were daily looming larger while the administration looked on helplessly, the need to find an explanation for parting with a prime minister who, whatever his shortcomings, had [...] given peace and security to the people so long as he held office became more and more imperative.

[...] Events moved very fast indeed in those days. Within three weeks of my relinquishing office, there was open rebellion in Poonch, where the Muslim population was fighting the state troops. Poonchies, particularly those residing in the tehsils of Sadhnuti and Bagh, formed a substantial proportion of the Muslim element of the pre-Partition Indian Army. In this district, there are always available many thousand people who have received military training and have actual experience of fighting. Fighting the state troops, therefore, was not a thing outside their experience or beyond their capacity. They carried modern fire arms and pressed the state troops hard.

Unfortunately, after I left, the Maharaja thought it fit to remove all officers of experience who might, perhaps, have saved the state from the mortal peril, which now faced it. Among those so removed was Major General Sir Henry Scott, chief of staff; R.N. Powell, inspector general of police; the Revenue Minister Pandit Anant Ram; Chief Secretary Niaz Ahmed, the governor of Kashmir and a number of other officers, high and low. In their places were appointed favourites of the moment, mostly belonging to the Maharaja's clan whose community of interest with the ruling dynasty was considered a greater asset counterbalancing their lack of experience and ability. The only consistent policy at this time appears to have been to place the Maharaja's clansmen and dependents in positions of responsibility and power. As a majority of these people were men of low calibre, it was inevitable that in the face of a critical situation, such as those presented by the Poonch rebellion and eventually by the incursion of raiders from outside, [...] the administration should crumble down.

The Maharaja seems to have realised that his protégés now entrusted with the reigns of the government were not the men to ride the storm. In the beginning of September, he allowed himself to be persuaded to send for [Sheikh] Abdullah, still in jail at Bhadrawah, so that parleys might be held with him.

Accordingly, Abdullah was brought to Srinagar Cantonment under the pretext of having his teeth attended to. Here the intermediaries met him. Eventually, the Maharaja, who had hitherto reacted violently to any suggestion of Abdullah's release, ordered his release, his hope no doubt being [able] to purchase, thereby, his peace with Mr Nehru and the Congress.

[In the] meantime, it appears the Kashmiri authorities were carrying on some negotiations with important persons in New Delhi. A set of papers was seized at the Lahore airport by the Pakistan authorities from one of the Maharaja's emissaries, which, as published in the *Civil and Military Gazette* of Lahore exposed these negotiations and caused a furore in Pakistan. This was probably the principal contributory cause of the raids which took place subsequently.

General Janak Singh, the prime minister, had a most unenviable task. Wisely, he took to his bed on the day he assumed office and continued occupying it until he handed over charge on 15th October, to Mehr Chand Mahajan. The de facto prime minister was Ramlal Batra, who had been a minor official in Punjab Provincial Service before he retired. But he had been appointed private secretary on the recommendation of the Swami, who found him a useful and subservient tool. The Maharani's brother, Nichint Chand, who had been an NCO [non-commissioned officer] in an Indian Cavalry Regiment before the Maharaja married his sister acted as the chief link between the Swami, the Maharaja and Batra, conveying messages from one to the other. He was almost illiterate and his experience and outlook were only those which could be expected of [someone who was] 30 years of age. The Swami was credited with superhuman powers. The Maharaja and the Maharani actually believed it when the Swami told them that the Maharaja was destined to become the ruler of northern India with his capital at Lahore. In fact, the Maharaja was so convinced in this belief that he had a special crown made to put on at the ceremony of his investiture as the ruler of his new empire. On one occasion, he produced the crown and showed it to the British Resident, Lieutenant Colonel W.F. Webb, remarking, 'This may be the future crown of Northern India.'

Such was the administrative set-up when the crash came. The release of Sheikh Abdullah, combined as it was with complete paralysis in administration and absence of policy, set forces in motion both within and without the state which overwhelmed the Maharaja and his government at the very moment of impact. Except for a single military officer who gave his life in a vain attempt to storm the raiders, no officer of the state did anything. Every one of them, particularly the non-Kashmiri military trucks, loaded with his entourage and property. To the last, his thoughts were for his clansmen. He collected as many of them as he could and transported them to safety in Jammu.

Mehr Chand Mahajan assumed the office of the prime minister on 15th October 1947. He gave a press interview immediately after. Among other things, he stated that he would devote his attention and energy to the development of the state during his tenure of office (five years under the terms of his agreement with the Maharaja) and finally that (by way of a hint to Pakistan) if anybody thought that they could coerce the state, he would call upon his friends for assistance.

On the 8th of October, the Sub-Divisional Magistrate of Muzaffarabad was reported to have sent a telegram to the Prime Minister indicating that information had been received that tribesmen were collecting in large numbers in Hazara with the intention of invading Kashmir and requesting assistance and instructions from the government. On this telegram, the Deputy Prime Minister Batra was reported to have noted that this officer was creating panic and should be given a warning. On the 21st, the raiders entered the state territory at Muzaffarabad and one of the first to lose his life in the doomed town was the unfortunate Sub-Divisional Magistrate.

The Maharaja, his court and a large number of officers left Srinagar at the midnight of 25th and 26th October. The next day was Sunday. Being under detention, though still in my own house, I had no knowledge of the momentous events until, on Monday morning, my gardener came up and told me that he had seen rider-less horses running about in the parade ground near our house. Even this did not convey the truth to me. A little later, I was told that a Sikh peasant with a little boy was downstairs looking for our Sikh servant. They had come all the way on a bicycle from Sopore, a town about 40 miles from Srinagar and had been travelling the whole night as raiders had reached Baramulla and were indulging in an orgy of arson, loot and murder. Throughout the district, Sikh villages were silent, as the inhabitants had either been killed and had left their villages and sought refuge in Srinagar for safety. Among the latter were the man and boy waiting downstairs.

The season was very cold and I asked that the refugees be given hot tea to warm them up pending the arrival of the servant they had come to see. It happened that this man's own family was also in the refugee convoy, the remnants of which reached Srinagar. A few hundred men, women and children out of a reported 6,000 had left their homes for safety.

My anxiety at this stage was for my daughter who was expecting a baby and my family (my father and brothers and their families who were living over the way). Though we had in fact two large cars and two lorries of our own, we had no petrol and there was none to be had except through official influence. At this time, we had no influence, official or otherwise. So, as a result, even if any of the family had agreed to leave, which they did not, the lack of transport presented insuperable difficulty. There was nothing to do but to wait on events which I was powerless to influence or control. At 2.00 p.m., my son unexpectedly walked in. He said he had brought an aeroplane from Delhi and wanted me to leave immediately, as the plane had to take off by 5.00 p.m. and could not stay longer. At this time, I could have left Kashmir if I had wanted to. There was no one to question my leaving, since the administrative machine had broken down.

But I decided that it would not be right, now that the country was in its death throes, for me to escape surreptitiously. Whatever fate was in store for the rest of the people for whom I had worked all my life, I would share. So I told him to take his sister and such other members of my brothers' families that he could transport to the airport. Unfortunately, however, only one of the cars had any petrol and that was just enough for one trip to the airport and back. So, only a few of the girls and children were able to leave.

Next morning, Indian troops started arriving by plane and in a few days' time, the danger from the raiders to the valley of Kashmir vanished. The havoc wrought in the villages of the Kashmir valley was the work more of the local populace than of the raiders. Among my own non-Muslim servants, one had his uncle and aunt shot dead on his own threshold and the third his house and granary burnt and these were in three villages situated at long distances from one another. Such cases were numerous. One that came to my notice was that of a Sikh boy who had, two years before, been a peon in my office. He came to my house and asked for assistance. His story was that he—with a large number of Sikh men, women and children—had been marching to Srinagar having abandoned their villages in Souget under the impending threat of tribesmen's incursion. Actually, they had an encounter with them near Sopore and, though they only suffered casualties, held their own until the Indian troops arrived opportunely and chased the raiders out. In this melee, many of their women had thrown themselves into the ruined well to save themselves from dishonour. Among these was his unmarried sister, 17-year-old, and his wife, whom he had married last year. He said he knew where the girls were and if he had a few policemen, he could still recover them. I asked him why he did not go to the authorities. He said he had done so but without avail.

An even more poignant story was that of the villagers of Vadipure, which contained a considerable number of prosperous Hindu families, including the Zaildar. No raiders reached this village but the local Muslim villagers came and told the Hindus that the raiders were coming and they would make short work of them. Their only safety lay in handing over their gold and silver ornaments and possessions to their Muslim brethren, who would keep them safe until the raiders went away and then hand them back. The raiders, they argued, were bound to search Hindu houses and would carry away not only the gold and silver but the search was certain to entail danger to their persons. The Hindus, accordingly, collected all their valuables and handed them over to their Muslim friends. A little later, some of the worthiest men came and told the Hindus that it would be best to tell the raiders that there were no Hindus in that village but that could not be done unless the two temples with their images were destroyed and no vestige of them remained. Accordingly, the temples were destroyed. Having thus far proved amenable, two further demands were made: the first was that since the Hindus had already agreed to be known as Muslims, they should have no hesitation to set the seal on their decision by eating beef and secondly, their marriages with their wives having become null and void, since they had married under Hindu rights but had now become Muslims, they must now remarry according to the Muslim law. As regards the first demand, the victims said they would think over the matter and as regards the second, they said they would not mind until they were told that the remarriages would not necessarily be between the same people that had been husband and wife hitherto. While they were still deliberating, the neighbouring Muslim jagirdar and a minor forest officer, who had been a Hindu but did not become a Muslim, arrived on the scene by chance and to these the harassed Hindus narrated the story. They turned on the Muslim villagers and threatened them with dire consequences if they did not leave the Hindus alone.

The Maharaja, having fled for safety to Jammu and the Indian Army doing the fighting, Sheikh Abdullah's party possessed themselves of power and civil authority in the valley of Kashmir. It must be conceded that Sheikh Abdullah's party permitted no physical violence except what they themselves inflicted on the people they did not like.

So far as the raiders were concerned, they were pushed as far as Uri by the end of the first week of November. Therefrom, the Indian Army proceeded no further and when the ceasefire was declared on 1st January 1949, Uri was still the limit of the Indian Army's sphere of operations on this side. Most of the district of Muzaffarabad continued to be in possession of what later came to be known as the Azad Kashmir [known as Pakistan occupied Kashmir in India] government, and so did most of the district of Poonch and the entire district of Mirpur. The territories north of Gurais, including the political districts of Gilgit, also fell off and were taken over by Pakistan. The Indian Army never penetrated there.

[...] On the morning of 30th October 1947, I found my

house surrounded by a large number of National Conference volunteers, about 25 or 30 of whom were standing on top of the compound walls. Not understanding why they were there, I asked two or three of them who were nearest to get off the walls. They replied that they were on duty viz., to watch the house, and the house was going to be searched. Later on two of their leaders came and asked me whether I had any complaint to make. I asked them, even assuming that the house was under surveillance, why it was necessary to send several hundred people to keep on shouting and howling all the time and being rude even to the police who were already in possession of the house and had been for a month and half; and finally, why it was necessary to post them on top of the walls. One of these gentlemen replied that they had information that there was a large quantity of sugar in the sarai, and they wanted to ensure that it did not disappear. Hence, the large number of volunteers to keep watch over the entire area. To this, I gave the obvious reply that though the sarai was in fact my property, it was a separate building in a separately walled compound, and separated from my compound by a large orchard as well as a lane. In any case, it was a trade mart occupied by a number of traders who stored their goods there. Therefore, it was quite likely that there might be sugar stocked there but that did not explain why my house had been surrounded and volunteers were making a nuisance of themselves. Both the leaders looked a bit shame-faced, but the second gentleman now stated that they had information that there were firearms in my house. They wanted to verify this. I replied that it should be no matter for wonder if there were firearms in my house. After all, I had until lately been prime minister of the state and, as the prime minister, I could keep firearms without license. But if they wanted to make sure whether there were such arms in the house, the simplest course would have been either to ask me and to take my word with regard to their existence or non-existence, or to satisfy themselves by forthwith making a search. In any case, there was no need to post a horde of the volunteers and cause unnecessary annoyance. They gave no reply and in due course went away. In actual fact, there were no firearms in the house, and the object underlying this show of force and power was simply to prove to the Kashmiri world that the National Conference were masters of the land and could do anything they liked to anybody, including those who, until then, had held the highest positions.

In the evening, another party of the [National] Conference bosses came and took away one of my cars, threatening to take the other one in the next few days. The plea on which the car was taken was that the country had need of it. No receipt was given, it being stated that it would suffice if an entry was made in the official register that the car had been requisitioned. This was said to be enough both for the car as well as the tools and the loose fittings. The car was not returned for four months and when it was returned, it was in a state of total collapse. Similarly, a brand new lorry, which was at the workshop to have its body completed, was taken away without any notice or authority. Months later, it was left derelict on the roadside with its battery removed and important parts of the machine broken.

Henceforth my house was under two different sets of guards: the official police posted during the Maharaja's days of rule, and the National Conference volunteers who functioned quite independently of the police and were far more numerous and some of whom were with rifles and swords. They searched everyone who came into and went out of the house. From 16th September, I had not left the house. I left it eventually on 17th February 1948, when I was removed to the Kothibagh sub-jail.

On 16th November 1947, my younger brother and his family, as also my sister and her baby left Kashmir as refugees. An hour or so after they had left, Ghulam Mohiuddin Kara, one of the particularly extremist leaders of the National Conference, who, since the start of the Quit Kashmir movement had remained underground, called at my house. On going down stairs to meet him, I found him in the drawing room with four persons dressed in military uniform; one of whom was carrying a rifle and was standing at attention in the room. The others carried revolvers. With them was also a head constable of the regular police. After a little casual conversation, Ghulam Mohiuddin left with his satellites. To this day, I do not understand why he came, unless it was that having heard that some of my family had that day left Kashmir, he wanted to make sure that I had not been one of them.

At this stage, all who were left of my family in Kashmir were my father, my elder brother and his wife and myself. From the time I was put under detention—16th September—most amenities, including medical aid, had been unavailable to members of my family. This created a very difficult position with regard to my father, who was suffering from advanced diabetes and was, therefore, in constant need of medical attention. The only medical advice he could get for nearly 10 months was that of a compounder, who had been coming to give him his daily injections.

Meanwhile, nothing was heard of the commission the Maharaja had appointed with regard to the allegations against me and though these allegations were later made the occasion of a prosecution and trial, to this day I do not know what the findings of the commission were. Even during the trial, Sheikh Abdullah's government refused to make available, even for my defence, either the report of the commission or their recommendations.

Except for the fact that I continued to be detained, I was left completely alone from 16th November onwards until my removal to jail on 17th February 1948. During this period,

> I led a quiet life while autumn turned into winter and the winter snows began to thaw and traces of incipient spring manifested themselves. My father had become bedridden, and his eyesight was badly deteriorating, so he could not come to see me and I could not go to see him. My brother came every evening and stayed for an hour or so. Now and again, so long as the planes could come and go, I got a letter from my wife. For the rest, most of my time was occupied in reading and introspection.
>
> I reviewed the events that had, after I relinquished office, culminated in the tragedy of Kashmir. I asked myself whether, given the same opportunity again, I would have acted differently to what I had done as prime minister. I was not conscious of any miscalculation, except the one I had made in respect of the Maharaja. Undependable though he was generally known to be, I had believed that there was one matter in which he could be depended on and that was his personal interest. For that I knew he would sacrifice everything. The palace clique had, however, so worked on his superstitious character that he really believed the Swami possessed occult powers of such great potency that he had it in his gift to enable him to carve out a new and vastly enhanced empire for himself out of the ruins of the British Empire. He also believed, as he often remarked, that to achieve this there would be no need of armies and aircraft. The procedure as outlined by the Swami was simple: a few soldiers with rifles in their hands would march at the head of crowds of people who would be shouting and beating drums and instruments capable of producing the maximum noise with the minimum effort. Therefore, city after city in Punjab would fall to the 'conquering' host. Hearing this seriously stated by the Maharaja, I could only conclude that those whom the Gods choose to destroy, they first make mad!

I imagine that this maxim applied not merely to the Maharaja and his palace courtiers but to the entire populations plunged into a frenzy of hate and destruction of life and property. The nation was subject to unimaginable chaos, uncontrollable violence and plumbed the depths of grief and tragedy during Partition.

Figure 18: The Maharaja and his entourage leaving Srinagar for Jammu in the dead of night on 25 October 1947 in about 85 vehicles, including bullock carts and his polo ponies

Illustration credit: Kashmira Tembulkar

The escape from Kashmir brought scant satisfaction to the Maharaja and his family, who initiated the great misadventure of the empire, emerging severely burnt from the flames of Partition as a family divided. The Maharani went on to make Kasauli her home, where she lived her life separately till the end. The Maharaja lived alone in Bombay, bereft of his prestige and power, resentful of his son, Dr Karan Singh, for aligning with his bitter foe Nehru and the Congress in usurping his authority and taking over as prince regent of Kashmir.

Sheikh Abdullah stayed back to enjoy the fruits of his office, but he soon alienated his friend Nehru and was himself externed from Kashmir, spending 12 long years under house arrest at Kud in Jammu. Perhaps it could be seen as poetic justice, but the orders for his arrest were given by Dr Singh.

Meanwhile, my grandfather bore his lot with fortitude alone, facing detention and house arrest, followed by nine months of jail under severe and unhygienic conditions in bitter cold, sustained by occasional letters from England, till he was himself externed from Kashmir while the case against him dragged on for more than a decade, resulting in a Pyrrhic victory. After 33 years of loyal service to the Maharaja of Kashmir, it was an unexpected end to a pinnacle of effort in serving his people.

18

Exile in England[27]

While we were in Delhi by the end of September 1947, my father remained detained but safe in Kashmir. We stayed with Sura Kak and his wife, Sarla, in Delhi. Siddharth was just a few months old then, having been born on 9 July 1947. He had no idea of the stress and turbulence in the family or in the nation.

A few days later, from Delhi, we moved to Mr B.K. Shah's kind and welcoming house in Vile Parle, Bombay. Mr Shah, Bhaiji's friend, and his wife welcomed Mummy and I with great kindness. The added bonus was that their children were very accommodating and friendly with me. Decidedly older, they included me in their games, and, I suspect, actually adjusted them to keep me happy and give my mother a break.

So, we spent a pleasant enough fortnight, at least for me, in the Shah household, with trips to Juhu beach and games at home. Despite the incidents of violence let loose across the country by Partition, I was in a happy oblivion. Even Mummy attested to the pleasant stay in Bombay:

> I'm very happy to look back on the fortnight at Juhu. I dreaded it so much beforehand and thought I should never get on with them all without Ramji, but actually I found myself welcomed and accepted and everything made easy. The Shah family is as large as our own and it is an experience

---

[27] This section of the chapter has been narrated by Lila Kak Bhan.

> to see it from the inside. The riches and solidity of their houses and possessions are something quite unlike Kashmir, but at the same time the simplicity of their way of life is very similar. Everything at Vile Parle is scrumptiously clean and the food I think is delicious.

Finally, it was time for our ship, the *Strathmore*, to set sail for Tilbury. Our voyage across the sea was uneventful—following the usual route to England, across the Indian Ocean to Aden, where we stopped before entering the Red Sea. I vividly remember the Red Sea because of the flying fish, which I recall gracefully 'flying' halfway up the side of the deck height. Mummy carried me out to watch this amazing phenomenon of nature late one evening. The scene is still vividly etched in my mind. When we reached the Suez Canal, we had to await our turn to enter. Thence to Port Said, Egypt, before we entered the Mediterranean Sea. There, the highlight was the young boys diving for coins that the passengers threw into the water from the decks of the ship. The divers are another of my indelible memories of that voyage. They were so fish-like and dexterous as they dived into the water shouting something that sounded like 'Gilly, gilly, gilly,' to me! We went from the Mediterranean Sea to Gibraltar, with its massive rock ridge, and then to the Atlantic, through the Straits of Gibraltar. Finally, we went through the Bay of Biscay, famed for its stormy waters, and reached Tilbury on 3 November 1947.

When we arrived in England, my grandfather, whom I called Grandaddy, and Mummy's older sister, Aunty Nancy, were there to meet us. We spotted them from the deck. As the process of disembarking was lengthy, it was arranged that they would go for a quick lunch and be back in time for when we would be let off the boat. Finally, when our turn to be released arrived, greatly excited, we walked down the ramp, only to be met by a flood of people all clambering to embrace their family and friends. Nowhere could Grandaddy or Aunty Nancy be spotted! I just clutched my mother's hand. Weary of combing the crowd, hoping to spot a familiar face, Mummy finally decided we should take a taxi to 15 Denman Drive, my aunt's house in Golders Green, a London suburb. I clearly remember the scene as we rang the doorbell. There was my family, in a celebratory mood and not at all surprised or apologetic about having missed us and seeing us arrive unescorted. They almost took our arrival for granted, it seemed, like it was quite a normal occurrence. I am sure some discussion and mild irritation must have taken place, but it went over my head! I was wildly excited to see so many unfamiliar faces with names that had become very familiar due to my mother's wonderfully detailed stories.

On 5 November 1947, we went from my aunt's house to Belton, near Great Yarmouth, where Grandaddy and my great-aunt Tantes or Tantie lived. On my bed upstairs, the sweetest doll lay with its eyes closed, set in its bone china head placed on a rubber body. Dressed in hand-knit clothes, Tommy Handley, for that was his name, lay wrapped in a cream shawl waiting for the youngest girl grandchild to take it. I couldn't believe my luck and still remember the awe with which I was filled. Tantie couldn't have made my entry into my life in England easier or more exciting. Tommy Handley travelled back to India and was very much loved and even played with by my children for at least 30 years till, eventually, his beautiful porcelain head broke.

Belton was to be our base till my father came the following year. My mother's family had a charming house called The Laurels and a wonderful live-in companion, Barbara, with a young toddler son, Roderick. Barbara was a godsend in every way and a very important person for both Mummy and I in those two years. She was amazing with children and had an artistic bend of mind. She, Roderick and I spent hours at the kitchen table—a large wooden top with innumerable scratches and blemishes—working on magical projects together. She would allow us to do things ourselves, never demanding we watch her doing all the fun stuff because we might make a mess. I adored Roderick and we were virtually like siblings. My mother admired Barbara and was so grateful to her for the help and support she provided with occupying me while she was busy corresponding with many dignitaries and family, trying to get my father released.

The year without my father was very difficult for my mother as can be seen in her diary entries. She was a very strong and courageous woman, though she would never admit that, preferring to describe herself as the shy and timid one who always stuck to her mother, rather like I was with her. Despite her claims, she spent a lot of time writing to a host of influential people, going up to London to meet them while looking after a five-and-half-year-old to boot. During one of her trips to London to meet Lord Ismay, I briefly boarded in Fritton Hall. I would receive a daily letter from my mother written in capital letters so that I could read it myself! Fritton Hall is another vivid memory. I sensed there were important jobs my mother needed to do in order to try and get my father released.

Meanwhile, in January 1948, while detained at Bagh Sundar, my father learnt that there was an assassination plan afoot to eliminate him. This information was given to him by his elder brother, Bab.

Bab had defended Kashiram, a goon of sorts, accused of murder, and had got him acquitted. Kashiram who was living with Swami Sant Dev in Chashme Shahi warned Bab that there was a plot to assassinate Bhaiji, and that he should sleep upstairs in the Red House, lock his doors and windows and keep two men on call nearby. My father had also heard a broadcast from Bakshi Ghulam Mohammad over the radio while sitting in the White House at Bagh Sundar that he was to be tried for treason and if proved guilty, shot. My father recalled that his friend K.T. Shah could not eat for three days when he heard the news. This was another warning that Sardar Patel had passed on to my father in Delhi, asking him not to return to Kashmir, for fear of being shot, which, fortunately, did not come true. But it was a period of enormous tension.

Back in England, as of March 1948, Mummy got a lot of

solace from prayers and philosophic thought. She was deeply spiritual, respecting the many unfamiliar ways of worship she had encountered as she integrated, with amazing alacrity, in her land of adoption. Yet, she continued reading her Bible, psalms and hymns. She made sure I learnt about both Christianity and Hinduism. I, too, have a Bhagvad Gita and a charmingly illustrated Book of Common Prayer for children, acquired in 1948, by my bedside, like Mummy always did.

One day, a letter from Nana Kak arrived, telling Mummy that Bhaiji and Bab had been arrested on 17 February. My mother looked up the Psalm for that day, 'My hand shall hold him fast and my arms shall strengthen him,' and felt greatly comforted.

It was a time of unbearable stress. My mother would meet people in high places, anxiously trying to secure Bhaiji's release, feeling harassed in the process. Confused by her reactions, I once angrily remarked to my mother, 'Why are you nasty to me? Have they killed Bhaiji?' I did not realise then that this was equally trying for her.

Although my mother wrote to many of the family members—Sura Kak, Brija Kak, Nana Kak—and Lord Ismay during this time, her collection of letters preserved by her family ceases once we reach England. She had no need to write to them anymore and was unable to write freely to Bhaiji. Her letters to other family members and important personages in the Government of India and Britain are lost to time. However, around this time, she started keeping a diary.

To my great good fortune, I have preserved with me my mother's original weather-beaten beige diary from 1947, in which she wrote her neat and meticulous entries in an elegant prose that spoke of her qualities of head and heart. The diary was chiefly a record of her observations and her attempts to help with the release of our RCK. In addition, there are extensive descriptions of our daily life in England, something she knew my father would enjoy reading later. She wanted to make sure he shared, albeit vicariously, our life while he was in prison.

Figure 19: Bended writing her diary in England while a 5-year-old Billy watches, 1947–48

Illustration credit: Kashmira Tembulkar

Though a man of few words, who might even seem somewhat detached to some, RCK was the most tender, emotional and sensitive of people. Highly moral, loyal and down to earth, he was a unique personality who was not impressed either by position or wealth. 'Money can come and go,' he used to say 'but a good education, *vidya*, is yours forever.' He was well-versed in Sanskrit, Persian and English—a true scholar. Importantly, Bhaiji had a great sense of humour, which was sometimes misunderstood, and a terrific sense of child-like fun which had us in splits of laughter, especially when Mummy decided to ask him to be less raucous but then couldn't help join in the uncontrollable merriment! As I turn the pages of her diary, I feel her presence beside me, her arm around my shoulder as she tells me gently, addressing me by my nickname, 'Billa, do you know what happened today?'

> The Sunday before we left India, the Psalm was 'The increase of faith, hope and charity.' It looks as if it is a duty to trust and hope and yet I feel scared to do it, lest I do it too easily and then fall into disillusionment. I cannot get settled. Either I worry or I hope and trust and feel guilty for being cheerful when I don't have the privations to bear. Billy is a bright spot of rarity and bloom.

Hope and despair alternate in my mother's diary entries from this period, which have been quoted below chronologically, as she wavered over the pros and cons of going back to India and the dilemma of conveying the depths of her feelings through letters that would undoubtedly be scrutinised. Letters were all Mummy had to hold on to. She clutched at straws, even political straws that may have been unfamiliar, until, finally, a letter arrived from Kamla, Nana Kak's wife. As Bended recorded in her diary.

> Letter from Kamla. She said Preya Kak [RCK's younger brother] had visited Sheikh Sahib [Sheikh Abdullah] who was cordial. I don't see why he even went, or why Sheikh Sahib even saw him unless he was really cordial. I rather wonder if his power is slipping or has slipped. Wouldn't be surprised at any developments in Kashmir, however contrary to previous tendencies.
>
> **14 April 1948**: Two letters from RCK—a wet and dreary month [in Srinagar] and he was moved to a set of rooms unoccupied all winter and unfurnished. Sent off some magazines, *Times* and one *Punch*, as RCK said they had little to read.
>
> **20 April 1948**: The radio at 1.00 p.m. mentioned speeches at Lake Success in which both representatives of Pakistan and India disapproved of the proposals put forward. The deadlock doesn't seem to loosen up. If only I could convey all that passes through my mind and when it passes [to RCK]. There was a news report on the main news page of *The Times*

called 'Little England in Kashmir', describing in somewhat lyrical terms the life of the 70 English people who refused to leave Kashmir. I can't quite understand the reason for giving it so much prominence.

26 April 1948: A batch of gloomy news on the 19th. RCK was moved from Badami Bagh to Kothi Bagh jail and reports in newspapers of an impending trial. I took the children, Roderick and Billy, for a walk but felt very worried all day.

I must write to Sheikh Sahib and Sardar Patel. Nana Kak wrote again on the 20th suggesting writing to Sheikh Sahib. But what? And how to help? Had a thumping headache by evening.

27 April 1948: Another letter from Nana Kak, this time of April 22nd. No more definite news, but he wonders and Mr B.K. Shah wonders whether it would be better for me to return. People of communist ideology had told him that Bakshi Ghulam Muhammad was at the back of it and they may go to any extent as regards punishment [to Bhaiji]. I feel in a panic, but my common sense tries to remind me that such people are glad to scare, and NNK [Nana Kak] and B.K. Shah are prone to take a gloomy view. Still bad enough in all conscience.

Another letter from Preya Kak on the 21st, more buoyant in tone. He suggests it is a war of nerves. I wrote to Nana Kak today and enclosed one [letter each] for Sheikh Sahib and one for Sardar Patel. I have been worried every day. Billy, sensing it, was very clinging. I should have thought a political trial with the UNO [United Nations Organisation] Commission there, or coming, and anything of a sensational or violent nature they would have wished to avoid just now. But it is impossible to assess what the position actually is. Thought [I reminded myself] that the family has before gone through hard times, as Bhaigash and RCK tell so often, but the family goes on. We belong to the same army and must go forward bravely as those we've heard about, like the lady who lived for 12 years with only one pheran! [Mummy is referring to Ganga Ded, Bhaigash's grandmother who—after her husband died, to save expenses—wore only one dress till her sons grew up.] A reminder that it is the strong spirit that helps people to survive.

Thinking all day of possible and impossible explanations of the latest move about RCK, and my brain goes round and round but has not sufficient grist. It would certainly be a great advantage to be in India and more in touch, but on the opposite side are the practical difficulties of living, accommodation and expenses. I think I should hear again by the mail that comes in at the end of the week.

30 April 1948: By evening, for some reason, perhaps merely reaction, I was more hopeful or rather less worried. Possibly because *The Times* had a leader and a report on the Kashmir and Hyderabad questions, saying that within the next few days, the two dominions would have to define their attitude to the UN resolution and that there was to be a cabinet meeting in Delhi today. The situation is, after all, still fluid.

In this sort of trouble, the hill is hard, that is to say if RCK had been a different sort of man, if he had been intimidated and not stood up to Nehru, if he had been less loyal, he might have been untroubled in the way he is and we are, and he might have suffered mental pain through feeling he had failed himself.

I try to think of the sort of letters I could write to RCK which would interest him, yet not seem unfeeling. Perhaps try to give him more idea than I have before, of the sort of village Belton is.

If only I could distil the last 10 years into some semblance of what it has seemed to me. The richness of the mind, the detail, the photographic exactitude with which I remember,

> how can it be transferred into writing? Like the despair of one who hears on the wireless a marvellous violinist, and dare not try again to play his own instrument.

These diary entries display the depth of Mummy's thinking, steeped in poetic comparison, which draws on one's innermost feelings. She was desperate to share every experience with my father. Most importantly, she wanted to let him know how special and unique her 10 years of married life had been. She couldn't have asked for more. With all its trials and tribulations, the positive experience and love permeated all her being. She felt full of gratitude for having him in her life. Meanwhile the trial dragged on.

> **3 May 1948:** Letter from Nana Kak this morning that the charges are: 1. the silk factory; 2. insurance; 3. Dara land. So far so good, and I felt more hopeful. As for my going back, they are for it, in any case, but are writing to Bab for his advice. *The Times* reports today that the attitude of India towards the UNO proposal is still uncertain but Pandit Nehru's tone is more conciliatory.

> **5 May 1948:** Latest from Kamla, Bombay bank, and best of all, one from RCK for me, and one for Billy, posted in Srinagar on the 27th, the following day after the first hearing. He sounded much more cheerful and it seemed to convey all he is. Next hearing on the 7th. Bab had written to Nana Kak that I should wait here in England, for the present.
>
> So, with Kashmir, if we have to leave it for good and settle elsewhere, the fundamentals are everywhere. It is only if one insists on having them in a certain shape and form that one is liable to be deprived of them.

It was such depth of feeling that helped my mother deal with so many similar situations. Many years later, in 1990, she once again had to flee Kashmir in the early morning, as it had become unsafe for Hindu families to remain in their homes. She described that journey out of the Valley with the same love and awe she had felt while leaving in 1947, despite the circumstances that now necessitated this exodus. I feel she refused to become embittered about the place she had adopted in 1937. Instead, she focussed on the incomparable beauty of the rows of poplar trees, the paddy fields just catching the rays of the rising sun and the snow on the Pir Panjal, a glow in the morning light. She was determined that her last glimpses of Kashmir would be of its incomparable beauty.

Meanwhile, my mother's diary entries from May 1948 reveal her frustration at politics continuing to overwhelm attempts to free Bhaiji from an unjust jail sentence.

> **10 May 1948:** No letters. A statement by Sir Muhammad Zafarullah Khan seems to suggest that neither side have been so outright in their refusal of the UNO terms as at first suggested, and, in any case, the commission is to go. Letter from WPJ, Aunty Nancy's husband, in the afternoon, says that Rahimtoola, Ahmed and Lateef had all expressed personal regret and wish they could help—not so with the Indian people. But that is understandable considering the politics of the affair.
>
> **11 May 1948:** Letter from Nana Kak this morning. Nothing fresh except it [the hearing] has been postponed again to 13th. Apparently, the question of [the] lawyer has not yet been settled, i.e. on 6th. The letter was rather incoherent, but I think on the whole he sounded more hopeful.
>
> **18 May 1948:** Letter from Brija Kak and Prema, but they had not heard for several days from Delhi, so no new news. Air letter from Preya Kak; the lawyer is a Mr B.B. Tawakali. The first hearing was on May 12th—sounded guardedly cheerful. Nature blooming—May blossom is at its height, bluebells in patches by the roadside, cow parsley coming into flower and the bracken uncurling fast.

As I reread Mummy's diary, I could not help but notice how much strength she drew from her deep interest and involvement with her surroundings, be it nature burgeoning in the seasons, the daily life of different people she came across or from her visits to towns and cities. She always found interests in and, oftentimes, distractions from the mercifully transitory moments of the troubled times she had to face, often single-handedly. Her deep spiritual faith and wisdom was a rock of comfort and saw her through her adversities, enriching and strengthening her beliefs further and giving strength to her family. Examples of these are manifest in her descriptions of her life, which she always said she would go through again with my father by her side—evidence of the happiness and understanding they shared. Hope bloomed in my mother's diary entry from 24 May 1948: 'Letter posted in Srinagar on May 17th from RCK, and one of 17th from Nana Kak. Apparently, the silk case was almost disposed of.'

A few days later, my mother again became philosophic with the turn of events. Her forced separation and, with it, the political uncertainty surrounding her husband's confinement over which she had no control, gave rise to a thoughtful acceptance.

> **25 May 1948:** RCK letter yesterday, he speaks of his 'new experience and knowledge' derived from what he has gone through this winter. This is something bought at a price and perhaps not to be grudged. Ten years so close together and now forced to experiment regarding the behaviour of the bond during separation. I wish I had Tagore's *Gitanjali*. 'I am uneasy at heart when I have to leave my accustomed shelter. There also thou abidest.' So with Kashmir, if we have to leave it and settle elsewhere. The fundamentals are everywhere—it is only if one insists on having them in a certain shape and form that one is liable to be deprived of them.

This, to me, was an amazing capacity to cope with the direst of situations with acceptance rather than despair and resentment. Despite being in a minute prisoner's cell, my father told me several years later, when I was a teenager, he would walk in the restricted space, counting his steps and completing his goal every day. He said it helped him keep his sanity. Rather than wallowing in self-pity, both my parents continually drew strength from seeing eventual hope in the dire situation and forging ahead for each other and me. In fact, Bhaiji told me on more than one occasions that having me, his barely six-year-old daughter, was a great incentive to tide the situation. I clearly remember feeling very elated and special, when he told me in my teenage years, that the responsibility of bringing me up was a driving force that pushed him on. Though he was not demonstrative in conventional ways, his deep attachment and emotions manifested in very special and unique ways. He was a very emotional man.

Every day in England for my mother was a test of endurance as the trial proceedings dragged on. She pored over the cuttings from *The Statesman* forwarded by Government House with regards to the political situation and decided to meet Lord Ismay in London at his office on George Street.

Despite her shy and modest nature, Mummy must have been deeply motivated, convinced and strong to gain the momentum to be constantly approaching dignitaries of the highest rank, seeking audience and presenting my father's case. Neither she nor my father were ever disposed to seek favours from my own observations as an adult too. Hence, her actions during this time speak of her courage and conviction. I know she proved to be a very convincing representative for my father.

Meeting Lord Ismay was a great step for my mother. It lifted her spirits just to speak to him, hoping he might be able to facilitate my father's release. Lord Ismay was outstandingly cordial, sympathetic and sincere, which was a comfort to my mother. He seemed to have understood the situation and relationships of the Maharaja, Nehru and Sheikh Abdullah. She felt Lord Ismay was balanced and sincere towards the situation. She wrote in her diary after meeting Lord Ismay:

16 June 1948: Lord Ismay had written more strongly than he had told me, 'Too much like the Gestapo and open for him, Lord Mountbatten, to have anything to do with it.' [He said he would] write again today to Lord Mountbatten that he had seen me but the difficulty was that they were leaving shortly [on 21 June 1948]. Would try to arrange that the incoming staff should continue to keep an eye on it [RCK's case] but danger of making things worse. So arrogant that they might say here's this Lord Ismay again, free self-governing teaching us what justice [is], etc.

Would write to America to Sir A. Cadogan and ask him to put the American delegate wise. I gave him the papers which he was glad to have and I said I left them with him and to his discretion how he used them. He said Lord Mountbatten had made a great mistake not knowing Hari Singh, who told him he looked tired and that two days [of] fishing would do him good and we can have a good talk on the last day. Last day, Hari Singh had a temperature of 104. Refused to say a word to Lord Ismay when he was in Kashmir, called me by my nickname talking this and that and leaving no opportunities [to discuss RCK].

Said RCK's name hadn't come up at Lake Success Security Council, a useless body always occupied with procedure and working in public. Indian delegation furious because they refused to keep to the isolated point of the tribesmen's entry into Kashmir. Sir Zafarullah Khan spoke for three hours and brought in everything.

Said he would point out that these charges against RCK surely were bailable. Seemed surprised that nothing political had been mentioned. Said I was to feel at liberty to keep in touch with him, and he would do anything to help and only wished he could do more. A quote from Lord Ismay: 'Nehru is a wonderful person and all that, but he has a completely blind spot on Kashmir and Abdullah.'

∽

My grandfather never made much of his privations in jail in Kashmir.[28] He may have spoken about his experiences to my grandmother, but the first time I ever heard of what he went through was more than 25 years later in the 1970s, when I began keeping notes of my interviews with him, and then too he made light of it.

Bhaiji spent a year in incarceration in different jails. His elder brother, Bab, was also jailed with him for some time. While Bhaiji never wrote or described the situation in any official memoir, he did mention to me about the unspeakable conditions and unbearable life in the local jails.

From September 1947, Bhaiji had been under house arrest for 'crimes against the state'. On 17 February 1948, at 10.00 p.m., he was taken away along with his elder brother and put into a sub-jail. Bhaigash came up to the door to see them off. He bore the humiliation of his two grown sons, distinguished in their service, being unceremoniously escorted to jail by an army general who came to take them away—their careers cut short and names blackened. It was snowing and the ground was layered with it. It was bitterly cold. Bhaiji never saw his father again. Slogans and jeers accompanied their arrest.

Bab was eventually released and detained in his house at Zaldragar, so he could be near Bhaigash as he neared his time. Bhaiji was not released and he was too proud to ask for any relaxation. Bhaigash passed away on 7 September 1948. Bhaiji received the news while he was standing trial in court without flinching or comment, giving no outward indication of his personal grief. He was only more silent than before.

Bab and Bhaiji shared the sub-jail room and the commode was so dirty that Bhaiji hired a sweeper to clean it out before he went in and thereafter every day on his pay. Rahat, his barber, visited the jail during Bhaiji's nine months of imprisonment and gave him a shave and a haircut, even when he was in the central

[28] This section of the chapter has been narrated by Siddharth Kak.

jail at Hari Parbat. Food and tea would come daily from the house for them both.

After a month, orders came to shift them. They didn't quite relish the idea of being moved very far out of Srinagar, as they would lose contact with their friends who were helping fight the case and carrying messages. So, Bhaiji quietly asked the head constable where they were going and he whispered into Bhaiji's ear in a thick Kashmiri accent, 'Alamonds' i.e., 'almonds' or the Badami Bagh cantonment nearby. There they were kept for another six weeks till Bhaiji was again moved back to the sub-jail around April–May 1948 and stayed there till 8 October when he was arrested on certain criminal charges and put into the central jail.

The sturdy Sikh police constable Surjit Singh was unable or unwilling to handcuff Bhaiji and merely walked shoulder-to-shoulder with him to the lorry from the court to give the impression that he had handcuffed him. At the central jail, Bishambhar Nath, the warden of the jail and former subordinate of Bhaiji, was too ashamed to open the gates of the prison and let him in. They were only opened half an hour later when Bhaiji, out of exasperation, told him that either they let him into the jail or he would go home.

The double barred cell in the central jail was 9 feet × 6 feet wide, where he was given three blankets and a *kadhai* for defecation and urination. It was an open utensil mounted on three or four bricks in the corner of the room. Bishambhar Nath asked him if he would apply for a higher category of criminal detention where the daily food allowance would be ₹1 and 12 annas rather than his allowance then, which was 6 annas. Bhaiji refused and Bishambhar Nath remarked sadly, 'I know, Sir. I have already told the higher authorities that you would not apply for the higher category.'

Bhaiji did ask Bishambar Nath if he could, on his own authority, arrange for a *chulha*, a *lota* and some tea leaves, as Bhaiji was used to drinking tea in the mornings. Bishambhar Nath said he would do what he could. However, at about 5.00 p.m., Dr Pichin, the director of jails, came and apologised to Bhaiji that he had been put into the wrong cell, and he was removed to a larger room with a tiny compound with 30-feet-high walls. There Bhaiji would pace up and down all day, refusing all books and reading material.

Sheikh Abdullah and Afzal Beg came the next day as Bhaiji was cooking food on the chulha and protested at his treatment. Bhaiji made no comment. Abdullah said he would arrange for a *durrie*, sofa, chairs and table, which he did, but Bhaiji said he wouldn't sit on them. Instead, hourly, he would drum the durrie up and down the tiny grass patch outside his cell, wearing it thin.

Once, while trying to figure out how to cook, Bhaiji asked a local labourer how he should eradicate the bitter taste from *gogji*, since he was cooking food himself for the first time. The rustic stared at Bhaiji in amazement before saying, 'Boil the turnips first, that's all, then drain the water away before actually cooking them.' He went away, shaking his head at Bhaiji's lack of this commonplace knowledge.

One day, a carpenter, who was painting the inside compound jail wall, began singing a Persian song. Bhaiji, lying inside on his bed, called out and complimented him on the verse. The carpenter came up to the door and said simply, 'I sang it for you.' The words of the song were:

> 'My heart, though you are full of pain
> Do not lament do not wail
> A wise bird when it falls into a snare
> Must lie still and be patient.'

∽

Meanwhile, in England, my mother had little idea of what her husband was going through, since he never disclosed his suffering.[29] The following excerpt from her diary is a particularly striking and a remarkable insight into her way of looking at difficult situations and coping with them through meaningful distractions, her juxtaposition of the difficult situation with the simple joys

[29]This section has been narrated by Lila Kak Bhan.

of daily life and, above all, her admiration for my father and recognition of his worth. Her diary entries offer a deep insight into her philosophical mind.

> **24 June 1948:** Dockers strike and Russian manoeuvres in Berlin and in Europe make my own worries more uneasy. Above all, there is time and peace to think about things. Recurrent rays of comfort are:
>
> 1. Our troubles are because our RCK is the man he is—if he were of lesser calibre, he might still be in the high position, having learnt to trim his sails. The man he is, is the one who is worth so much to us all and to himself.
> 2. That there may be and probably is purpose in everything.
> 3. That even in the smallest things—cooking, eating, washing, walking, seeing—there are minute satisfactions and joys, which fit together to make life.
>
> **29 June 1948:** At last, a piece of good news reported that Nehru had been again to Kashmir to see the situation first-hand. *The Times* correspondent says impartial opinion is that owing to economic plight, a plebiscite would be, for Pakistan, simply an escape from present troubles.
>
> **3 July 1948:** Reported that henceforth no European pilots to be allowed to pilot planes on the India–Kashmir run, and all visitors to Kashmir to have permit from the defence department. This was put at the end of a column describing the increasing difficulties between Hyderabad and India.
>
> **13 July 1948:** Considering the possibility of writing to Lord Ismay and asking him whether he thinks it desirable for me to write to the UNO Commission.
>
> **14 July 1948:** Letter from RCK dated July 8th 1948. Bab again interned, this time in the central jail without a servant.

As I grew older, I became more articulate about my feelings.

I missed my father and began to know he was going through a very difficult time. My mother wrote in her diary about me: 'When she was reading her letter from Bhaiji this a.m., she sat with it open for a moment. I found her like that when I came from the bathroom and then she said, "My heart bleeds to think of Bhaiji there."'

On another occasion, when Mummy asked me what I was thinking about, I had replied: 'Guess what I'm thinking about? Who's in India? Who's my daddy?'

My mother and I shared a lot from my earliest days and that sharing continued for life. We were friends and she never talked down to me.

My father finally arrived in England in November 1948. There are no more entries in my mother's England diary about that landmark event. We must have been in London for the momentous day that Bhaiji finally arrived. I could find no reference in the diary but can imagine the joy and relief on his release and the anticipation to hear he was finally on the boat and had set sail from Bombay. The utter relief my mother must have felt needs no words. Her actions spoke for themselves. She could not have cared for anyone more than she did for my father. On his arrival, we were briefly with Aunty Nancy in Denman Drive before leaving for Belton to see my mother's family. It was decided we should move to Hampstead Garden, a suburb where I attended the PNEU (Parents' National Education Union) school and from where it was easy to access London for meeting people and contacts who might be helpful to my father.

∽

Based on Bhaiji's accounts of the jail, it appears there was a very lax notion of security there. On 21 October 1948, the day Bhaiji was to be released, his Kashmiri Pandit cook, a young boy, came into the room. He looked around to see that no one was watching before opening his mouth and taking out a piece of paper on which was written 'You are to be released today'.

And, indeed, he was—the order was given by Sheikh Abdullah himself at his bungalow over a cup of kahwa or Kashmiri tea. Perhaps after his visit to Bhaiji in the jail earlier in the month, he was convinced that Bhaiji had suffered enough. Bhaiji was externed from Kashmir and given seven days to leave. By early November, he set sail for England to rejoin Bended after 14 tortuous months of separation. A new life awaited them.

19

Exile in Bombay 1950–52[30]

In 1949, we returned to India, on the *SS Jal Jawahar*, to start a new life. After a few months in Jalandhar with Siddharth and his parents, Surakak and Sarla Bhabhi, we moved to Bombay in 1950, as my father had been offered business opportunities for which it was a suitable hub. The next phase of our life was to be there. My mother recorded our new journey thus:

> I have now been married 18 years, which means I have been living in an Indian family for 18 years. For the first 10 of these years, we were prosperous and influential and though many of my most painful adjustments took place during this time, I lived a very sheltered life and had little or no concern with the mechanics of living. I sometimes longed for my own food and more of my own habits and wished that I could arrange the household differently, but at that time it seemed beyond the limits of my knowledge and ability to do so. Those first years were spent in an effort to conform as much as possible, so that, being inconspicuous and unobtrusive, I could absorb and assimilate the personal side of family life. 'Family' is used in the Indian sense, and it included several generations and many branches, all living very close together, and in innumerable ways inextricably intertwined.

[30]This chapter has been narrated by Lila Kak Bhan.

> The upheaval and dislocation which destroyed the old order came after 10 years. There followed an interlude in my English home, the first after a decade. Looking back, this time marked a landmark in my understanding of the Indian side of my life. It showed me how far and in what directions I had moved since I had left and checked my memories of England with the impressions I received when I went back. They were vivid and strange, for not only had the war years intervened, but we had moved from the Midland countryside, where we had been brought up and our parents and grandparents before us, to a remote village in Norfolk.
>
> When we returned to India, as we did after two years, it was to an entirely different life. Kashmir was behind us. There, though I had been a stranger, my husband's family had been so deeply rooted over many generations that in 10 years, I had come to regard myself as equally identified, and now, for the second time in my life, I felt the pangs of exile. We went to live in a tiny cottage on the beach at Juhu in Bombay. The family in the larger sense was widely scattered, and my husband, myself and our eight-year-old daughter were alone with an elderly Kashmiri servant [his name was Balbadar Bhat but we called him Balji], who was as strange to Bombay as we were ourselves.

My mother's circumstances on our arrival in Bombay in 1949, after two years in England, as she described them, were very different from what they had been just a few years before—she was no longer the memsahib wife of the PM of Kashmir. The cottage in which we now lived in Bombay was a converted servants' quarter. A close friend of Bhaiji's, Sir Manilal Nanawati, who lived in a luxurious sea-facing mansion up the road, offered this abode to us. My parents had no car, no furniture, no bank balance and no amenities beyond one pleasantly opinionated servant who was not adept in negotiating the devious ways of a hard-bitten city he considered inferior to his own. Yet, my mother's approach, as is evident from her reflections on Bombay, is buoyant and cheerful.

Siddharth's abiding memory of Bombay as a four- or five-year-old child, while visiting Bhaiji and Bended along with his parents, was of wrestlers on the Juhu beach and sand artistes creating images of Hanuman, the monkey god, for passers-by to worship.

The sea was close to our house. Once, Siddharth rushed in with a small glass tank to capture, with great concentration and luck, two small, unfortunate fish, which he proudly showed off to Bhaiji and Bended. They smiled and nodded kindly. Unfortunately, next morning, both the fish died. Siddharth can still recall the sad fishy smell on his fingers when he threw them back into the sea!

Figure 20: Bended and Billy buying vegetables outside the gate of their house in Juhu in 1951

Illustration credit: Ira Tuli

My mother's reflections and observations about a Bombay from nearly a century ago paint a telling and sympathetic portrait of a bygone era. She was a keen observer and had a wonderful way with words. As a young girl, someone had suggested that she be an author. She told me that this petrified her timid nature, as she had read the biographies of many writers and they all seemed to have lived tragic lives. That was something she didn't want—to have her writing stem from misery. So, she had firmly decided that that profession wasn't for her. However, her vivid accounts of our time in Bombay tell a different tale.

> My first conscious attempt to master the intricacies of Indian housekeeping was just before we left for Bombay when I got my daughter-in-law, Sarla [Siddharth's mother], to describe to me how to cook a few things in the Kashmiri way and put it down in my recipe book. But, for some time, I made little use of her instructions. The Juhu cottage had two storeys, both very small; but whereas the upper one was tiled and clean, the lower one had been left as it had been when the building had been converted from its original stage as a line of servants' quarters. Our old servant lived below and there, he rigged up a kitchen and produced our evening meal. Ever since I had first arrived in India, I had come to the conclusion that if one did not know and could not do, the best thing was not to see, but to eat one's food and be thankful. So, I left him alone, but upstairs, there was a small room with a sink and a cupboard, where we made breakfast and tea, [...] and, in course of time, it was here that my early experiments in Indian cooking were done.
>
> The cottage leaked more violently than any house I could ever have imagined. Its roof was fundamentally faulty and, in the monsoon rains, a fine spray came through the ridge, which rapidly set the terrazzo floor awash. Fortunately, its level sloped, a relic from the days before the upper storey was built, and our floor was the superstructure of the huts below. We soon discovered that in one corner, furthest from the ridge where the slope was favourable, we could rely on having a dry island, and there we spread out our communal bedding,

duly sheltered by all our mackintoshes and even umbrellas.

[...] In the hot weather, the sun beat down mercilessly on the same inadequate roof, driving us out of our two-and-a-half small rooms to the narrow shade of the back verandah. But, just because it was so inadequate, it was the nearest approach to living out of doors that one could wish for. The views on all sides were open and magnificent. To the west was the Arabian Sea, fringed with palms, and to the east, a great stretch of marshland, backed by the fantastic-shaped hills of the ghats. Even if we were wet and salty, the monsoon skies were magnificent and we could watch the storm clouds sweeping over the hills and clashing in great bursts of thunder and lightning. We could see the rain squalls rushing in from the sea and ran to close our windows before they reached us with an impact like the rattle of bullets.

The glories of nature were not our only interest. Just below the upstairs kitchen window was a cluster of huts where the *malis* and servants of the big houses by the sea lived with their families. These were all Mahratta [Marathi] country folk and we rapidly came to know them intimately by observation, if by nothing else. On our other side was a house newly built by a Gujarati millionaire. It had been built to the owner's taste and design and was adorned with marble and coloured tiles and neon lighting. Within, the family lived comfortably, simply and in homely style, in strange contrast to the expensive whims of its building.

We had no car and travelling far or often was not only hot and uncomfortable but also expensive. So, I spent most of my time at home, gazing to the right and left of our little domain whenever I needed interest or diversion. I soon learnt many things.

The six yard length of [...] material, which is a sari—though I had worn it ever since I had first arrived in India—had always seemed to me very hard to manipulate. I had, in England, preparatory to returning to India, washed and

> ironed those I had with me, for laundries in those post-war days were chancy and difficult. It took me a long time and cost me a lot of nervous wear and tear in a small kitchen with a small table before I got them folded and pressed to my satisfaction. But now I have learnt the art [...] anyone who looks beneath my mattress will generally find three or four neatly folded saris, undergoing their final press...

I can imagine my mother alone at home, when Bhaiji was away at work and I was away playing all day, looking down from her first window and observing life around her in cinemascope as it were. The red buses lumbering past, the constant bustle in the little slum colony below, the drama of life in passing and the distant hum of the sea were a kaleidoscope that she observed with great curiosity, sensitivity and literary grace, which I dare say is difficult to surpass.

> How much of the supple grace of Indian women derives from their habit of doing their household work at floor level? And is it the absence of bending and stooping and squatting that betrays me even now after years of sari-wearing as an Englishwoman who can walk long and far—but not with the grace that even the lowliest Indian possesses. My knees are less stiff than they were. I can sit cross legged on the floor I strive—but I have not arrived.
>
> When I look back and remember how closely we used to watch the little settlement below us, I sometimes question our motives. Was it pure inquisitiveness or a sort of 'bird watching' instinct—reprehensible when applied to men and women—or, more hopefully, was it abounding interest in human nature? To do my husband justice, he was interested only at second hand. He listened to the saga that Billy and I concocted and appeared to relish it, but never gazed, as we did, from the kitchen window or dropped bananas or packets of small titbits into a crowd of quarrelling children, like manna from the skies.

As I write, I see, once more, our little world laid out before me. There is the bus stop, the scene of our departures and arrivals, the focal point where our individuality ceases and merges into the anonymity of Bombay. Behind it is our way down to the beach, so near that the children can run across in their bathing suits. It is a broad gap between two large houses, overshadowed by palms and flowering shrubs bending over the garden walls on either side. Our rich neighbour has built his house directly facing this gap, so that no future building shall ever bar him from the breeze that blows from that precious glimpse of the sunlit ocean, but his house, as is ours, is set back from the road by 200 yards or so. The unmetalled road which leads to his door also leads to ours and to the huts next door after which it peters out into a rough track through palms and scrub, so that our attention is quickly focussed on any stranger, man or vehicle, that crosses the road and comes towards us. But all other traffic passing up and down only serves with the little red buses, more sharply, to define the limits of our rural life. It does not concern us, even on holidays and Sundays, when an unending stream of cars pushes and hoots their way to the main beach, and the stragglers park themselves on every inch of our tiny by-road.

Immediately below our windows lies our own compound, showing, like the rest of the cottage, a certain inconsistency of intention, for though it has a very handsome front wall of pierced and ornamented concrete with two gates, one double and one single, its remaining sides are inadequately marked by a few strands of wire through which dogs, fowls and children frequently make their way from the adjoining waste in front of the huts.

Separating us from the Beach Road is a vacant building plot, where flocks of sheep on their weary pilgrimage to the Bandra slaughterhouses add a rural note, whilst they snatch what meagre pasture they can find. The irate old man with the grey hair, a Goanese Christian, who lives in the depths of the palm grove adjoining, comes rushing out to abuse the herdsmen and send them packing. As often as not, he carries an old gun beneath his arm, which adds an agreeable note of excitement, especially as we are comfortably aware from observation that his bark is far worse than his bite. His legitimate interest is only his hedge that separates the plot from his grove, but his curses and gesticulations leave the whole field clear. This brings the children out to watch the old man's blustering. They too suffer when the berries that they love are ripe on his hedge, and their depredations are constantly interrupted by the sight of his grey head bursting through the trees.

But now, the wretched sheep have passed on and the old man stumps back to his hut, and Shantia, the young girl with her littlest charge on her hip and the toddlers straggling behind, comes back to the playground beneath our kitchen window, and to the kitchen I too must go, and unless I plug my ears and blindfold my eyes, our intimacy grows.

At sunset, when the shadow of the palms was lengthening and deepening and the distant hills were touched by the afterglow, [...] Shantia's mother, her good nature uppermost, would sit with her little daughters on the little platform before their hut. The baby would be at her breast, the toddler fussing and fretting but content if she could find an inch of lap where she might also lay her head. Shantia would comb and examine her mother's hair with exploratory zeal, or present her own head for her mother's attention. The bold, bad sister would skirmish around, teasing and calling.

The coconut palms, amidst which we lived, watched over them and brought them comfort. Shantia's father made floor matting for themselves of the woven strands of the leaves. When the monsoon came, by way of umbrella, he made a little travelling shelter in the same way, like a large and elongated hood. When the children used it, it came

> down to their toes, and from behind, it looked like a small moving hut. With the husks of the coconuts, they made their cooking fires, and a month before the rains were due to begin, they were busy thatching their houses and barricading their verandahs with the great, fan-like leaves.

I will never forget my first realisation of my mother's strength and convictions. We had been living for some months in the cottage. It was mid-afternoon and the mali next door was home and must have had an altercation with Shantia's mother. He lost control of himself and started beating her mercilessly. Before I knew it, Mummy had left my side at our watchtower–window, and the next thing I saw was her atop the low separating stone wall, leaning over, in her muslin sari, getting closer and closer to the miscreant and beating his glistening bare back. Soon, a small crowd gathered to watch this most unusual spectacle. The beatings ceased and Mummy said what she could in her version of Marathi and Hindi interspersed with English. I will never forget the scene and am not quite sure what my father thought, but Mummy was quite sure a woman should never be beaten.

Even braver than this was my mother chasing a thief out of the bedroom. Next to Mummy's pillow, on the marble-chip floor, was a candlestick. It not only held a candle and a box of matches but also a large Rolex watch with a gold-plated wrist band, which belonged to my mother. Well, one night, I was woken up to her screaming, '*Kaun hai*, who's there?' Before I knew it, I heard a door bang and a bolt being shut. The 'thief' had rushed to the bathroom, locked the door and slid down the drainpipe outside the window and run for dear life across the wide marsh that was behind the house. The distant lights of the Santa Cruz airport twinkled on the horizon in contrast to the full moon that clearly illuminated the bare back of the miscreant wearing a short checked dhoti. The only other witness, beside my mother and I, was the tall papaya tree growing gracefully near the verandah. Soon, Bhaiji awoke and discovered the watch was gone. Mummy was convinced the fugitive's fleeing back looked surprisingly like the one she had recently beaten! Regardless of these difficulties, Mummy continued to maintain a mostly positive record of our time spent in Bombay.

> At that time frugality was what I most needed to learn, for Bombay was strange. The cottage was small and unfurnished, and as our resources for the time being were unavailable, we had to make do as best we could. I do not pretend that we lived anywhere close to the same level as the huts [below], but even then, it was salutary to be perpetually reminded of how much could be achieved by good housewifery with infinitely less resources than we had. Eventually, my eyes became so accustomed to sparseness and simplicity that I used to breathe a sigh of relief when I returned to Bombay from the [...] houses of well-to-do friends. I think it must surely be untrue that the poor always envy and covet possessions.
>
> The breeze that blew from the sea at Juhu quickened the senses with whispers of cool springs and golden autumns that Bombay would never know—false whispers but nonetheless siren sweet. Our uncurtained windows stood wide open to receive it. We had no furniture to block it. Our bedding was rolled up neatly against the wall. Boxes were arranged to make a long, low seat opposite. The white-chip terrazzo floor was bare except for one or two mats of woven grass. The breeze blew straight through to the open door and away to the vast stretch of marshland and the hills, where winking beacon lights ringed the aerodrome. No, I was always glad to get back, and though we grumbled when it was too hot, and more urgently when it was too wet, when it was neither, it was indeed a place to dream of—a 'lodge in the wilderness', beautiful beyond compare.

It is astonishing to discover in my mother's observations, acceptance, empathy and a felicity of expression in describing what was essentially a record for personal perusal. For her, this simple home bordering a slum colony in Bombay held as much beauty and diversity as our beloved Dara in the beautiful valley of Kashmir. In a particularly sensitive portrayal, she referred to this space as her 'listening post' to India. Diwali was one such occasion.

> It was Diwali, the festival of lights, the greatest day in Bombay's year. Lila and I had put out the light and were kneeling at the window in the dark. Beyond the arc of the street lamp, where the little red buses halted noisily, we could see the thick darkness of the passage that led down to the sea. But what attracted our gazes was the big house adjoining this dark passage. Outlined against the lighted doorways and the dusky edge of the upper balcony, we could see the figures of children, their faces lit by tiny points of flame from the small earthenware lamps they shielded in their hands as they ran to place them on the edge of the balustrade. Soon, it was all aglow, and the children came running out with sticks of sparklers, which they held over the side in bright cascades of bubbling light. We could faintly hear their shrill voices and laughter. Our mood was wistful. Only two days ago, we had arrived in this strange place. The little flat, bare and unfamiliar, had not yet revealed its possibilities and the holiday, which made our neighbours so gay, made our preliminary arrangements even more difficult.
>
> 'I wish I knew those children, Mummy,' this was Lila's refrain that agitated the early days of our unpacking and settling in. But Lila's instinct was right. Contrive to know them she soon did, and it was with them that she established the first listening post in her new territory. They were not [as] rich as we had thought at first. The big house, requisitioned during the war and now dilapidated, was let off in portions. They were refugees from Sind and disorganised like ourselves. In two or three large rooms, two brothers and their numerous children lived. In the usual manner of big families in India, they did not seem to crave or expect

such privacy, and Lila, who had been used to her own large family in Kashmir, soon ran in and out from early morning until we called her in at nightfall.

Balji, whom we had brought with us from Kashmir, was our only servant. This is how he preferred it to be. On our arrival, a kind friend had engaged a local servant for us, but after two or three days, he failed to appear and we never saw him again. That same morning, Balji lost two rupees from under his pillow and the coincidence strengthened his already firm conviction that the world outside his native Valley bred strange and undependable men.

Strange, in the sense of unlike, they certainly were if the contrast of Balji's own appearance among them was any proof. Every day at noon or soon after, he used to set out to walk the two miles to Santa Cruz to do our marketing. His reverend looks belied his years, which, in the face of all probability, he stoutly maintained were only 35 or thereabouts. In deference to Bombay's climate, he had abandoned his turban, and a wave of grey brown hair curled up from his brow, emphasising a distinction of expression born of his Brahmin ancestry, which his homely circumstances and country upbringing could not entirely overlay. He used to wear a kurta bequeathed to him by my husband, a loose white shirt-like garment, considerably larger than necessary, which flapped and ballooned in the breeze as he walked. He looked exactly what he was—a bird from temperate climes venturing among exotic tropical species with the firm conviction that he was the norm and they the aberration.

Several years later, it was the same opinion Gula, our young helper, had when he came to Kasauli with us for the winter months. Nothing could equal Kashmir, neither the people nor the beauty. As Gula would say, '*Panun Koshir katye bane* [Where can we ever find our incomparable Kashmir]?'

Meanwhile, all my father's attempts at business in Bombay failed miserably, as he was taken for a ride multiple times. As he told Siddharth, apparently, some Gujarati partners had appointed him managing director of a company dealing in manganese ore and obtained an order from the American branch of Rothschilds' for manganese ore worth ₹36 lakh—a huge sum in those days. The representative of Rothschilds', who met Bhaiji in Calcutta (now Kolkata), had placed an order on the strength of Bhaiji's name, as he had read a book on the plane in which Bhaiji had figured prominently.

Unfortunately, the Gujarati partners planned to cheat Bhaiji. Having spent more than a year in futile negotiations in Bombay, Bhaiji realised he was quite unsuited for business. He now wanted to shut his company. His solicitors from the firm Romer and Dadachanji could offer no help. So, he wrote to his elder brother, Bab, who suggested he meet the Registrar of Companies in Bombay, a gentleman named Bhide, and quote a certain section of the Companies Act to him. Surprisingly, despite the Registrar's initial reluctance, Bhaiji successfully closed down the company based on that particular clause. When he mentioned this to his solicitors, they were surprised. They opened their tomes and looked for the section, which indeed was there. After a pause, one of them said, 'Why don't you ask your brother to come to Bombay? He could command any salary that he may desire here.' In fact, Bab was earning a goodly ₹3,000–₹4,000 a month even as far back as 1947.

After this disappointingly unsuccessful and unfortunate experience, my father became very unwell. It was decided that we leave Bombay. The hills were considered the best option for my father to recuperate and provide a cool climate and familiar terrain. The hill station of Kasauli was unanimously selected. Thus began a new and exciting phase in our lives in which Siddharth and I began participating.

20

Exile in Kasauli[31]

With its salubrious climate, endless walking trails and mystical quality of drifting in and out of the fluffy, low-hanging clouds, Kasauli was surrounded by range after range of mountains. This immediately attracted my parents, who had found the heat of the plains unfamiliar to say the least. My brothers set up a house in Kasauli for my parents. In addition, and significantly, Kasauli was very close to the Lawrence School, Sanawar, a boarding school where two of my nephews had already been admitted and where, it was suggested, I join them.

Kasauli ended up being a veritable haven for us and was our home for almost 25 years. For me, the most amazing decision was to send me to Sanawar, using my father's provident fund to pay the fees. He was determined that I should be well-educated and equipped to follow a profession and earn a livelihood. He often reminded me, 'Money comes and goes but a good education is yours forever.' What a wise truth!

Shyam, the son of Nana and Kamla bhabi who were living in Japan, and Krishen, the son of Prema bhabhi and Brijakak who was an officer in Hodson's Horse and was constantly posted to different army stations, were the first of us to join Sanawar. Both boys had been sent to a boarding school for stability in their education a year before we moved to Kasauli. For my father, it was imperative to move to a cool place and peaceful environment, both factors

---

[31] This chapter has been narrated by Lila Kal-Bhan.

conducive to helping him recover from his illness. We arrived in the charming hill station in late February 1953. A comparatively small hill station, it was also a brigade headquarters, founded in 1850 with strict rules related to building and expanding. Hence, it succeeded in maintaining its quiet, spotlessly clean and unique ambience.

The Lawrence School, with its red roofs, was spread across a picturesque hilltop just opposite Kasauli. The family unanimously agreed it was a great idea to make Kasauli home. Its pleasant climate and Bhaiji and Bended being so close by to the young children, who would then be able to come home for weekends and short breaks, clinched the decision. My mother often remarked what a bonus it turned out to be to have five of us youngsters spend so much time together in our childhood, getting to bond and know each other well. It was here that Siddharth spent several years with us—starting at the age of six, before he joined Sanawar at 10. He was, thenceforth, veritably, my younger brother.

In addition to family bonds, Kasauli produced an amazingly eclectic group of residents that became our good friends. It was a very positive era of my life, where I spent my formative and most important years with my parents. Lovely cottages of all shapes and sizes were nestled on the two main roads—the Lower Mall and the Upper Mall. In addition to the two main roads, there were other winding offshoots, often leading to endearing dwellings hidden, secretly, in groves of fragrant pine trees. They were all charming homes, many of them bought and occupied by famous Indians. Each house had a story that fascinated me. People with an artistic bent, like authors and artists, seemed particularly attracted to Kasauli.

We occupied five different houses in the 25 years spent in Kasauli and enjoyed every one of them, including the period piece furniture that belonged to each rental. Fair View was our first house in Kasauli. After our exiguous quarters in Juhu, it seemed like a mansion to me. Rambling, with a large garden and a tennis court to boot, it was the lap of luxury! We were able to host several members of the Kak family in this house and reconnected with them after getting separated from them during Partition. In addition, I vividly remember how exciting it was to have Bhaiji's Jeeves and our erstwhile retainer, Kashinath Mulla, visit us in his familiar orange turban. His portly figure is so clear in my mind's eye even six decades later. It was a wonderful reunion.

From Fair View, we went to Killarney. Mummy was charmed by the vast spread of romantic Irish, Scottish and British names of the houses. They must have been given to remind the residents of the far-off climes they had come from. We read them out as we went on our walks, guessing where each original owner hailed from!

Killarney was a two-storey house, but we had just the top floor. However, we used the common front door to climb up the stairs. Under the stairs was a cupboard, which later proved to be a very useful hiding place when, on one occasion, a swarm of locusts descended upon us during a short break while we were playing outside. I clearly recall the relief when the missing grandson, Krishen, was found in the cupboard hiding from the diving creatures.

Killarney saw a lot of boisterous holidays, as Sanawar had three 10-day breaks in 1954—not long enough for the boys to go back to the plains. Instead, we were all together in Kasauli and had a ball, ate like horses and played together for the week. My parents loved being the matriarch and patriarch of the Kak clan. I never thought twice, however, of all the cooking that Mummy did, which was required to feed five hungry, growing children! It was amazing how she managed, albeit with the assistance of a young helper called Anant Ram, an addition to the ravenous brigade!

Our next move was to another rambling house, Shrublands. This was located below the Lower Mall on the Cart Road. It had a wild garden and a little fountain. I got mumps and was quarantined there along with Siddharth and Krishen. The latter was delighted to miss a couple of weeks of school. They would visit me at my window and we would giggle and chat.

Subsequently, Dunedin Lodge took us to the Upper Mall, just next door to the club. It was wonderful for me to make the acquaintance of the young subalterns and play tennis, badminton and learn squash with them. The club became the hub of social activities, including the occasional army dance. Siddharth was my faithful escort and was chuffed with that duty! We lived there for about four years before moving to one of two flats of Ellisville, just above the Jai Mull and Jakki Mull complex. This final move came when my parents returned to Kashmir after Bhaiji's exile ended. Then, they only spent six winter months each year in Kasauli, rendering the accommodation adequate for us, with always room for an extra bed for visitors.

Kasauli helped us forget the privations and humiliations of the previous few years. After insular Kashmir, it had a cosmopolitan flavour. Mentioning at least a couple of our friends from this time is very important, as they were invaluable and another reason why Kasauli still means so much to us.

Most special of the Kasauli friend circle are Dr Thomas and his family. He was the Director of the Central Research Institution (CRI), famous for its research and production of numerous vaccines, and his wife Leela, a much-loved teacher at Sanawar. I consider their three children, Anil, Anita and Eapen, as my siblings and we continue to be in touch, even 60 years later. Dr Thomas was instrumental in bringing my father out of depression and back on the path to total recovery. It was a remarkable recovery, and his support has never been forgotten. In addition, he was most filial, visiting my parents nearly every evening for a cup of tea and a chat. We spent Christmas together, making our own traditions that we looked forward to each year. The Thomas children were as integrated in our family as their parents, and we spent a lot of time together. The family visited us in Kashmir in later years, such was the connection.

Mrs Chesney was another Kasauli staple. She was a very dedicated, retired nurse who had stayed on from British times. She became a special friend of Mummy's, as they had a lot in common to talk about, sharing experiences as expatriates. She was probably one of the very few English people my mother got to know well. Interestingly, Mummy had few British friends, and she never appeared to hanker for them. Basically, she had totally submerged herself in Indian culture in a remarkably seamless way, but it was nice when she found a kindred spirit in Mrs Chesney, who loved Kasauli and India in the same non-judgmental way.

Hanni Spahn, a trained nurse, was another pillar among our Kasauli friends. Through her, I was exposed to voluntary service in a big way. Hanni worked with the Tibetan refugees housed below the Lower Mall as a volunteer of Service Civil International, a Swiss organization. My first memory is of her coming to the door to answer my knock, cradling a tiny baby in her arms. She said she couldn't put the infant down because of its frail conditions. Needless to say, she nursed it back to good health over several weeks. She became an intimate friend and remains in touch from her home outside Zurich. She would visit often during her spare time to have a snack and a chat. She claims to have opened her view of the world because of her interactions with my parents and the people she met in our house. She is still in touch with us and was, for me, a window to a larger world.

Our social activities in Kasauli were very different from the conventional ones. Many might consider them non-existent but I didn't. In addition to our family walks, my mother and I would visit a local resident most evenings. There were scarcely any people of my age, but I loved listening to the variety of conversations, be it with the Bennets, a friendly Anglo-Indian couple, or Mrs Pasricha, an Englishwoman who had married an Indian officer. I also enjoyed the variety of snacks each home had to offer. I learnt a great deal about people, different cultures and ways of life from each one's stories. I was imbibing an understanding of a diverse world first-hand by absorbing the different ambience of each home. In a way, these visits were first-hand, living history lessons from many perspectives. My father excused himself from this activity, preferring to relax at home after his two daily constitutionals.

Kasauli became a favourite for us all. Clean, sparsely populated and with beautiful khudsides, decked seasonally with pink thunder lilies, dahlias and berries planted by English predecessors, the seeds and bulbs having been brought from far-away gardens, were treasure troves of colour and variety, along with the unique atmosphere of Kasauli. Spring brought snowdrops, hyacinths, primroses and daffodils, followed by summer delights, each with their special fragrances. Bulbs to replicate distant gardens were brought all the way from England. Gradually, they spread across the gardens and became (native) beauties. Kasauli was like an indigenous mini-England. It made the English poetry and books we read seem not alien as it must have to the students of the plains. Kasauli immediately brings to mind Wordsworth's lines: 'When all at once I saw a crowd, a host of golden daffodils!' They fluttered and danced in the Himalayan breezes as they did for Wordsworth in the Lake District!

My life in Kasauli would have been incomplete without our all-important walks. They were a daily occurrence, probably a vestige of a British tradition from my mother's side of the family. They were times of sharing, bonding and always had a therapeutic effect on me. I have continued this family tradition with my children whenever the opportunity has arisen, particularly during our summer holidays.

I associate Kasauli with the indispensable conversations that took place on our long walks at least twice a day, usually before and after lunch. The winding roads of Upper Mall and Lower Mall, being totally vehicle-free, were perfect for the occasion. Instead of cars, we shared the road with villagers from the surrounding hamlets carrying scientifically stacked loads of wood, foraged from the idyllic pine-covered slopes, on their backs to sell locally. Never would we pass each other without a greeting of 'Namaste' or 'Ram, Ram'. These indigenous dwellers of the hills, with their rustic but charming dialect, were as much a part of the charisma of Kasauli as were the quaint houses with names to remind the occupants of their distant lands. Roscommon, Killarney, Waverley and more—each with different architecture and beautiful blooming ablaze with familiar flowers that grew in Kasauli because of its cool climate.

My father walked every morning for a little over an hour, coming back in time for a cup of coffee at 11.00 a.m. I would often go with him while Mummy would potter around the house and cook lunch. Those were the times Bhaiji held me captive with his mesmerising tales, most of them ending with a subtle lesson embedded in its twists and turns. I imbibed, albeit vicariously, an amazing amount of knowledge and philosophical wisdom from him. The quote that has stuck with me after all these years is about the importance of vidya:

> *Vidyā Nāma Narasya Rupamadhikaṁ Pracchannaguptaṁ Dhanaṁ*
> *Vidyā Bhogakārī Yaśaḥ Sukhakarī Vidyā Guruṇāṁ Guraḥ* |
> *Vidyā Bandhujano Videsha Gamane Vidyā Parā Devatā*
> *Vidyā Rājasu Pujyate Na Hi dhanaṁ Vidyā-Vihīnaḥ Paśuḥ* ||

> (Knowledge is the beauty of man, it is a secretly hidden wealth.
> Vidya gives us many pleasures. Vidya is the Guru of the gurus.
> If we ever go abroad, then vidya is the biggest Goddess.
> Vidya is worshipped in kings, not their wealth. Therefore, the person who is without education is an animal.)

Very occasionally, when I was younger, I wanted a day off from a walk, so that I could have a 'lazy morning', absolving myself by saying that I knew most of Bhaiji's stories. But, my mother would always encourage me to go, saying he loved my company and it was good to breathe the fresh air. In retrospect, I am eternally grateful that I didn't miss a day, for my father was a fount of knowledge, being a Sanskrit and Persian scholar, in addition to being very well-read, wise and knowledgeable. It seemed to me he had a quote for every situation. Through his discourses and by observing him and interacting with him, my philosophy of life came to be heavily influenced by him. He had no airs and graces despite all he had achieved. He stressed the importance of being modest and comfortable in one's skin. As he rightly pointed out, no one can be someone else. He cut a stately, if sometimes quaint figure, in a woollen *pattoo achkan* and matching *churidar*, which he wore in solitary splendour. Kasauli had probably never seen such an attire!

'Let them say what they say,' was his favourite adage as an antidote for people who made fun of our differences. This helped me survive the teenage tensions so common in the middle school years. We walked round the Upper and Lower Malls while chatting away, savouring nature's rich bounty that enveloped Kasauli. Many a times, Bhaiji would stop in the middle of the road and, characteristically, point his walking stick in the direction of the first red dahlia of the season, high up on the khudside, or the sunlit Shimla against the backdrop of the mighty Himalayas. Shimla evoked stories of his sojourn there in his younger days, with descriptions of the Jammu castle and his days there. Nothing escaped him. It was wonderful how interesting a quiet hill station could be—not only the flora and fauna, the breeze gently whistling through the stately pines or the beauty of the first snowfall but also the discussion about diverse topics, from family ancestry to poetry, literature and history to more contemporary matters about our current situation. Many lasting friendships were nurtured in that idyllic hill station.

The walks were very varied and the length depended on the day's circumstances. For instance, if we were in the midst of a long discussion, we might choose to go round The Mount and right to Monkey Point and thence take the footpath to join the tarred part of the Lower Mall. When we were expecting a visitor for elevenses, we went down the 'cut' next to Charles Law's Groombridge and then along the Lower Mall. There were innumerable routes. The Kasauli Club was a major landmark where the young subalterns and varied members would congregate for tennis, squash, the library and dances. It always managed to spark conversations and gave me insights into many aspects of my father's liberal yet sensitive thinking. It was my first foray into a more adult world, where I was treated as an equal by the officers and their families.

My walks with my mother were as significant to the development of my outlook as those with my father. In addition, these were a treasured time of bonding, a feature I recognised and coveted early on. It was a different relationship with her. She would tell me details of her life, letting me into her innermost being. Likewise, I would regale her with all the happenings in my life and introduce her to the latest pop songs, details of my friends, crushes and life in college and school. She had a knack for listening without being judgmental, yet she would advise me if she thought it necessary. She was my best friend, a friend whom I still sorely miss. Observant and accepting, she had a great sense of humour that helped us tide over many tricky circumstances. Most importantly, she would laugh at herself, something I have found very useful to emulate. Our walks along the gently winding paths of Kasauli, with its Arcadian atmosphere, are a part of my being. I did not realise till much later what special experiences I had, not because of any 'privileges' but because I had two unusual parents whose unique lives enveloped my development, teaching me the value of simplicity and open-mindedness.

Simple incidents excited us. We learnt to entertain ourselves. Being bored was taboo. My parents, both avid readers, received a regular supply of books from my grandparents in England, often as a result of a review in *The Times Literary Supplement*. The parcels took a good three weeks to arrive, and the smell of the brown wrapping paper and string became a welcome and familiar presence.

Looking back, Kasauli, with its beauty and simplicity, symbolised a catharsis for my parents. It was, indeed, a major cornerstone of my upbringing that, along with being an overriding influence on my outlook to life, fostered lifelong relationships.

21

Fairyland called Kasauli

More than half a century ago, in 1953, I went to stay with my grandparents in Kasauli. Unlike Billy, who, being older than me, was better able to appreciate Kasauli's local society, my experience was of childlike delight at the fairy-tale atmosphere of the place itself and the different houses we stayed in, created by my grandparents through their sheer love, imagination and family bonding.

We initially rented a large beautiful bungalow named Fairview, on the Lower Mall of Kasauli. What I remember of Fairview is that it had not much of a view, curving as it did, round a bend in the woods on the Lower Mall, but it had a beautiful lawn, airy rooms opening out into the garden and a disused tennis court beyond. Billy tells me that Bhaiji rented it for ₹1,000 a year from a very affable retired Major Charles Law.

Fairview later became a landmark in Kasauli, when it was bought as a retirement home by the erstwhile Lieutenant Governor of Kashmir, B.K. Nehru, a cousin of Jawaharlal Nehru. His Hungarian wife Shobha (née Magdolna) loved the place so much that she continued to live there, even after B.K. Nehru passed away, until the end of her life at the age of 109 in 2017. Shobha Nehru was famous as the oldest resident of Kasauli, where most residents knew her as Aunty Fori. Rahul Gandhi, a frequent summer visitor to Fairview, attended her last rites. She was cremated at Mashobra. Kasauli was full of such famous homes.

Ivy Lodge, owned by an Englishman, was bought by artist

Vivaan Sundaram's father. Vivaan's mother was the sister of the internationally famous painter Amrita Sher-Gil. Raj Villa, owned by author Khushwant Singh, previously belonged to his father-in-law Sir Teja Singh Malik. The Mohan Meakins house and brewery were owned by the sister of General Reginald Dyer of the Amritsar Massacre. She was a gracious hostess hosting tea parties once a week where she served crumpets, sandwiches and cakes.

While in Kasauli, Bended contemplated taking on a matron's job in Sanawar to supplement the family income. Fortunately, around this time, Bhaiji's trial ended in a victory, preventing a further separation for my grandparents after retirement, which would have happened if she had taken the job.

As a child, I had no inkling of these dire forebodings. Billy told me that in the early years of Fairview and Killarney, Bhaiji was keeping unwell. He would feel weak and breathless and suspected he had heart trouble. As Billy narrated, two people in his life helped him recover—one unknowingly and the other knowingly. Knowingly, it was Dr Thomas of the CRI; unknowingly, it was me!

One day, when I had come to Killarney, while walking along the Lower Mall with Bhaiji, something caught my attention. Perhaps it was a rabbit scurrying through the underbrush or the rare sighting of a bird, which I had just seen in the illustrated books in our library, but I suddenly rushed up the khudside in pursuit, ignoring Bhaiji's calls for caution. In desperation, Bhaiji was forced to climb the khud himself to find and bring me back. When he reached the top of the hill, he suddenly realised, as he told Bended later, if he could do this without any side effects, there was nothing wrong with his heart. He was not physically ill but, perhaps, depressed and psychologically unwell. From that day, he regained his energy. After his chance meeting with Dr Thomas, who started him on a natural therapy of processed charcoal sticks, Bhaiji recovered completely. Dr Thomas became a good friend for life and his children, Eapen, living in Coonoor, and Anil and Anita, now based in the US, remain close friends of the family.

Kasauli was full of adventure for a youngster. When Krishen's father, Brija Kak, an army man, was shot at by dacoits while travelling from Patiala to Sangrur in Punjab and escaped narrowly with a fractured leg where a bullet had hit him, he came to the Army Hospital in Kasauli for two months of recuperation. Krishen got permission from school to visit his father and stay with Bhaiji and Bended. Looking at Brija Kak, who was always jovial and full of fun despite his crutches and leg being in plaster, it was difficult to imagine what he had gone through on that fateful night his car was waylaid and he had to use his revolver to fight his way out.

Our next move, in 1955, after Killarney, was to another rambling house, Shrublands. This was located below the Lower Mall on Cart Road. It had a wild garden and a little fountain. Shrublands was owned by Doris Rivett, a spinster who lived with several dogs for company and talked to them fondly. Kasauli, with its open spaces, was a haven for dog lovers.

Below Shrublands was the main road connecting Kasauli to Sanawar via Garkhal and, of course, winding further down to the railhead at Kalka. There were thick woods around Shrublands and a steep pathway up to the Lower Mall, which I used to climb every morning to go to Mrs Bell's School at Waverly on the Upper Mall, a strenuous short-cut from Shrublands. Mrs Bell was a strict but kindly Anglo-Indian lady who lived with her husband in a small annexe in the compound below the school. I remember beautiful strands of cosmos grew in her garden from where there was a good view of the Sanawar hill.

I quickly established myself in her good books. Though not an exceptional student, I got permission to stay back after hours to colour pictures in drawing books. Those were among my happiest hours. Two years later, when I was turning 10, I was admitted to Sanawar and lost touch with kindly Mrs Bell.

Bhaiji and Bended spent most of the day hoeing and trimming the garden. I remember Shrublands had a large lawn with a bird bath and *champa* trees with fragrant pink and white flowers, which Bhaiji would trim with large garden shears. It was a change of pace for both of them and they were immersed in living life close to nature. Beyond the garden was a dense pine forest, ominous in its dark sighing recesses. I used to often hear the cuckoo calling but never dared to venture into the forest to spot it. The sun would disappear over to the other side of the Kasauli hill. By about 4.00 p.m., the evening chill would settle in and the pine woods around Shrublands would turn darker.

Dunedin Lodge brought us to, perhaps, a livelier part of Kasauli on the Upper Mall in 1956. While not a very large house with four rooms plus a small lawn and outhouse, it was right next to the Kasauli Club—the centre of Kasauli's social life. Before I joined Sanawar, I would play badminton and table tennis here, and Billy, being friendly by nature, would be the toast of the young army officers with whom she played tennis and squash. I suspect I was often given a game by virtue of being Billy's unofficial escort and insurance policy.

It was a carefree time, and I made good use of the club reading room during quiet mornings. I had become fascinated by cars across the world and had made a large scrapbook of pictures. It was a glimpse into an unattainable lifestyle, from the romance of a Wolseley standing outside a stately British country home or a flamboyant Lincoln Continental on an American highway or perhaps an exclusive Mercury with the steering gear shifts that were popular in those days. I dreamt of the good life while surreptitiously tearing out a magazine page or two in the reading room and quietly pasting the car cut-outs in my scrapbook, stored safely in Dunedin Lodge. After 70 years, I must apologise to the Kasauli Club for having misused their trust and desecrated dozens of beautiful magazines to feed my fantasies.

From Dunedin Lodge, it was an easy walk to Monkey Point, our favourite evening stroll after tea. I looked forward to it not only because I loved walking but also because conversations with Bhaiji and Bended, covering any subject, were illuminating. We could speak about anything at all, from the habitat of the black-bottomed langur or the glimpse of a fox or a rare butterfly to, perhaps, a headline in that day's papers or even an oddly shaped pine cone. Particularly interesting were the stories of the long-term residents of Kasauli, whom we might greet or pass occasionally on the sparsely traversed paths. Seven decades ago, Monkey Point was a fairly isolated place, and one only occasionally met a human soul along the way.

At the base of Monkey Point, lending it an eerie air, was an abandoned gravesite, called Lady's Grave. There were a few broken tombstones scattered under the sorrowing pines and the Lady's Grave itself had a carved Gothic font on it, which was broken. Its brass sundial had long vanished. The story went that Lady Anne Robertson, who lived in the bungalow named Padre View (later renamed Pahar View), overlooking the Kasauli Club on the Upper Mall, died of consumption in 1856, and her husband, Captain Robertson, of the 10th Lancers, a red-headed, eccentric fellow, prepared her grave at Monkey Point. But, the evening before she was to be buried, he took her in a coffin to the grave and burnt her there late at night. Perhaps, he could not bear to be parted from her. The pallbearers were terrified, but he had them put her ashes into a casket, which he took back to England and wore a locket containing her ashes for the rest of his life. Over 100 years later, in the 1950s, the derelict memorial he had erected in her memory gave the deserted broken down cemetery a ghostly appearance.

Depending on what time one reached the Lady's Grave, one had the option of continuing all around the base of Monkey Point and coming back once again to it half an hour later from the other side of the hill. This side of the hill had a spectacular view of the valley through the pines, beyond which lay the Shivalik Hills and one could discern the faint outlines of the city of Chandigarh. The evening sun literally poured down in an incandescent torrent as we walked. This side of the hill had a small but well-defined path full of flowers, birds and bees, which, for the most part, flourished without any disturbance. Few people ventured out along this path that we trod daily. At a few points in the clearings, someone had thoughtfully put a concrete bench to sit and contemplate the view. The hillside echoed with birdsong. It was as if nature showcased its prodigious orchestra for anyone who cared to observe its magnificent symphony. It was free and we partook in the magic every evening.

∽

Attending the Sanawar School Founders Day 60 years later, I found the Upper Mall leading to Monkey Point closed off by the army. In fact, Monkey Point does not exist in its original form anymore. It has been cut away to install an army radar facility and a television tower, taking advantage of the unique location of the hill overlooking the plains.

I did get permission to take a walk along this path once more, but it was now overgrown. No one walked here anymore. The benches had broken down. The hillside was being reclaimed by nature. Thorny bushes grew across the path and blocked it. Tall grass camouflaged the narrow pathway. There was a danger of slipping down the khudside with one false step. This was now a restricted area and as I retraced my steps alone across the jungle path in growing darkness, for the first time, I felt a tinge of fear.

∽

Bhaiji and Bended came to finally settle at Elise Ville in Kasauli—the smallest of all the houses they rented—just two small rooms, a tiny lawn and an enclosed porch with a mostly unused medium-sized drawing room with a separate entrance. The enclosed porch was our favourite space in the evenings. The evening sun would warm the room. Bhaiji and Bended would read. Billy and I would listen to music or chat. It was a small, intimate and comfortable space, conveniently situated opposite the imposing gates of the CRI. Dr Thomas found it easy to drop in. Jakki Mull, the store, was two minutes away. Daily Needs was another two minutes away, a different short-cut down the slope to the Lower Mall. The convenience and simplicity suited Bhaiji and Bended, and they adopted it as a winter base till 1975, even after they returned to Kashmir from exile.

At Elise Ville, I first realised, with great shock, about what my grandparents had had to endure as pawns of a political chess game played between the Maharaja, Sheikh Abdullah and Nehru before and after Partition. I was 14 years old then. Bhaiji had never revealed much unless asked nor complained about the treatment meted out to him. I remember chancing upon the newspaper reports and articles in a trunk at Elise Ville and was aghast to see my grandfather painted as the villain of Kashmir with particularly bitter reports by D.F. Karaka in *Current* magazine, criticising his decision to stop Nehru from entering Kashmir at a time when passions would have been inflamed. Knowing Bhaiji's integrity and loyalty to the Maharaja of Kashmir, I was shocked to read these accusations and vowed as a schoolboy to right this grave wrong done to my grandfather. It has taken me more than 60 years to fulfil that vow.

After he resigned from prime ministership, Bhaiji led a life of genteel poverty for nearly 15 years, until his pension was restored. He tells me that he could not bear to look at his bank account because of its constantly dwindling balance, with no income of any consequence for over a decade. This is why, one of the highlights of my memories of Elise Ville is perhaps the only restaurant lunch I ever had in nearly 20 years with my grandparents at the posh Alasia Hotel. Perhaps the occasion was winning the case at last after 12 years. What did we order? Perhaps something as mundane as grilled chicken with potatoes or perhaps a cauliflower soup with a spinach cheese bake, but the pleasure was in the unfamiliar luxury, after decades, of being served.

Recently, I visited Alasia Hotel and discovered it remained a popular, if somewhat run down, destination with its continental menu still intact. And the houses we lived in still exist as I remember them from 75 years ago.

For Bhaiji, Kasauli may have symbolised a period of healing, where he rediscovered his health and the joy of living with Bended, free from the excruciating stress and uncertainty of political life. Bended was able at last to live her life with her husband, not only free from political stress but also the obligations and expectations of conservative Kashmiri society! One of my handwritten notes in the mid-1960s perhaps sums up the way in which our grandparents became an example of democratic living for us:

> Since 1947, Bhaiji polishes his own shoes, even irons when necessary, keeps an account of the *dhobi's* clothes and sometimes helps in the washing up or the shelling of peas. He eats with relish the simple fare dished out by Bended, who does the cooking, serving and washing up herself, also the dusting, cleaning and making of beds. For the prime minister's family, this is dignity of labour.

I was at Ellis Ville when Bhaiji received the news that his pension of ₹700 had been granted, though not the approximately ₹3.5 lakh of arrears accumulated over the years.

Billy believes that Kasauli was, in many ways, her mother's favourite place because of the proximity to her grandchildren. The freedom from politics and the absolute joy of grandchildren made the lack of funds pale into insignificance. This was the peaceful and engaging life that we children had with Bhaiji and Bended in Kasauli. This was the prototype of the humble paradise that they then created at their summer home in Dara when they returned, after years of exile, to Kashmir, bequeathing us indelible memories of a lifetime.

22

The Exiles Return to Kashmir[32]

While I was in my first year in college, the exhilarating news of my father's return to his beloved Kashmir, for the first time since 1948, was announced. It was 1959. He had spent 12 long years away from his beloved home. His brother, Pandit Amar Nath Kak or Bab, an eminent lawyer, had taken the case in his hands, as it was a delicate matter involving many prominent people in important positions in the Government of India. So, anyone with true legal acumen hesitated to take on the case and, with it, the risk of losing their jobs. It was a great irony that Bab passed away soon after winning the case for Bhaiji. It was as if the elder brother had lingered long enough to successfully defend and exonerate his younger brother from the great humiliation that he had unjustly suffered with stoic resolve for 12 long years but was unable now to take part in the celebrations that followed.

I remember my mother describing the people who thronged our family home, Bagh Sundar, in Srinagar, to welcome him home. My mother said it was an amazing sight and these visits lasted for several days. Women of all ages, resplendent in their burqas, men with beards and turbans as well as children tagged on to see the *tamasha*—Hindus, Muslims, Sikhs, it mattered not, all were Kashmiris and they wanted to see Kak Sahib with their own eyes. Some of the younger ones must have come out

[32]This chapter has been narrated by Lila Kak Bhan.

of sheer curiosity to see who this person was that had been banished from 1948–59.

One sentence my mother told me people chanted as they thronged the garden at Bagh Sundar was, 'You threw gold on our roofs, but we threw mud back at you.' This was apropos his plans for how to deal with Partition in 1947. The welcome was overwhelming and very touching, according to my mother, who said it made Bhaiji quite emotional, particularly after spending 12 years in exile. Unfortunately, his ailing father Bhaigash, who had watched him being taken to prison one wintry night a decade earlier, and his elder brother, Bab, who had been imprisoned with him and fought the Kashmir state 12 long years for his younger brother's rights, were no longer in this world to share his joy.

Figure 21: Bhaiji and Bended being greeted by people in the Bagh Sundar garden after returning to Kashmir from 12 years of exile in 1959

Illustration credit: Kashmira Tembulkar

Both Bagh Sundar and Dara had gone completely back to their primeval form during my parents' long exile. The beautiful gardens were overgrown and unkempt, not a sign of the erstwhile flowerbeds or manicured lawns. However, the two stately chinars still stood tall over the tangled shrubs and saplings, overlooking the property like two loyal sentinels.

It was a time for reflection, rapprochement and reconstruction. It took my parents the best part of the decade to fully find their feet, particularly in reviving the Dara cottage or, as my father fondly described it, Daman-i-Kosar, 'the skirt of the hills'.

It is, therefore, revealing to read my mother's descriptions of Kashmir, which offer rare insights not just of Kashmir in the last century but also indeed of my mother herself, shaped indelibly by the land of her adoption to which she was finally able to return after being suddenly and cruelly plucked without warning a decade earlier.

> Many people who travel to holiday resorts of many different lands have spent some of their precious time trying to imagine the holiday, as it appears to no one of those who live there and who call it home. How often as a child, sitting in the parlour of the farm at Shortcliff, where we stayed summer after summer, surrounded by the objects which seemed to me so notable, the clock which had a musical box in its case which played three tunes when wound, the pictures, the ornaments, and the china teacups with flowers embossed so high upon their sides that they felt rough to the tongue, have I struggled to imagine the rock as it was when we were not there; when the farmer's family were sitting round the fire with a winter world outside, instead of the fields flooded by the hot August sunshine which we know.
>
> It is more such feeling that prompts me to write about Kashmir, or rather about that aspect of Kashmir which I know. To me, it has been home, a home of adoption it is true, but where I have felt fire beneath me, the foundations laid

generation after generation by my husband's family. Apart from this privilege, there is no justification for adding to the innumerable accounts that have been written of Kashmir, of the hills and valleys and lakes of the holiday makers. The Kashmiri people appear in these books also. Intelligent and handsome, they say, often picturesque, but lazy and easy-going and not over particular about the cleanliness of their persons or of their surroundings; suave and pleasant spoken and humorous, it is true, but always with a keen eye to their own profit. It is the usual cry of the tourist who meets, as a rule, only those whose job it is to make their living by ministering to his needs.

Kashmir occupies, in regard to India, a position very similar to that of England in regard to Europe, and it is not surprising, therefore, if her people are in rule and outlook, often misunderstood by and misunderstanding the people of the great peninsula to which she is attached. The Kashmiri, by nature, is rooted in Kashmir. Srinagar is the centre of his world. His country, his climate, his way of life is the norm. It is the visitor of whatever kind or race who is strange and unaccountable, who needs to be humoured, like a child, if he is to provide the profit which supports his home. Kashmiri is a language that nowadays is rarely, if ever, written and is completely distinct from other Indian languages. It is highly inflected and possesses many modified sounds which the unaccustomed ear finds difficult to hear, let alone distinguish. This also serves as a protection for their reserve, for though they speak with the outer world in Urdu, among themselves they speak Kashmiri.

So, the Kashmiri people live a private life, which very few penetrate. Only they themselves can assess the intricacies of their politics, of their divisions and their jealousies, and those who meddle in their affairs may often find themselves pixie-led, pursuing will o' the wisps which bear no relation to the aims they intend to follow.

What then of the Kashmir landscape as it looks from Srinagar to those to whom Srinagar is the prototype and model of all cities?

When he first saw the Midland countryside, where I was brought up, my husband criticised, 'It is too lush, too fat, too overgrown.' When, in due course, I went to Kashmir, I understood what he meant. Indeed, for some years, in my heart of hearts, I longed for the easy softness, the moist greenery and the innumerable birds that, in Kashmir, are found only in the higher valleys. The main valley is an expanse 5,000 feet above sea level, once probably a lake, varied with plateaus, most of them waterless. It is about 90 miles long and from 10 to 20 miles broad, surrounded on all sides by a mountain barrier, varying from 8,000 feet high to be pierced only in the south-west, where the Jhelum flows out into Punjab. The winters are colder than in England, and the summers hotter. The land is closely cultivated. Wherever there is water for irrigation, there are rice fields. In early spring, they are bright with yellow mustard flowers. The mustard crop is harvested and the fields are full of standing water shining over the dark earth. Soon, the water is threaded with vivid green shoots, the rice springs up, and in July and August, there is a variegated carpet of russet and many different shades of green, according to the type of rice seed sown. After the rice harvest, the fields are palest dun, touched with the faint yellow of the stubble. Autumn in Kashmir is a season of pastel colours and deep tranquillity. The skies are the tenderest blue, the ring of peaks is etched in silver and grey and blue, the earth is pale and dry, the grass yellow and sere after weeks of mellow sunshine. Only the trees flame in orange and gold and red, their glories often undisturbed for weeks together by the wild winds and rain that we associate with autumn.

Above the fertile land of the Valley bottom, stand the unirrigated plateaus, which, in spring, if the season has been kind with timely rains, are green with wheat or gay with the blossom of almond orchards. But by June or July, they are dry and pale, except for little clefts, where a spring or a stream have nurtured a few chinar trees.

The Valley is pleasantly dotted with groves of trees but almost invariably they shelter villages of tall three-storied houses of timber and thatch and, picturesque though they look in the distance, they are mostly rough and untidy on nearer view, for the peasants of Kashmir have not yet developed the modern idea of preserving and displaying their countryside for the benefit of visiting urban dwellers. If they need earth for mortar or for bricks, they go to the nearest slope and cut out what is required and are quite unperturbed by the gaping hole which mars the green bank. If they need wood, they cut it from the nearest suitable tree and so on. The earth is there for their use. Precious it is, but precious in so far as it serves their needs.

This then is the landscape of Kashmir; dotted with groves of majestic trees, green and fertile wherever the life-giving waters reach, elsewhere green only until the summer sun has scorched up the tender growth of spring. But on every side is the horizon, a horizon surely the most majestic of any land. So numerous are the peaks that for the dwellers in the Vale, they are mostly nameless and impersonal, as though they belonged to another plane of existence. Ridden in mist, wreathed in moving cloud garlands or etched in silver or ebony against the sky, one is always conscious of the mountain barrier enclosing the vale. Even in the centre of Srinagar, one has only to lift one's eyes to see it—remote, unapproachable, austere, brooding over all the temporary and fevered activities of mankind.

It presents an eternal paradox to those whom it shelters. It hems in and constricts the land where they live, but by its form and nature forever demonstrates the illimitable, the infinite, the immaculate, only to be apprehended by mind and

> spirit. This paradox is reflected in the Kashmiri mind itself. The typical Kashmiri is fiercely self-opinionated, parochial, mischievous and ready to cause his neighbour the maximum amount of irritation and annoyance short of real injury. But at the same time, he is deeply sensitive to spiritual values, not cruel, and mysticism, especially of that type which disregards considerations of worldly appearance so entirely that it can scarcely be distinguished from madness, is held in the greatest reverence by Hindu and Muslim alike, quite irrespective of the faith to which the mystic officially belongs.
>
> In this horizon, the true Kashmiri has gazed so long that he finds it difficult to regard as important the world beyond and is secure in the confidence of his own intelligence, is apt to be contemptuous of the capacity of them who live outside and the conditions under which they live. '*Kati bani Kashiri*?' is always his cry, 'Where will you find another Kashmir?'

It was this Kashmir to which my parents returned to rebuild their lives and homes. It was not easy. Bagh Sundar had to be repaired; lawns, gardens and vegetable patches reconfigured. The ancient well in Bagh Sundar was also rejuvenated. This took several years. Side-by-side, travelling up as frequently as possible to Dara and rebuilding the modest bungalow again, restoring the spring and the waterfalls to their original beauty, repairing the side walls and regularising documents and lands, reviving orchards and making them productive again took more than a decade. My father was not young. He was already over 65 years old in 1959. My mother could help with the home and run the house, but she could not help him rebuild his business among the people. My father was alone and not really a businessman as the unfortunate interlude in Bombay had proved. But this was a matter of the land that he understood better. In due course, the cherry orchard at Dara began to yield a crop that could be leased out as did the apple orchard and some of the rice fields and orchards in other parts of Kashmir. Though not significant, it was a respectable living for my parents and comparatively stress free.

I was, by then, teaching, sometimes abroad and sometimes in India, and my friends from India and overseas simply loved to visit and live close to the beautiful land, partaking of the simple and frugal lifestyle that had evolved for me and my parents in difficult times, which they continued, in their wisdom, to live as their lands returned to fertility and fruitfulness little by little. My mother was very firm about the spiritual dimensions of Kashmir for her. This is a remarkable demonstration of how fully she had integrated into the land of her adoption.

> This attitude of mind has been fostered by the reverence in which Hindus from time immemorial have held the valley of Kashmir. All the mountains of Himalaya are held sacred, but the sanctity of Kashmir is unique, a sanctuary within a sanctuary. In ancient times, every place of pilgrimage in India had its counterpart in the Valley. The old text says: '*Yani kani cha tirthani, tani Kashira mandala* [Whatever holy places there are anywhere, Kashmir contains them all]'. Therefore, the pilgrim visiting the little land of Kashmir could in epitome apprehend the grandeur and sublimity of all that Hindus held sacred. The land itself was a living temple, Sharada Pitha, the sanctuary of Parvati, daughter of the mountains and the bride of Shiva.
>
> Consciousness of this proud position added to the complacency born of a good climate and a fertile soil and had brought about a shift of emphasis in Kashmiri thought as offered to that of India. Unlike their fellow Hindus outside the Valley, they were not obsessed by the futility and deceitfulness of earthly life, for life in their own experience was good. The Gita says:
>
> 'He who shall draw
> As the wise tortoise draws its four feet safe
> Under its shield, his five frail senses back
> Under the spirit's buckler from the world.
> Which else assails them, such a one, my Prince!
> Path wisdom's mark!'

> The senses are to be distrusted, and the mind, undeceived by the veils of maya, must penetrate the shifting forms of human life to find the reality that lies behind. But Kashmiri philosophers, the greatest of whom were Utpal and Abinavgupta, regarded life differently. For them, every manifestation of life, wheresoever and howsoever exhibited, was to be regarded as a revelation of some aspect of the divine nature. 'Wherever the mind runs, there it should be fixed.'
>
> Among Kashmiri Brahmins, to become a *sanyasi* was a thing almost unknown. Many devoted themselves to the contemplative life and acquired great spiritual powers, but they considered this could be done without abandoning house and family. 'It is hardly likely,' my husband's grandfather used to say somewhat scathingly, 'that a man will make a success of the spiritual world, if he is unable to make his way successfully through this one.'
>
> This attitude of mind, with its uninhibited interest and concern with the events of material life, sharply differentiate the Kashmiri outlook from that of Hindus outside the Valley, and viewed from this angle, their interest in the history of their own land is not surprising. This interest is what distinguishes them...

The Kashmir that my mother and father returned to in 1959 corresponded, in large part, to the descriptions in my mother's writings. Alas, not for long. Before the century was over, Kashmir suffered a shock to its ancient cultural coexistence, transforming the fabric of its society yet again, never to return to those halcyon years again.

But the years before the 1990 terrorism, these serene days constituted our world. For more than two decades after the return of the exiles, beauty and optimism reigned as we rediscovered the Kashmir of our imagination.

23

The Bus Journey to Dara

After 1947, once the Kak family left Zaldragar and the property was sold, Bhaiji went into exile and there was a hiatus in the presence of the Kaks in Kashmir for more than a decade. Dara and Bagh Sundar, even though they had caretakers, fell into gentle disuse. The Kak family began settling elsewhere. Jalandhar was where Bhaiji and Bended stayed with us for nearly a year in 1950 before going to Bombay. Nana and Kamla Kak returned from New India Insurance's Japan headquarters to the Bombay office. Brija Kak, who was posted in an army cavalry regiment, and his family were based out of Jhansi in Uttar Pradesh.

Bhaiji and Bended's return to Kashmir in 1959 changed that. For one thing, when my father, a lieutenant colonel in the Army Corps of Engineers at Delhi Cantonment, got a posting in Kashmir in the Border Roads Organisation, he began to stay at the White House on the ground floor. He used to attend office on The Boulevard opposite the Dal Lake, near Nehru Park. Then Nana Kak, after he retired, came to live on the first floor of the White House. Thus, the Kaks started to return.

With the magical experience of Kasauli fresh in my mind, I used to spend part of my holidays every summer in the 1960s in Kashmir with my grandparents, even if my parents were still in Delhi. The attraction for me was the idyllic retreat of Dara, with its private spring, nestled in the hills next to the Dachigam Sanctuary. Often, Billy, who was teaching in a public school in Nabha, and later Indore, was able to join me. We used to travel by bus from Bagh Sundar to Dara, which was an adventure by itself. Here is how it used to happen, as recorded by my young self:

Figure 22: Young Billy and Sid on a crowded bus to Dara, surrounded by babies, peasants, sheep and hens
Illustration credit: Kashmira Tembulkar

> It is a pleasant June morning in Srinagar. The countdown has begun for our Christopher Robin moment. Billy and I are travelling to our own 100-acre-wood in Dara. It is our key to the magic kingdom of Daman-i-Kosar!
>
> It takes us about half-an-hour to reach the Kashmir bus stop at Amirakadal in the centre of the city. And then an hour by bus to Harwan. And finally, another 45 minutes or so of walking uphill to our kingdom in Dara!
>
> In the crowded central market area across the bridge and over the Jhelum river we sway with the tonga, holding on to our bags while the high stepping white horse trots smartly, weaving among the pedestrians, scornfully overtaking

another tonga while our charioteer shouts cheerful invectives at jaywalkers who narrowly escape being crushed under the galloping hooves! At Amirakadal, we take leave of our charioteer, Rahmana, and search for our carriage in the rows of haphazardly parked buses bound for various destinations outside Srinagar—Gulmarg, Pahalgam, Anantnag, Qazigund, Sopore, Baramulla, Ganderbal... In this melee, we are looking for the local bus to take us to Harwan, about 15 kilometres away. The bus stop is full of excitedly scurrying passengers, honking buses with scores of bus attendants in their flapping pherans shouting invitations to the crowds, sometimes pulling passengers physically into the moving bus to make sure every seat is occupied. '*Pak se*! *Pak se* [out of the way]!' they yell, haranguing the crowds to get a move on. '*Pakyu mahra* [out of the way, sir]!' The bus attendants yell more politely at senior citizens in a piercing cacophony that forces us to shout at each other to be heard!

Each bus, however full, stops at stations along the way to take on even more passengers till it is stuffed to three times its capacity. There is money to be made from extra passengers over and above the official seat count.

We find what we were looking for just in time. Hidden in a corner, the bus to Harwan is getting ready to leave. If we miss it, we shall have to endure the pandemonium for another half-an-hour before the next bus. Billy excitedly shouts and gestures to the attendant before the bus pulls out. The attendant, seeing a memsahib wishing to board, hangs out from the footboards and pulls us in, squeezing us into the back seat, bags and all. He quickly collects our fare of an anna or two, of course without a receipt. With a lurch and shudder, the bus pulls out of the stop, taking us past the venerable SP College, the famous Nedous Hotel, the golf course and the tourist reception centre before turning left for its first stop at Dal Gate.

Dal Gate is a narrow channel, which flows via a sluice

gate into the Jhelum, at the congested mouth of the Dal Lake. It is full of skiffs ferrying supplies to a cluster of houseboats, opening out into the Dal Lake, skirting The Boulevard crammed with shops selling curios and hotels offering rooms, chock-a-block with traffic. A few youths clamber onto the bus and hang by the footboard. The attendant bangs on the bus door and shouts to the driver '*Pak sa lamb* [Get along quickly]!'

We are all squeezed in, staring at the backs of a battalion of passengers standing in the centre aisle. There are a couple of youths wrapped in blankets hunched on the floor. They fix us with unblinking, unabashed stares. We are indeed aliens in the back seat with our quaint pidgin Kashmiri!

Now, we are on the wide Boulevard Road, skirting the famous lake. Shops have given way to poplars, the crowds have vanished. The vistas are expansive, with shikaras and boatmen plying on the shimmering lake. In the centre are the romantic outlines of the two artificially created Char Chinari islands with chinar trees at their four corners visible like distant sentinels.

At the Char Chinari stop—where the road diverts upwards to what are now the tulip gardens, and the former Maharaja's outhouses converted by the Oberoi Group into an exclusive 5-star hotel (now Lalit Hotel)—a vendor is selling *bhutta* but without salt or a squeeze of lemon as in Delhi or Bombay. Still, the cob is fat and sweet. Not many folks are getting on or off. The locals wait for the Nishat or Shalimar Garden stops further down, where substantial villages have grown around the tourist trade.

Now, the whole bus and centre aisle is occupied by standing or squatting passengers—four or five to a seat meant for two, the last few of whom are sitting facing us. One of them is holding onto an indignant squawking hen.

The bus screeches to a halt at the Nishat village stop. A passenger enters holding a bleating lamb. There is a buzz of high-pitched conversation punctuated by squawks and bleats. The two youths facing us get off here and the crowd pours into the vacuum, like the sea. Nishat is famed for the best *nadirmonji*—a local variety of crisp salted lotus stalk fries tossed in red chilli powder and rice batter. This is a local speciality, but I cannot risk vacating my precious inches of space on the bus for a newspaper packet of crisp and crunchy nadirmonji! Oh well, I dream of the treats awaiting me at Dara prepared by Bended on her two faithful stoves—perhaps shepherd's pie and home-made rocky buns with kahwa!

The bus halts at a nondescript village stop. A stream flows next to the road with willows bending over and touching the waters. A gaggle of geese waddle across. It could be a zen painting from the edge of time.

A few passengers get off to be replaced by a buxom, rosy cheeked woman wearing a pheran, a typical knotted kerchief around her head, carrying a snotty child on her hip. She smiles at Billy, who gushes back. My grouse with Billy is that she is far too friendly and trusting with everybody and practises her Kashmiri unashamedly while I cringe. Having her around, however, makes us acceptable in the bus. Billy makes place for the snotty child and laughs at me apologetically. I am not amused, but people in the bus smile and nod, our exotic status forgotten!

The buxom woman asks Billy in Kashmiri in between lurches, 'Where are you going?'

'Till Harwan,' replies Billy. Short sentences in Kashmiri are easy!

The woman smiles and responds, 'I am going there too.'

'*Av, av* [yes, yes]!' claims briskly, volunteering as she does in her trusting way, 'Then we are going up to Dara.'

'*Yi cha Kak sahibun jai* [Is that Kak Saheb's place]?' asks a sharp old man who has been listening intently. All conversations in the bus are public.

I am a bit surprised but not too much. Bhaiji is somewhat

of a legend in the area. Everyone examines us with renewed interest. I pretend not to notice.

The old man says loudly in Kashmiri, referring to Bhaiji's prime ministership, '*Aasmana's layyum thok. Vapas peyam paanas peth* [We spat at the sky. Now that spit has fallen back on us!]'

Billy and I look at each other and manage a little embarrassed laugh. It is an unpleasant memory. This was a time literally when the people of Kashmir had, more than a decade earlier, abused Bhaiji after he had resigned as prime minister.

A political discussion is fortunately averted as the attendant shouts, '*Harwan chu vyothmuth! Vasiyu* [We have reached Harwan, get down! Get down!]' The burly driver swerves across the Harwan Bridge to come to another shuddering halt.

The Harwan stop is in a picturesque clearing. One side leads to the Dachigam Sanctuary, famous for its barasingha and the red bear, in a valley adjacent to the hills of Dara. Behind us is the Harwan Reservoir that supplies water to Srinagar. Straight ahead, a path winds up through the sleepy village of New Theed (commonly known as Theed) to Dara and the high mountains beyond.

Bhaiji's retainer, Lassa, has come to carry our bags up from Harwan. He has a shy smile and doesn't speak much. He takes our bags without a word, straps them on to his strong shoulders and begins walking. [This kind of service, being a relic of a bygone time, is no longer common.]

The Harwan clearing is a large, tree-filled meadow that extends up to the village of Theed from where the climb begins. Theed's quiet steep pathway is lined with shops on either side. Many of the shopkeepers are suppliers to us at Dara—the vegetable and fruit vendor, butcher and grain and dry fruits merchant. There is a little post office here too. Dogs lie in our path, unmoved. The shopkeepers acknowledge us with a brief smile or a salaam. They know who we are. Everyone knows everyone. We acknowledge their greetings and stumble on. We are a little out of breath by now. We have been climbing for half a mile. At their age, Bhaiji and Bended walk up this same pathway too, if slower. Although, this time, they had come by taxi earlier that morning, as we also had a lot of luggage. Above the lane of shops, the incline eases and widens past a clump of walnut trees. We pause for breath. Lassa passes us with a smile and goes on ahead to alert Bhaiji and Bended.

The path curves past a few thatched homes. Women are washing clothes in the tributaries flowing down from the Malhouri river. We smile and exchange greetings. We can hear the distant rush of the stream beckoning us home. Our steps quicken. Ahead is the quaint bridge that crosses over the foaming Malhouri to Dara village. We are almost home.

From here, it is a short climb, stumbling over the rocks that litter the sloping pathway. We pass the water mill still busily grinding. The miller, a flour-covered ghost waves and shouts his greeting, 'Salaam!'

'Salaam,' we exclaim, waving back. His is the last outpost of habitation before our cottage. Now, we can see the retaining stone-covered wall of Dara and our cosy home perched on top of the hill. On our right, the waters of Malhouri gush and pirouette gaily. We can feel its spray sting our faces.

The sun is still high, but, at this elevation, the air is cool. We can see the cherry trees peeping above the retaining wall of stones running parallel to the ascending path. Just ahead is the ancient wooden entrance gate to the cottage. Bhaiji and Bended are already there, waiting for us by the open gate. Bhaiji has a gentle smile. Bended welcomes us with open arms. 'Billaa,' she calls out fondly to Billy. 'Hoof,' she exclaims, my nickname from the Dr Doolittle series. We embrace. We are finally home for the summer holidays!

24

Memories of Dara[33]

To transport myself to Dara, all I need to do is close my eyes, so vividly is it etched in my mind. I can travel up the rough mud and stone path winding up to this little paradise, remembering each turn, the fragrance of the pink and white roses tumbling down the grey stone walls dispelling the stronger but familiar odour of cow dung cakes drying in the village courtyards.

Unless we happened to be coming by a taxi or car, we descended the local bus at the bottom of the ascent opposite the Harwan reservoir near a large grove of horse chestnut trees. When the trees around were blossoming, their familiar scent greeted us as we walked along a well-beaten path, which was shaded and led to a bridge, made of mud and wood, on to the rougher 'main' road going through the sleepy village of Theed. A diversion from the Telbal river rushed under the little bridge, providing water for the residents of the area.

Theed was characterised by several sleeping dogs who invariably decided to plonk themselves in the middle of the path, opening one disdainful eye to see who was stomping past them, disturbing their morning siestas. Shops, festooned with coloured scarves and dupattas, lined the path on the left, whereas village houses bordered the other side. In addition to the colourful scarves, pretty earthenware containers held the yogurt that made it famous as far away as the capital city of Srinagar. Theed's zamadod made its

[33]This chapter has been narrated by Lila Kak Bhan.

mark as being the sweetest and purest, made from the milk of cows that grazed on the delightfully flavoured mountain grass in the surrounding pastures. It truly was creamy sweet and scrumptious.

Greeted with smiles and salaams, we started our climb, awaiting the first, magical, glimpse of the cottage a mile up the hill. En route, we passed several small villages with their stone walls put to use for drying clothes and cow dung cakes, interspersed with the delightfully simple but gorgeous, five-petalled *aharabal* or rose creeper indigenous to Kashmir. In each village, we ran into acquaintances. Akbar Kuth lived in Barich, the first hamlet after we left Theed. Turning the sharp corner from there, several welcoming salaams emanated from unseen faces. Lokut Lassa, Raaji and Ali shouted out gleefully to herald our arrival. The event was easily as exciting for the village folk as it was for us. We were a sort of entertainment, an ongoing series from a literary work, providing interest and a glimpse into another way of life, yet sharing a common thread of being partly rustic, like the viewers.

Finally, a rather long stretch led us to a more modern bridge with bright red wooden railings, which spanned the tumbling Malhouri in whose valley we lived. All along, willow trees spread their beautiful maroon roots that clung to the rocky terrain and dived into the trickling streams that gurgled over rocks wherever they found a slight descent. The bridge heralded the final stretch of our journey to our cottage. It was also a crossroads and meeting point for the villagers, where four roads intersected. If we continued straight, we reached the main village of Dara, the left took one through several villages and finally to Danihome and to the right was the way to Dara Chak, with the breathtaking climb up the valley passing several picturesque Gujjar settlements and finally to the sacred mountain of Mahadev. Our home was on this route and not too far from the bridge. To get there, we had to go over boulders and rocks unless we chose a narrow rocky path beaten down by the constant footsteps of the villagers, Bakarwals and Gujjars, who traversed this route.

Passing the flour mill was always a thrill. It continued to grind sacks of wheat as it had done for decades—two large stones, a flume with gushing water that came from the spring in our garden all in a lantern-lit mud room, neat and tidy, powdered with flour. The flour-covered miller often sat outside, basking in the sun, puffing on his hubble-bubble, entertaining anyone who wanted a puff, a rest or a jolly chat, inviting them to perch on the rocks around him or sit on any slightly moist patches of grass they could find. As we passed the mill, the dialogues exchanged were always the same punctuated by excited smiles from both sides.

'*Salam hassa* [Greetings],' we would say.

'*Kota kaal chu rozun* [How long will you stay?]' the miller would enquire.

'*Retus khandus* [A month or so!]'

'*Jaan gao. Sallaam hassa* [That's good. Bye!]'

The most memorable part of our home in Dara was this delightful ever-flowing spring that my parents discovered in the garden that was as good as the springs in the public gardens of Chashme Shahi or Anantnag. It even survived the long years of my parents' exile.

There is a romantic story of how Mummy and Bhaiji arrived upon the land where the cottage was built. Bhaiji owned a lot of the land in the Malhouri valley—mostly rice fields and a few orchards. After they got married in 1937, my mother shifted to Kashmir and my parents would go for picnics to the orchards and walk from the bus stop up to the area. On one occasion, in the later 1930s, they sat down on a rock and as they partook of a snack while looking around, Mummy noticed a small area of grass amid the otherwise rocky terrain. She scratched the area with a pointed stone to dig a little and saw it growing moister.

On removing some stones, they spotted the smallest trickle of water. Being adventurous and curious, they decided to buy an acre or so of the land surrounding this bit and to excavate and see if their guess that there might be a spring hidden deep down was accurate. The land, it turned out, belonged to an ancestor of the miller. So, the deal was clinched and, much to their delight, digging

Figure 23: Damin-i-Kosar—a view of our home in Dara.
Illustration credit: Anjum Siddique

the land produced more water. So, their surmises had been spot on. People from the nearby villages were hired to dig further and line the channel with a stone wall within which gracefully entered the cleanest, sweetest water you can imagine from a little cavern—the opening of a spring. The architect of the pool, under my parents' guidance, was a village elder from Dara Chak called Khazr Woin. His family had a long association with ours. He, scandalously for those times, took a Gujjar woman for his second wife, I believe, and had a beautiful daughter named Shammi, who was about my age, lively, vivacious and the belle of the district.

Dara was a rocky jungle of acacia saplings that spread like wildfire, their tenacious roots growing like tentacles. The resuscitation and resurrection of both Dara and Bagh Sundar proved to be the focus of the next quarter century for my parents. Transforming them into havens for us, particularly for Siddharth and I, was a labour of love for Mummy and Bhaiji. This project was binding in purpose and aim and, in the bargain, all consuming. It was their joy and pride to see both properties in Srinagar and Dara develop into the vision they had jointly shared. The transformation of Dara, with its sacred spring, charming waterfalls and vast informal yet well-ordered tract of garden, was particularly magical. Each nook and cranny had a purpose and often also had a charming tale to go with it. The lavender beds were a result of seeds sent from England. Each year, the swaying stems were pruned, dried and sachets were made of the fragrant flowers. Butterflies and humming bees always hovered over this sea of purple, adding a characteristic vibrancy.

Each waterfall and pond of water the spring created served a special purpose. The spring was sacrosanct and, apart from being used to cool milk or custard near its maidenhair-decorated mouth, it was not polluted, for it was our source of drinking water—the sweetest, purest water we had ever tasted. It gurgled down a channel bordered by leeks and ferns, tumbling over the stones we had collected to make a waterfall. This was where we came, swinging empty containers, to fill them with water and carry up to the kitchen to refill water pots for our consumption. Each time anyone came down, they would linger and gaze at the waterfall, listen to the songs and sounds in the garden, savour the sunshine and the natural beauty all around. No one could avoid the ritual of absorbing the atmosphere. From here, the water danced its way down a longer channel, purposefully built by several caring hands under the auspices of my parents. The second waterfall tumbled into the utility tank. Here, clothes were washed and rinsed in a basket that served as a washing machine. You just had to place the woven basket under the strong waterfall, changing the position of the clothes occasionally till all traces of soap disappeared. Then came the fun part of wringing out the larger clothes in pairs and laying them out on the warm clover and buttercup dotted grass. The clothes had a special Dara fragrance. We would also gambol and play in this pool, as also in the bottom one, which then escaped into a channel outside our wall, reaching the waterworks' hut just beyond the boundary and thence onto the miller's, where our water turned his ancient millstones, producing flour for the villagers around us. The essence of life in Dara was sharing and interdependence, a concept we imbibed early on. The place meant a lot to my parents and my mother wrote about the planning for the house, bearing the community in mind, with deep feeling.

> We spent the whole Sunday superintending the building of the wall that encloses the spring at Dara. When we took over the land, it had been almost obliterated and one scarcely knew it was there except for the beds of watercress which marked the site. Now, we have built for it a little almond shaped pool about 20 feet long and 5 feet wide with a 4 foot dry stone wall round. The main spring gushes out under a huge block of stone and two or three subsidiary springs run in at the sides, so it is a lovely sight! It's shadowed by two mulberry trees big and bushy on the steep slope above. The slope was thick with huge boulders. These have now been rolled down to make the wall and we have cut out a flat platform in the slope just above the spring for sitting out.
>
> We are going to plant the crevices with ferns of every sort. The water is to flow out of the pool into another, where we are to have watercress. The idea then is for the stream to go on again in a cascade to another pool where we should have a small stone hut built for keeping milk cool. The third pool will be sheltered by a hedge and used for cleaning kitchen utensils and the fourth and lowest will be a bigger, deeper one for bathing. There is another mulberry tree where we can sit in the shade after bathing. The house is going to be the simplest cottage with two bedrooms, a pantry, a bathroom, a sitting room and an 8-foot verandah. But there is to be a raised area, like a platform, outside which we can put up tents if we like the view! The Pir Panjal range with the valley, the lake and Srinagar in the foreground at a distance of 20 miles or so framed by two arms of hillside, which come down on either side of our valley. The kitchen

is separate behind with service rooms above and a little corner of land to grow herbs. Behind the house we mean, eventually, to have a store.

This spring is the most priceless possession—such glorious water. It's like drinking nectar! The house is a mile and a half from the car road so, if HH needs RCK, we can, at a pinch, be in Srinagar in an hour, so it's ideal for us and I think should make all the difference because if we have bedding and utensils ready, we can easily come up for a night and go down again to attend office the next day. RCK says when the twin bedroom gets more complete, we will spend July and August here, and he will go up and down to the office every day. We have ideas for a village uplift to improve the cattle and sheep and encourage home industries.

Across the way from the house, we have a piece of land on the banks of the Malhouri, which has been planted as an orchard. The land there is silt and very rich and the trees are looking fine!

Figure 24: A boy guarding the Dara cherry orchard for a contractor

Illustration credit: Kashmira Tembulkar

Dara's magic and sanctity was shared with many. One of the most touching scenes was when Mummy observed Hanni Spahn going down to the spring every morning silently gazing at it and walking around it. When she was about to step down to the first waterfall, she folded her hands in deep prayer and bowed her head before she proceeded to the waterfall. Later, she mentioned how spiritual and special she found the daily experience and how enlightening and inspiring she found Dara to be. We had a regular flow of volunteers, from the American Peace Corps and the British Voluntary Service Overseas, visiting from my school in Punjab. They were extraordinary young men and women with whom I have continued to remain in close touch. Many have become very close friends. We pitched tents for them in the garden just outside the bungalow or when a larger group came in our orchard, Sekhi Chal, just outside the gate. It was an amazing bonding and sharing experience. To this day, the young volunteers, now in their seventies, turn misty eyed while recalling the evenings after dinner, the community washing up and then gathering on the verandah with a kerosene lamp on a table. With the moonlight shimmering on the Dal Lake, visible through the trees at the bottom of the garden, and the orchestra of the tree frogs filling the night air, we all shared stories of the day past and plans for the next.

Outside the garden walls and down a rocky slope tumbled the Malhouri, its soothing sound a constant backdrop. Its level was seasonal, lowest in the season when water was diverted to flood the rice fields on the other side of the bungalow and along the Mahadev Valley. The larger rocks were exposed and lovely little pools formed—a haven for paddling children and exciting to catch some fish that had been carried down from the Malhouri's source. When there were thunderstorms, the river showed another face and muddy water roared down, crossing over the banks and almost flooding Sekhi Chal. My favourite face on the Malhouri was how it was for most of the time between May and September. Pristine water winding round corners creating foam over rocks and allowing us to make pools where, as youngsters, we could swim about four strokes in each direction. Hours were spent paddling in the water, warming ourselves on the rocks while chatting or reading. It was a utopian existence.

Our other unique entertainment was the evening walks along the very narrow mud dividers between the paddy fields. We challenged ourselves to come home with clean sneakers that were not mudded in the fields! Local children who found our household to be a constant source of entertainment would pull up their loose pherans and burst into convulsions of laughter. I can well imagine their amusement to think we made so much of keeping our shoes unsullied by squelchy mud, something their agile limbs could do without any effort. I often wondered what the locals thought of us. It was cinema at its best. Seeing many Western people for the first time and at close quarters. 'Salaam!' they would exclaim at us, followed by uncontrollable giggles. 'What is the time by your watch?' or 'What is your good name?' they would ask, testing the rote learnt sentences from their little government school in the village. Much to their joy and satisfaction, they would always receive an answer, and a smile of a newfound confidence would light up their faces.

The simple joys and pleasures of life in Dara were endless and paramount in shaping our attitude and understanding of the depth of life. Watching the Bakarwals passing by our wall, year after year, was an excitement we looked forward to. They followed a way of life that was simple and ancient yet intriguing and colourful. The clothes the women wore were beautifully and intricately woven and their hair was braided in dozens of little plaits, looped under attractive headgear, highlighting their gorgeous eyes and simple beauty. Young children, babies and pregnant mothers rode along atop horses, always with a couple of attendant mastiffs guarding them. The sturdier crew walked along, emitting the familiar whistle through their teeth, keeping the athletic goats and sheep from straying too far. These shaggy animals loved putting their front hooves on our wall to get a mouthful of branches of whatever trees they could reach. We were very tolerant of sharing our leaves with them unless we heard some stones from the wall tumbling down. Then Lassa and his minions would dash to the breaking gate, open it and harangue the crown. For us, these events were better than a showing of the latest movie. One needs to experience this oneness with nature to totally understand its impact; it was not only a visual delight but also a living lesson in anthropology and history rolled in one. I remember Bhaiji explaining the coming and going of the Bakarwals to alpine pastures above our valley from the passes leading to what is now Pakistan, and how they needed no visas. They simply came and went year after year, each flock to its special pastures. Their language was a blend of languages—bits of Pashto, Gujari, Kashmiri and Pahari. We could understand each other was the bottom line.

Bhaiji's statement to my mother, 'If you want to see life, I can show you!' is epitomised by the daily round at Dara.

Sometimes, our visitors would ask me, 'Billy, don't you get bored here?'

It was pointless saying too much. One either had lots to do or was at a loose end. It was each one's inclination. When my father was once offered a phone line by the Maharaja, his instant reply had been, 'Then I will have to go further up the valley. I want to have a couple of quiet days with my family when I am not on duty!'

We did get a transistor radio in the late 1960s, used for news and mostly select worldwide and musical programmes, but our days flew by, exploring the valley with its myriad villages, going on long hikes, often with picnic lunches, evening walks, reading, helping with household chores and soaking in nature. No place could be more conducive to building close relationships and bonding. It was because of the shared understanding of the enchanting effects of nature in its entirety.

Mixing humour with scholarship was another unique feature of Dara. Bhaiji had been director of archaeology and, after working under Sir John Marshall, had become an adept and outstanding archaeologist himself. Among the several historic sites he found, the one that was the most famous was the excavations at Harwan, about three miles from our cottage in Dara. This was where Kanishka held the fourth Buddhist Council in the second century.

More than half a century earlier, the relics and potsherds with inscriptions from an earlier age could be found in plentiful numbers in the streams and pathways around Dara. Bhaiji always had a story to tell about them and a large cardboard box in the verandah grew with the collection, adding to the charm and significance of Dara.

We last saw this house in 1989 when my daughter, Renuka, was married and came for a reception with Mummy, my in-laws, the Bhans, and other family in Srinagar. In the 1990s, it was ransacked during militancy. Siddharth visited it in the early 2000s and saw the impact of the blasting for himself. It fell into disrepair and was finally acquired by the descendants of our faithful retainer, Lassa, who now lives there. The spring still flows today, a legacy of abundant times. One can imagine that even two thousand years ago, Dara must have been considered a patch of paradise by the people of now forgotten civilisations.

25

Buddha's Golf Course or the Lost Buddhist City

I woke up early that pleasant June morning in Dara in the 1960s and went out to the porch to breathe in the cool morning air. It had rained overnight. I felt a sense of peace. I could see the red cherries ripening quietly in the garden. The sun was rising over the Dal Lake dispelling the morning mist. The steady hum of the Malhouri river tumbling downhill had a lulling effect.

To my left, the sun had just touched the top of the hill overlooking the Malhouri. Two large domes gently sloped down towards the ancient Buddhist settlement of Harwan, which had been excavated nearly 50 years earlier by Bhaiji.

My eyes were arrested by a strange sight. Yesterday, the hillside had been rocky and featureless, but today, perhaps because of the overnight rain, one of its flanks appeared suddenly exposed. In this gap, only a few feet wide, I could see the remnants of an ancient brick wall lying deep inside the mountain. I was astonished at the sight and rushed in to alert Bhaiji about this discovery!

Bhaiji took a look at the exposed ancient brick wall, a sight that he must have seen many times in his archaeological career, and nodding sagely, said in his imperturbable manner, 'Yes, that wall must be 2,000 years old.'

It was my turn to be astonished as I asked, 'Is there an ancient settlement inside the mountain?'

'We are living in the middle of the ruins of an ancient

Buddhist city,' said Bhaiji calmly, 'about 2,000 years ago, the Fourth Buddhist Council of the Emperor Kanishka was hosted just around here, where we are living! This must have been one of the grandest locations of any Buddhist monastery in Kashmir, framed by the majestic Mahadev Mountain, named after Lord Shiva and overlooking, as we are, the Dal Lake, the sacred Hari Parbat and the city of Srinagar beyond.' Bhaiji gestured to the large cardboard box on the porch full of potsherds with ancient Prakrit markings, which he and Bended had gathered during their walks around Dara. I nodded. I had picked some potsherds myself. It was not uncommon to find them in the streams and pathways surrounding Dara white strolling.

'I had discovered the Buddhist ruins of Harwan a few kilometres away in a similar fashion,' said Bhaiji, going back to the time when, as a young archaeologist in the 1920s, he would explore the hillsides on foot. 'I was puzzled to see a large tract of the Harwan hillside bare, with a single stunted tree while all around were fertile fields. When I asked a local cowherd grazing his cattle by a brook nearby, he pointed to the barren patch and simply answered '*kitur-i-darj* [field of potsherds]'. His words resonated in my head and I ordered an excavation. Sure enough, the area below had the stone foundations of a Buddhist monastery under it, which is why nothing grew above it!'

I have visited the historic monastery Bhaiji discovered at Harwan, which he later wrote about in his classic reference book *Ancient Monuments of Kashmir*. I even filmed it for my TV show, *Surabhi*.

At that time, Bhaiji had thought he might find buried there, the copper tablets that codified the historic break between the old Hinayana and the new Mahayana Buddhism at the fourth and last historic Buddhist Council in the first century, held under the aegis of Emperor Kanishka and supervised by the great sage Nagarjuna. To his disappointment, he did not find them there. Perhaps the venue of the conference had been some other place.

At that time, he did not imagine that he was at the periphery of what was probably the largest Buddhist settlement in Kashmir. It did not occur to him that almost 20 years later, he would build a home at almost the exact spot where the rare copper plates he was searching for were probably buried, perhaps inside the very hillside opposite our home in Dara.

Bhaiji continued to muse, 'Look at these two hilly domes. They are bare and rocky. Nothing much grows on them. Probably there are two massive brick and stone stupas below these domes which is why they are barren. However, that rectangular section between them is covered with green grass. That's why we call it Buddha's Golf Course! It seems there is no stone structure below, inhibiting the growth. This might be where the rectangular tank between the two stupas existed 2,000 years ago!' A water tank was an intrinsic component of any large monastic establishment. It gave me goosebumps to realise that we were perhaps standing there at the edge of history, with the mountain finally deciding to reveal its secret to us! A secret that, alas, would be buried once more.

∽

Today, Dara is unrecognisable with ugly constructions up to the remains of the picturesque cottage, which was ransacked and blasted by militants. The damaged cottage itself has been demolished by the new owner, Akram, whose father, Lassa, loyally served my grandfather for many years. Akram has developed a flourishing trout farm next to the Malhouri, which has been reduced to a trickle but the original spring still flows strongly in the garden. Only about half the domed hill is left, destroyed by quarrying. But, in my mind's eye, I can see Malhouri's clean, cold water gushing as ever. I can see Billy and myself panting up the hill from the other side and hooting when we saw Buddha's Golf Course, a green, mysterious oasis between two apparently barren mounds. We would then wave to and shout at Bhaiji and Bended watching anxiously from the cottage below.

During militancy, it was next to impossible to visit Dara. Even recently, when I visited Kashmir, it was a daunting prospect, but, finally, the ASI has risen to the occasion and taken up the task of prospecting the site, with the Ministry of Culture holding an international conference on its historical potential. The ASI plans on declaring it a protected site, to carry out a full-fledged investigation, followed by an excavation. This would have greatly satisfied my grandfather, as he did his best to prevent quarrying in the region during his lifetime.

I recall that pleasant rainy morning nearly six decades ago when the mountain suddenly revealed its secret to us at Dara, making us realise it was not only a sylvan and wondrous place but also perhaps, because of that, profoundly historical.

Bhaiji's most significant discoveries a hundred years ago had been made at the nearby Harwan. More than 50 years after the first discovery of remains of a lost Buddhist city around our home in Dara, the ASI has finally launched a formal exploration of the region. If the lost Buddhist city and the rare copper tablets of the Fourth Buddhist Council that my grandfather searched for during his lifetime were to be discovered here, at Dara, his soul would be at peace again.

26

Epilogue

As this book ends, so does, it seems, the worst of the Covid-19 pandemic that disrupted the world. The future is uncertain, though, and we may have to suffer unexpected consequences for many years to come—perhaps forever.

But, in retrospect, I can say that the pandemic was, in its peculiar way, the best thing that could have happened to me. This book might never have been written but for the pandemic. The enforced layoff gave me the opportunity to look inward and choose, in the time available to me, to take up the things closest to my heart. Imprisoned at home, time stretched endlessly and the mind was set free. The motivation for completing long cherished projects was resuscitated.

The pandemic neatly divided my life, at any rate, into two phases, which I call before pandemic and after pandemic. Before pandemic, I was unthinking, pursuing imagined fame and success, which forever tempted me with higher peaks of attainment, the global rat race, with dozens of staff to provide or manage the smallest detail for me.

After pandemic, I commenced a long-postponed personal career, the fulfilment of goals articulated but never embarked upon—creative goals, unfulfilled ambitions, a bucket list of activities and things to see and do, unfettered by unwieldy teams and strategies. Very personal—very individual. This book is one of them.

I have, while writing this book, often been struck by the difference in personal and public stances. I have often wondered why Ram Chandra Kak, our Bhaiji, chose the difficult path of joining the Maharaja's administration, which was apparently so alien to his character and temperament. On this path, diplomacy was preferred to the truth, evidence was less consequential than royal approval and life was circular—one frequently ended up where one had begun in the first place, with no visible achievements even in a lifetime. And this happened to Bhaiji as well, even after 33 years of faithful service to Kashmir.

None of the reforms that he had far-sightedly introduced—like local self-help groups for irrigation, afforestation and development, or an initiative to bring professional industry to Kashmir through a joint venture with the Tatas—survived after he resigned. He was removed on a whim before any of his reforms could take root. He was disgraced and humiliated, imprisoned and ostracised in petty retaliation and eventually forced to spend more than a decade in exile, away from his beloved Kashmir.

Would staying back in the archaeology department have fulfilled him more? In tune with his apparently aloof and analytical nature, would he have been satisfied with writing books and excavating history as an end in itself? Or did he perhaps, in his heart of hearts, relish the cut and thrust of political life about which he has written with humour and insight, unlike his factual investigations and dry records of history?

It is as if his life too was divided into two distinct phases. The first, intimately connected with the hustle and bustle and politics of Kashmir and the second, closely interwoven with his family and nature. In this phase, he began living, as it were, a second life. In both, I believe, he excelled.

Margaret Mary Allcock, our Bended, also experienced two distinct phases in her life. The first was as a typical English girl brought up in an affluent but conservative English countryside home, and the second, by her voluntary adoption of a difficult and radically different lifestyle, separated from her family and home. Travelling to a land of extremes, where she knew neither the people and their customs nor was she familiar with their food, their habits or prejudices.

Was it the inevitability of her life in England that prompted her to plunge into this exciting adventure in an unknown land? Or were the qualities and nature of the man she embraced the source of her adventure and fulfilment? I believe here, too, the answer is both.

I believe Bhaiji surprised his entire family, perhaps even himself, by his choice of a bride so alien to the world to which he belonged. While his sons may have found him taciturn and intimidating, I believe Bended, when she first met Bhaiji, found him fun, with his tongue-in-cheek British humour and strong convictions, both qualities which she may have found endearing and which, perhaps, swung the balance in favour of her decision to spend the rest of her life with this unusual man.

∽

As children, we look up to our elders as role models. For us, they are ideal in every way. We scarcely imagine them as passionate lovers or swashbuckling heroes. We feel more secure when we see them as prosaic providers of affection and necessities, however lacklustre that service may appear to be.

Both Lila and I would like to hazard that while Bhaiji and Bended played their roles as the patriarch and matriarch of the Kak family, when they were young, they might certainly have been considered quite forward and indiscreet. We would imagine that Ram Chandra Kak, in his time, might have been found very dashing and that demure, attractive Margaret Mary Allcock, would have been quite the eligible catch.

Bended never looked back at the life she left behind with any sense of loss. She embraced her new world and, with it, the man with whom she forged a new destiny, never returning to England, the land of her birth, except cursory visits.

The world may not have quite known them for who they were. Over the years, many judgements were passed in absentia against our Bhaiji. He was accused of being a traitor, suspected of favouring accession to Pakistan, of being autocratic, stubborn and strong willed. Some lauded his contribution as a much misunderstood Kashmiri Pandit, an ironman of integrity, a keen intellectual or an able administrator. Actual facts were hard to come by. There were few documents, most of which reflected the prevailing bias of the time.

Bhaiji was a patriot and loyalist. He was true to India and the Maharaja, though, in the end, it was a difficult tightrope to walk. His vast learning, based on his extensive archaeological excavations and writings, meant that he knew and believed in the deep connection the rest of India had with Kashmir not only as a centre of Buddhist thought and philosophy but also as a centre of Shaivite learning, home to Sharada University, known as Sharada Pitha. Even today, some South Indian Brahmin sects ritually prostrate themselves in the direction of Sharada Peeth or take seven symbolic steps towards it to signify their desire to attain the highest level of learning, all the while reciting:

> '*Namaste Sharada Devi Kashmira mandala vasini.*'
> ('I bow to the Goddess Sharada, who lives in Kashmir.')

For a man immersed in this learning, reciting Sanskrit shlokas by heart, accession to Pakistan was farthest from his mind. In all this controversy, our dear Bended tends to be ignored. She seemed of no consequence in the drama of Partition and after Independence, it appeared that Ram Chandra Kak and Margaret Mary Kak vanished from the public gaze.

This book is, therefore, a tribute and a fact check regarding Bhaiji's and Bended's unseen contributions. It aims to correct how history has judged this reticent and modest couple. This book has been written to acknowledge the debt we children owe to them. A deeply personal story of how they made us who we are today—for gifting us a memorable upbringing despite the difficulties they were facing.

In writing this book, we realised the depth of their simple wisdom and unspoken legacy, the strength of the values they upheld till the end, which continue to influence later generations.

Figure 25: Bhaiji and Bended—our most unforgettable characters
Illustration credit: Kashmira Tembulkar

Bhaiji passed away in 1983 in Kashmir and Bended in 1996 at Billy's home in Indore. But our memories and love for their role in our lives and those of our children will survive forever. No matter what the world believes, for us, they were models of integrity, wellsprings of love and fountainheads of knowledge. They passed onto us their belief in the dignity and equality of civilised life. What we are today is because of who they were, inspiring us through conversations and by living their life with affection and sincerity. This book has been written to share with you how the simplicity of their lives brought incredible beauty and complexity to our lives and those of our children forever. Bhaiji and Bended are our most unforgettable characters and this is their untold story.

Appendix: Bhaiji's Career Graph

Year	Degree/Designation	Remuneration
1913	BA	NA
1914	Librarian	₹50
1919	Curator of museum and superintendent of archaeology	₹250–₹450+₹50 (honorarium)
1925	Assistant private secretary in addition	₹300
1927	Poonch residentship proposal by Watal	₹1,000
1928	Director of archaeology	₹400–500[34]
1929	Foreign secretary for four months	₹600–800
1929–31	Foreign and political secretary[35]	₹600–800
1932 (early)	Inspector general of customs	₹1,200–1,500
1937	Chief secretary	₹1,500+₹100 (allowance)
1941	Army minister and minister-in-waiting	₹2,500
1945	PM of Kashmir	₹4,000
1947	Resignation; pension frozen; restored in 1959; arrears denied	₹700

[34](50 per cent fall in salary; expected to be the cabinet secretary with a salary of ₹1,000, but Abdul Quayyum, Wazir Wazarab of Udhampur, was appointed instead)

[35]Replaced Colonel Hoshiar Singh, political secretary and a Pathan, a distant relation of the Maharaja's family, after foreign secretary's position was abolished.

Glossary

Achkan: Coat

Bagh Sundar: A complex of two houses—the Red House and White House—built by Bhaiji near Karan Nagar, Srinagar, in preparation for Bended's reconnaissance visit in 1936

Barasingha: Swamp deer

Batha: Rice

Belton: Bended's grandparents' house in Norfolk

Bended: A term meaning 'respected elder sister', used to refer to Margaret Mary Kak

Bhaigash: Keshavlal Kak, Bhaiji's father

Bhaiji: A term meaning 'respected brother', used to refer to Ram Chandra Kak

Bhands: Local folk artistes

Bhutta: Corn on the cob

Lila/Billy: Lila Kak Bhan's pet names

The Boulevard: The main road skirting the Dal Lake

Buddha's Golf Course: The common name for possible Buddhist ruins buried at Dara

Champa: The champa tree, also known as frangipani, has fragrant pink and white flowers, with Asian cultures believing in its many health benefits.

Chaprasi: Attendant

Chashme Shahi: One of the trio of famous spring-fed gardens skirting the Dal Lake, near Srinagar, along with the Nishat and Shalimar Gardens

Chinar: A tree similar to the maple, with distinctive, mostly five-cornered leaves. It grows to a singular height and width over the years.

Chulha: An indigenous stove that runs on firewood

Dachigam: A wildlife sanctuary famous for the red bear and the barasingha

Dak tonga: Relay horse tongas that delivered mail from Lahore to Srinagar and vice versa

Dal Lake: The principal lake of Srinagar

Dara: A village in the Mahadev Valley and hills overlooking Srinagar and the family name for the idyllic mountain cottage near Buddha's Golf Course, close to the village of Dara

Denman Drive: A suburb of London

Dharmarth Trust: The Dharmarth Trust, headed by the maharaja of Kashmir, was founded by Maharaja Gulab Singh in 1846 as an endowment for a religious charity and to manage and administer the temples and religious activities of the state, such as the annual Amarnath Yatra.

Dogra: The Dogras are an Indo-Aryan, ethno-linguistic group living primarily in the Indian union territories of Jammu and Kashmir and neighbouring Pakistan. They speak the Dogri language.

Doonga: A barge used to transport goods; sometimes a basic houseboat for local families

Double gilas: A large, juicy, red cherry

Durbar: The maharaja's court

Durrie: A rough rug made in India

Gabbas: Colourful rugs crafted out of *lois* or old woollen blankets, then dyed, embroidered and backed by waste cotton cloth

Gaddi: Seat of power

Gogji: Turnips

Gulmarg: Alpine slopes, about 30 miles outside Srinagar, where the Kak family had a chalet for holidays

Haak: Kale, a local staple in Kashmir

Hangul: Kashmir stag

Harwan: A village where Buddhist ruins were discovered by Bhaiji

Hisaab: Indian calendar

His Highness (HH): A formal way of addressing Maharajah Hari Singh

Kadhai: An indigenous utensil

Kahwa: A sweet Kashmiri tea garnished with almond slivers and cardamom

Kardar: A tax collector

Kangri: A small pot filled with lighted charcoal

Kasauli: A popular hill station in Himachal Pradesh

Khatamband: Typical Kashmiri wooden inlay work found inside houses, particularly on ceilings

Kikar: Acacia tree

Kut: Prayer room

Lota: An indigenous mug

Mali: Gardener

Marg: Meadow

Maya: Maya in Sanskrit means illusion, a fundamental concept in Hindu philosophy implying all that meets the eye is illusion.

Misri: Sweet black cherry

Nadirmonje: Salted lotus stem fritters fried in rice batter

Nag: Spring

Nyoth: Rock salt

Panak: A cannabis-based drink

Pattoo achkan: A knee-length coat—buttoned in the front, made of a homespun woollen fabric resembling tweed—mostly worn in northern India.

Pir: Local saint

Sanawar: Colloquial name for The Lawrence School, Sanawar, a famous boarding school

Sanyasi: A Sanyasi in Hindu philosophy is a religious ascetic who has renounced the world, abandoning all claims to social or family standing.

Sarai: A traditional halting or clearing place for travellers and goods along major movement corridors

Seer: An Indian unit of measurement for mass and volume equal to approximately 1.25 kg

Sharada Pitha: One of the holiest pilgrimage sites for Hindus, located in the Valley of Mount Harmukh, believed to be the abode of Lord Shiva. Sharada Pitha means 'the seat of Sharada'—'Sharada' being the Kashmiri name for Saraswati, the goddess of learning.

Shikara: Covered pleasure boat that plies the Dal Lake

Sid: Pet name for Siddharth Kak

Thal: Kashmiri metal plate

The Maharani: Maharani Tara Devi, Maharaja Hari Singh's wife

Karan Singh: Heir to the throne of Kashmir, Indian politician and former member of Parliament

Tonga: A horse-drawn carriage commonly used for transportation in the Valley

Tsaman: Cottage cheese or paneer

Tsotchavur: A kind of Kashmiri bun

Vidya: Knowledge

Vitasta: The original Sanskrit name of the Jhelum River

Vyeth: The origin of the Jhelum River at Verinag; also a small unit of measurement

Zaldragar: A colony in the heart of Srinagar on the banks of the Tsunt Kol, a canal connected to the Jhelum

Zamadod: Curd

Index